MEN OF LETTERS

—

DUNCAN BARRETT

MEN OF LETTERS

Published by AA Publishing, a trading name of
AA Media Limited, Fanum House, Basing View,
Basingstoke, Hampshire, RG21 4EA, UK.

www.theAA.com

First published in 2014
10 9 8 7 6 5 4 3 2 1

Map illustration by Nicola L Robinson

A CIP catalogue record for this book is available from
the British Library.

ISBN: 978-0-7495-7520-5

Printed and bound in the UK by Clays Ltd.

A04989

Our books carry the FSC label are printed on FSC
certified paper. FSC is the only forest certification scheme
endorsed by the leading environmental organisations.

For my mother Michèle
—

DUNCAN BARRETT is a writer and editor, specialising in biography and memoir. He grew up in London and studied English at Jesus College, Cambridge. In 2010 he edited the First World War memoirs of pacifist saboteur Ronald Skirth, published as *The Reluctant Tommy*. He is co-author, with Nuala Calvi, of *The Sugar Girls*, which was a *Sunday Times* top ten bestseller for eight weeks and ranked second in the history bestsellers of 2012. This was followed in 2013 by *GI Brides*, which also went straight into the non-fiction paperback charts.

Contents

—

FOREWORD BY ALAN JOHNSON 8

MAP 10

PROLOGUE: POST-HASTE 13

1. POSTMEN ON PARADE 19
2. A FORTNIGHT IN FRANCE 41
3. FESTUBERT 61
4. I REGRET TO INFORM YOU … 87
5. KILLING TIME 97
6. LOOS 117
7. SEASON'S GREETINGS 145
8. KEEP THE HOME FIRES BURNING 161
9. MAIL PRIVILEGE 175
10. THE SOMME 193
11. FROM HELL'S VALLEY TO HIGH WOOD 207
12. THE BUTTE DE WARLENCOURT 233
13. 'ACTION!' 251
14. AN UNPOPULAR HERO 263
15. PASSCHENDAELE 275
16. FAREWELL TO THE FIRST BATTALION 287
17. THE END GAME 303

EPILOGUE: THE LAST POST 317

ACKNOWLEDGEMENTS 327

TIMELINE 330

Q&A WITH DUNCAN BARRETT 332

FOREWORD

BY ALAN JOHNSON

Alan Johnson MP is a former Home Secretary and author of the bestselling memoir This Boy. *From the age of 18 he worked as a postman, and before entering Parliament in 1997 he was General Secretary of the Communication Workers Union.*

When a soldier on the Western Front wrote to a London newspaper in 1915 saying he was lonely and would appreciate receiving some mail, the response was immediate. The newspaper published the soldier's name and regiment, and within a couple of weeks he'd received 3,000 letters, 98 large parcels and three mailbags of packets.

Had that soldier had the time and inclination to respond to every letter, he could have done. Wherever he was fighting, his letter back would have been delivered in a day or two.

The story of how the General Post Office maintained an excellent postal service to soldiers and sailors in the First World War is an extraordinary one. What Duncan Barrett does in this book is to weave it in with the equally amazing story of how postmen fought in their own Post Office regiment throughout the conflict.

Servicemen had always provided a regular stream of Post Office recruitment. Postmen, like soldiers, wore a uniform and served the Crown. Post Office terminology was (and still is) militaristic. Postmen didn't go to work, they went on duty. They took annual leave rather than holidays, and were in a 'service', not a job.

So servicemen had always become postmen, but in 1914 postmen became servicemen. Whilst the Royal Engineers Postal Section (REPS) consisted of postmen who would deliver the Forces' post, the Post Office Rifles consisted of postmen who would fight the war.

Their story is an incredible one, as are the experiences of the women recruited by the Post Office to fill the vacancies left by the men who'd joined up.

Until now, this crucial aspect of Post Office and military history has never been properly examined.

Enriched by the personal stories of these men and women, this narrative will add to the proud history of a great national institution, and to the enjoyment of those who like their history reading to be about more than dates and places.

Alan Johnson, 2014

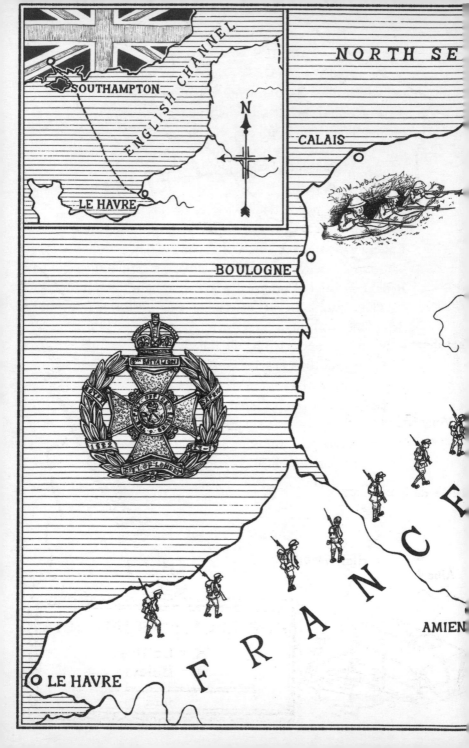

NORTH SE

ENGLISH CHANNEL

SOUTHAMPTON

N

LE HAVRE

CALAIS

BOULOGNE

FRANCE

AMIEN

O LE HAVRE

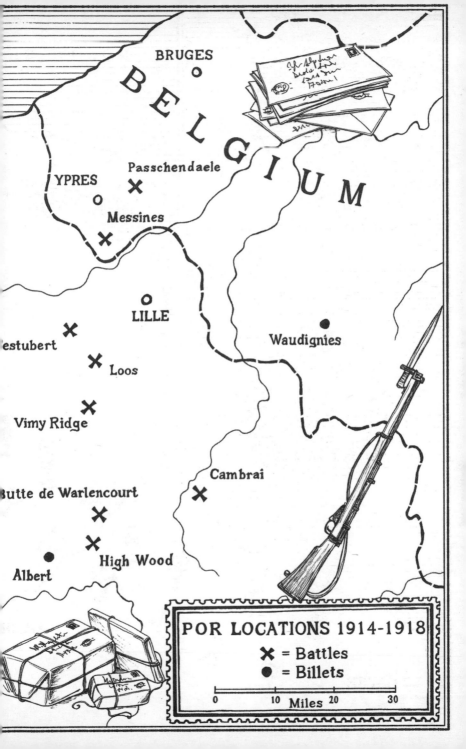

Prologue

Post-haste

—

Why did I join the POR?
  They thought that I must have been barmy.
  I joined it because
  It jolly well was
  The best in the ruddy old Army.

Poem written by Captain Eric Gore Browne, 1915

ON 3 AUGUST 1914, a sunny bank holiday Monday, Frank Seddon gazed out of the window as his train pulled out of Victoria Station. A Londoner born and bred, he was on his way to Eastbourne, for a fortnight at the annual Post Office Rifles summer camp. The train he was on – along with another just like it – had been specially commandeered to transport a thousand-odd Post Office workers to the seaside town, for what was to be the highlight of their year as volunteer part-time soldiers. As a new recruit, Frank had never been to camp before, and he was looking forward to it.

Frank was one of five children born to a working-class family in Bethnal Green, in the heart of London's East End. He had joined the Post Office not long after leaving school at the age of 14, and soon found himself pacing the streets 'Up West' in the blue-and-red uniform of a messenger boy, delivering telegrams to those who lived at the smart end of town. The job had proved an eye-opening experience – one morning, Frank had looked on in amazement as crowds of suffragettes paraded down the streets, smashing windows as they shouted 'Votes for Women!' It was a world away from the London Frank had grown up in, where the right to vote was the last thing that struggling wives and mothers worried about.

Frank had volunteered for the Post Office Rifles a week shy of his 17th birthday, in June 1914. A sporty type, he was attracted by the football and cricket matches after work in the evenings, as much as by the military training. Compared with the regular Army, the lifestyle in the volunteer unit seemed idyllic – the recruits would spend time camping in the grounds of their aristocratic officers' country estates, sleeping in tents or barns, and gathering round the fire to drink beer and sing songs together late into the night. It was a great distraction from the humdrum day-to-day life of the Post Office worker, and an opportunity to get to know fellow employees. Best of all, those workers who volunteered were entitled to an extra week's paid holiday every year.

The unit had been formed half a century earlier, in response to Irish acts of terror in London. Initially the volunteers were trained up as special constables and charged with protecting Post Office buildings, but after the Fenian threat passed, some of the men had requested to stay on as a part-time army corps. In

1899 they saw combat for the first time, when a force of Post Office workers was sent to South Africa to fight in the Boer War. But it was scarcely a baptism of fire – of the thousand-strong group of volunteers who went over, only two were unlucky enough to be killed in action, although many more succumbed to foreign diseases.

By 1914, the Post Office Rifles had become part of the relatively new Territorial Army, incorporated as the Eighth Battalion of the London Regiment. The men trained regularly, meeting in their evenings and weekends at the London Rifle Brigade's headquarters in Bunhill Row. They performed drill practice at the Tower of London, and gathered at Finsbury Circus or Somerset House for regular marches through the city. Every so often they would visit a shooting range at Purfleet in Essex to practise their marksmanship.

For messenger boys such as Frank, the military training was nothing new – as part of the Post Office's programme of educational activities for its youngest workers, telegraph boys were regularly taught drill using small carbine rifles. But not all of the Post Office riflemen were youngsters – many were seasoned veterans, Post Office workers who had served in the regular Army during the Boer War. This meant that new volunteers benefited from experienced instructors and colleagues.

As it turned out, Frank never made it to Eastbourne for the summer camp. As his train neared Three Bridges Station in Sussex, the driver suddenly slammed on the brakes. There were police standing on the platform, and they had been sent with instructions from the War Office: the two trains carrying the part-time soldiers from the Post Office were to halt their journey immediately, and await shunting back to Victoria Station.

The cause was a series of alarming events that were rapidly playing out in Europe. The assassination of the heir to the Austro-Hungarian throne a month earlier had triggered a major international crisis. Austria and Serbia were already at war, as were Germany and Russia. Now the German Army had requested passage through Belgium in order to launch an invasion of France, and the Belgians had defiantly refused. If Germany violated the smaller country's neutrality, Britain was treaty-bound to intervene. Already the regular Army had begun to mobilise.

By the time the Post Office Rifles arrived back at Victoria Station, London was in a mood of feverish anticipation. The riflemen marched through streets that were now thronged with people, many of them waving flags and singing patriotic songs. The eight companies that made up the battalion dispersed among the capital's larger post offices, and awaited further instructions. Some of them were put on military guard duty, protecting sensitive letters and telegrams from potential German spies and saboteurs.

Frank was one of several hundred men who spent the night at the General Post Office (GPO) headquarters on King Edward Street, a stone's throw from St Paul's Cathedral. (The stop on the London

Underground that we know today as 'St Pauls' originally went by the name 'Post Office'.) There they slept in the basement on a bed of empty mailbags, and wondered what news the morning would bring.

The next day a colonel arrived with some more information. The situation in Europe was not looking good. German forces had begun marching into Belgium and the British Prime Minister, Herbert Asquith, had issued an ultimatum: unless the Germans withdrew by 11pm Greenwich Mean Time (midnight in Berlin), Britain would declare war on Germany.

'When the ultimatum expires,' the colonel announced gravely, 'you will all be mobilised for active service.'

At this, a great cheer went around the room. The Post Office men were as excited as the rest of the country at the prospect of having a go at the Germans.

Frank was ordered to go home for the night and await further instructions. He returned to his parents' little house in Bethnal Green, holding his breath along with the rest of the nation. But by 11pm there had been no response to Asquith's ultimatum.

The next morning, a letter arrived for Frank, courtesy of his own local postman. He was ordered to report to barracks immediately. Britain was now at war with Germany, and the Post Office Rifles were joining the fight.

CHAPTER 1

POSTMEN ON PARADE

—

Strike, England, strike, and spare not! Lo, thy sons
Are rallying to thy standard from afar!
Strike for the peace that crowns a righteous war
'Gainst devils' lust and malice, till thy guns,
Thundering the foes' destruction, tell the birth
Of freedom and goodwill to all on earth.

From 'Armageddon', a poem published in the Post
Office magazine *St Martin's Le Grand*, October 1914

ON 11 AUGUST 1914, the Secretary of State for
War, Lord Kitchener, called for 100,000 new volunteer
soldiers. The nation didn't disappoint him, with more
than seven times that number signing up in the first
eight weeks – and the men who worked for the Post
Office were no exception. Up and down the country,
postmen, sorting clerks and messenger boys rushed to
the colours, their hearts filled with patriotic fervour
and a desire to help bash the 'Hun'.

Soon 11,000 staff had volunteered, some for the
Post Office Rifles and others for their own local
regiments. For a lucky few, a third option was a
position with REPS, the Royal Engineers Postal
Section, which was responsible for delivering mail to

men at the front and was formed largely from former Post Office workers. Compared with serving with a fighting unit, working for REPS was seen as a pretty cushy option.

It wasn't long before the effect of widespread volunteering began to be felt throughout the Post Office, which had been caught off guard by the sudden declaration of war. It was the world's largest employer, with more than a quarter of a million people on the payroll – and many of them were reservists, men who had already served a term in the Army but could be called on to return in an emergency. If too many workers left at once, the organisation would struggle to cope.

To begin with, the Post Office actually tried to hold men back from the Army. Less than a fortnight into the war, a row erupted when 52 telegraphists who were members of the Post Office Rifles were forbidden by their superiors from reporting for duty, on the grounds that they were needed at their posts. The Army hierarchy waded in, and the Post Office soon backed down, but as the men reported at Bunhill Row, the Post Office was left facing a serious labour shortage.

Soon the number of daily collections and deliveries was reduced, to cope with the shortfall in manpower. As volunteers swapped their delivery rounds for daily drill practice in Regent's Park, those left behind found themselves acting up to cover for them, and often struggling to juggle several jobs at once.

Bill Howell was a 19-year-old telegraph messenger at Willesden Sorting Office. When all the postmen there suddenly departed, leaving just eight messenger boys to keep things going, the whole operation was plunged into chaos. Some deliveries were abandoned and collections were frequently missed. As Bill later put it, 'We were led a rare old dance.'

Bill was made acting assistant postman, although he still wore his messenger boy's uniform. He and the other messenger boys were ordered out on the postal rounds, but when it came to heavy deliveries the lads were not physically strong enough. Their supervisor issued them with wheelbarrows and told them to get on with it, but the workload was almost impossible to keep up with, and they often found themselves trudging the streets late into the night.

The boys complained that they were being asked to do too much, but their supervisor was far from sympathetic. As far as he was concerned, it was the least they could do, after the postmen had volunteered for the Army. 'Those men are going out to fight for you and your country,' he told them angrily.

The boys huddled together in a corner of the Post Office and debated the best course of action. After a few minutes they came to a decision. The eight young lads marched out of the Post Office doors together, leaving their supervisor cursing. Then they went straight to Bunhill Row and volunteered for the Post Office Rifles.

By the time they arrived, the building was already packed with volunteers, and a long queue was beginning to form in the street. Inside, Bill stripped off his messenger boy's uniform with relish and threw it in a kit bag in the corner. Then he walked up to see a doctor for his medical exam.

'You're a very fit man,' the doctor told Bill, 'but you'll want to put on a bit of weight.' Then he added, as an afterthought, 'And height.'

Bill was only a little over five foot one and his nickname at the Post Office was 'Tich'. Unfortunately, the minimum height for the Territorial Army was five foot two.

Bill stepped up to a large scale to be weighed and measured by a corporal. The man shook his head sadly as he told him, 'Sorry son, you're half an inch under.'

Tears began to well up in Bill's eyes, and he did his best to blink them away. By now he was desperate to do his bit in the fight against the Germans, and he couldn't face returning to the Post Office and those long, miserable deliveries with the wheelbarrow.

Bill's obvious distress made an impact on the corporal. 'Perhaps I made a mistake,' he said kindly. 'Get on there again.'

Obligingly, Bill climbed back onto the scale and stood up as straight as he could. But strain as he might, he was still just under the requisite height.

The corporal leaned in and whispered, '*Stand on tiptoe, you bloody fool!*'

Bill pushed himself up onto the balls of his feet. 'You're in!' the corporal declared triumphantly.

Soon Bill was all kitted out, with the badge of the Post Office Rifles in his cap. He felt a wave of pride just wearing the brand-new khaki uniform. It was a couple of sizes too big for him, but he couldn't care less.

When Bill got home, however, he found his mother was less than enchanted with his new look. In fact, when he first arrived she didn't even recognise him. 'Get out, I'll call the police!' she shouted, at the sight of an unknown soldier marching into her home. When Bill took off his Army cap and his mother saw his face properly, she fainted.

Once Mrs Howell had come round, and had recovered from the initial shock, she began to berate her son angrily. 'You go back there and get your shilling back!' she shouted.

'I never had a shilling, mum, just a bit of paper,' Bill told her. 'It's no good. Nothing can take me out now.'

Although the Post Office Rifles was intended for Post Office employees, not all new recruits strictly fitted the bill. Tommy Thompson had already failed a medical exam for his local battalion, the Kensington Regiment, when he arrived at Bunhill Row hoping to join the London Rifle Brigade. There he ran into Sergeant Baylis, a friend of his brother, who was serving with the Post Office Rifles. 'What about joining us?' Baylis asked him.

'I'm not in the Postal Service,' Tommy explained sadly. But Baylis told him not to worry and brought him over to the attesting officer.

'And who is this man?' the official demanded, looking Tommy up and down.

'A clerk in Wimpole Street, sir,' Sergeant Baylis replied confidently. Wimpole Street was the headquarters of the Western District Post Office.

'Very well,' the officer replied, and Tommy was in.

As it happened, there was some truth to what Baylis had said. Tommy was indeed a clerk in Wimpole Street, but at Debenhams department store, not the Post Office.

The 'Why and Wherefore' is the paramount influence in the training of the Londoner, and differentiates him most from other classes of soldier. Born and bred in a large city, where his wits have been sharpened from his earliest days ... he is brimful of common sense, and quick to learn and respond to anything which appeals to his intelligence. The drill-sergeant's monologue of interminable detail bores him to tears; he requires to be shown how to hold his rifle, and why he has to hold it in this way or that ... Let him have a clear reason for any job that he is called upon to carry out, and why it has to be done in a particular way, and he can be trained for any enterprise.

Lieutenant Colonel Arthur Derviche-Jones, commander of the Second Battalion and author of the official history of the Post Office Rifles (1919)

With so many men rushing to sign up, the Post Office Rifles soon found themselves oversubscribed. By September 1914, they had reached their full strength of around a thousand men, but the volunteers kept coming, and soon a Second Battalion was formed, intended to recruit and train new members who could be sent out to the First Battalion as the need arose.

By the end of September, while the Second Battalion was mustering troops in London, the First Battalion had moved to an Army camp at Crowborough. It was a brand-new site and had yet to be equipped with fresh water or sanitary arrangements. The men slept 20 to a tent, sharing blankets – which were in short supply – as the miserable autumn rain lashed at the canvas. And to make matters worse, the Post Office Rifles were not alone there – they were sharing the camp's rudimentary facilities with three other battalions: the 'Cast Iron' Sixth Londons, the 'Shiny' Seventh Londons, and the London Rifle Brigade (the Fifth Londons).

But despite the less than ideal set-up, the mood was one of excitement and expectation, and the men made the best of the primitive and cramped conditions. Second Lieutenant Home Peel, a 19-year-old private secretary from the India Office who had been attached to the Post Office Rifles as a junior officer, wrote to his wife Gwendolen on 17 September:

We arrived here yesterday about 11, having left East Grinstead at 8. About 10 miles, pretty hot, but very pleasant march. In the course of the day we got the tents pitched. To-day it rained & blew like the devil all the morning, [but] it has been quite nice this afternoon ... I am thoroughly fit and really enjoying it. The other officers are an extraordinarily nice lot ... There are three of us in a tent, the other two very nice, & we get on quite comfortably ... The whole thing here is extraordinarily like going back to school.

Of course, as an officer, Peel's lot was rather better than that of the rank and file – he was sharing his tent with only two other men, not 19 – but his cheerful attitude seems to have been mirrored throughout the ranks. Many officers assigned to the Post Office Rifles commented on the men's easy-going disposition, and in a battalion drawn largely from London post offices there was plenty of traditional cockney humour.

In temperament, Second Lieutenant Peel was more of a scholar than a soldier. He was a thoughtful-looking man with a carefully trimmed moustache, and never appeared quite at ease in his Army uniform. With his slight frame and relaxed posture, he was far from a natural warrior, and he lacked the slavish deference to his superiors that was expected of recruits in the Army.

For an intelligent and independent-minded man, the chain of command could be very frustrating, and Peel was far from alone in resenting it. As he put it in a typically forthright letter to his wife Gwendolen, 'You have to say Yessir and Nosir like a beastly lackey to men who you despise.'

He was certainly not one to mince his words where the Army top brass were concerned, and was capable of some very colourful turns of phrase. 'We are having our lives made miserable by a brigadier with a mania for counting buttons,' he complained in one letter home, describing the man as a 'purple abortion' and a 'foul-mouthed mutton-headed fool'. In another letter, he told his wife about a colonel with 'the mind of a preacher and the imagination of a lump of pork' – adding, as an afterthought, 'Don't tell anyone I said so!'

To begin with, Peel had been highly sceptical about the war itself as well – 'I feel so horribly sad about the terrible suffering that will ensue,' he wrote to Gwendolen. But having read the 'Blue Book', a hastily printed pamphlet containing speeches given to Parliament by the Prime Minister and Foreign Secretary, he had come round to their point of view – and found himself with 'no more doubt of the justice of this war than of my own existence'. By the time he arrived at Crowborough Camp, his greatest fear was that he might be transferred to the Second Battalion to help train up new recruits, and would miss the boat when the First Battalion departed for action.

At Crowborough, training for war began in earnest. The men from the Post Office practised firing rifles and hurling bombs. They acted out mock engagements with imaginary enemies, and bayonetted endless hostile sandbags, arranged in a variety of approximately lifelike configurations. Over the course of six weeks, the ordinary postmen and messenger boys were transformed into bloodthirsty warriors, capable of butchering the most ferocious German soldiers.

Although most of their training was for old-fashioned open warfare, it was becoming clear that once they got to the front, the men would soon be spending much of their time in trenches. After the German retreat that followed the Battle of the Marne in September 1914, both sides had begun to dig in, and by November a pair of roughly parallel lines, over 400 miles in length, bisected France and Belgium from the Swiss border right the way up to the North Sea. The war that had originally been expected to be over by Christmas was shaping up for a much longer haul.

Meanwhile, the potential of the Territorial Army units had already been proven on the Western Front. Lord Kitchener had made no secret of his disdain for the 'town clerk's army', as he called it – he had far more confidence in his own 'New Army' of fresh volunteers. But after the first Battle of Ypres in October, the War Secretary was required to eat his words. The London Scottish Battalion put up a spectacularly brave fight, helping to hold the line against a German attack and losing more than half their men in the process.

Despite the heavy losses suffered by their Scottish counterparts, the Post Office Rifles were itching to join them at the front lines. So when their friends in the London Rifle Brigade were sent off to France without them, the men were understandably disappointed. 'We are fearfully sick to-day,' Peel wrote to his wife Gwendolen. 'We had always counted on moving with them.'

Fortunately, some good news soon arrived to boost the men's morale: the Post Office Rifles, along with the Cast Iron Sixth and Shiny Seventh London battalions, were being transferred to the 47th London Division, where they would form a new brigade with the Civil Service Rifles (the 15th Londons). The Post Office was technically a branch of the Civil Service – in its earliest incarnation, the Post Office Rifles had been part of the Civil Service Volunteers – and there was considerable overlap between the two battalions, with several hundred Post Office employees serving in the Civil Service Rifles, and civil servants such as Peel commanding the Post Office Rifles.

As the men from the Post Office prepared to leave Crowborough, they were visited by General William Fry, who announced that he was impressed with their progress and had recommended them for service on the Continent. Most flattering of all, he declared that they were every bit as good as the London Scottish, the brave men who had forever changed public perception of the 'Saturday night soldiers' of the Territorial Army – proving that they were a real fighting force and not just a poor man's substitute for the regulars.

For the Post Office Rifles, the general's confidence in them was encouraging. Now all they wanted was a chance to prove that they deserved it.

Leavesden,
Kings Langley, Herts

My darling,

I haven't had a moment to write before. We are more or less settled down here now – in the lunatic asylum! That is to say, my Company & one other are billeted in the big recreation hall of the huge asylum here, & we officers are billeted on the Superintendent Doctor. All around us are 2,200 incurable lunatics. A most cheerful atmosphere. I've been round with the Doctor looking at them this afternoon, and anything more depressing cannot be imagined.

Really, the billet is quite a good one, & we are very comfortable & well fed and looked after. The Doctor & his wife are very nice & have an amusing little daughter of 13 ... It is nice to sleep in a bed & have things dry & clean again ... I'm very fit and all is well – Best love to you darling & to Elizabeth – and the Birds.

Your very loving

Mister

Letter from Second Lieutenant Home Peel
to his wife Gwendolen, November 1914

The new brigade of which the Post Office Rifles made up one-quarter was based around Watford and St Albans. On their arrival, the Post Office men found themselves billeted in the theatre of Leavesden Lunatic Asylum at Abbots Langley, where they slept on a hard wooden floor, each man using his own boots as a pillow. A mental institution might seem an odd choice of location for a military unit, but given the number of men to be accommodated there was nowhere else in the village that was suitable. It offered ample floor space for the men to sleep on, and also had its own vegetable gardens and livestock, cared for by the inmates themselves.

The Post Office Rifles shared the lunatics' bathing and laundry facilities, the latter run by the female inmates. For some of these women, the sight of a thousand strapping young lads in uniform was an impossible temptation, and the men found themselves on the receiving end of plenty of unexpected hugs and kisses. But many of the female inmates were actually perfectly sane. One girl had been sent to the asylum by an employer who had got her pregnant – there was an orphanage conveniently located just across the road, where unwanted children were disposed of.

Even the most 'mad' residents were capable of moments of lucidity. One morning the riflemen returned from a gruelling 24-hour mock battle to parade in front of their commanding officer and wait to be dismissed. They had spent the night wading along a river and crawling about in the mud, and were in a terrible state, bedraggled and wrung out. As the men stood silently to attention outside the building, doing their best not to show how miserable and exhausted they felt, a voice came from one of the barred windows: 'Who are the barmy ones now?'

The Post Office men were dismissed and returned to their billets, feeling pretty wretched after a night spent out in the grounds. But the situation could have been a lot worse. The following January a group of 12,000 of Lord Kitchener's New Army recruits were marched to a parade ground near Woking for inspection by the War Secretary himself. But Kitchener arrived several hours late, and the 14-mile round trip through driving rain was too much for some of the men. Two of them died and many more were treated for exposure.

The Post Office Rifles did lose one man during their training period at the asylum: Rifleman Oliver Maitland, a 36-year-old former postman for whom a bout of flu led to pneumonia. Oliver died on 26 February 1915 at the local Voluntary Aid Detachment hospital in Watford, the battalion's first wartime casualty. He was buried in the local churchyard at Abbots Langley, where a plaque hangs to this day in memory of the Post Office Rifles who worshipped there during their training.

For many of the Post Office men, the training at Abbots Langley provided a first brush with inflexible Army discipline. E.J. Robinson had been counting his lucky stars since the billets were allocated, having found himself with his own bed in the home of the village butcher, rather than just a patch of cold floor in the asylum theatre. But he soon found that life in the Army was far from cosy and comfortable.

Soon after the Post Office men arrived at Abbots Langley, they paraded in the street for inspection. Robinson stood to attention as a captain strode past him and then stopped suddenly, murmuring to a provost sergeant at his side. He was sure he had heard the captain say, 'Take this man's name,' but had no idea what he had done wrong.

When the captain was gone, the sergeant came up and explained. 'You're charged with having your bootlaces done up contrary to regulation pattern,' he told Robinson brusquely. 'Parade outside Company Office at six this evening.' Robinson had threaded his laces crosswise, as he had done with every pair of shoes he had ever owned, not realising that in the Army a straight-across pattern was mandatory.

At 6 o'clock, Robinson arrived at the Company Office to hear his fate, escorted by the provost sergeant and a pair of regimental policemen. 'What have you to say?' the captain demanded.

Robinson opened his mouth to answer but before he could get a word out the sergeant bellowed, 'Shut up!' Then the captain declared, 'Six days confined to barracks. Dismissed.'

As punishments went, it could have been worse, and it certainly had the desired effect. For the rest of his life, Robinson never tied his shoelaces crosswise again.

As well as offering a chance for further training, the months spent at Abbots Langley provided an opportunity for a major reorganisation of the Post Office Rifles, and at times men seemed to be coming and going at an alarming rate. The battalion's adjutant, Captain Tom Morris, a smooth and handsome old Etonian who always wore a Bowie knife on his belt, was growing increasingly frustrated. As the officer in charge of the battalion's admin and communications, it was he who had battled the Post Office over the 52 telegraphists initially held back from the Army – and now that he had finally got hold of them, a larger number were volunteering for transfers to the Royal Engineers Postal Section (REPS).

Next it was the turn of the underage men – those who were not yet 19, and were thus ineligible for foreign service – to depart to join the Second Battalion at Cuckfield. Among them was Frank Seddon, the young messenger boy who had joined the Post Office Rifles shortly before war was declared. He ended up based on the Essex coast as part of a special underage unit made up of boys from the Fifth, Sixth, Seventh and Eighth London battalions.

The boys in Frank's unit spent their time patrolling the seaside towns of Southwold, Walberswick and Easton Bavents, on the lookout for a German invasion fleet, their heads filled with stories from *Boy's Own* magazines in which the Kaiser's soldiers launched bloody assaults on Colchester and other towns in the Southeast. They already knew the area pretty well since they had spent several days in Braintree practising their trench digging – the idea behind building mock trenches near the coast was that rather than filling them in afterwards they could simply be left in place, to be put to use in the event of a German invasion.

At Abbots Langley, the underage recruits were soon replaced by a draft of men from the Second Battalion, but the constant reorganisation made life difficult for those junior officers who were trying to familiarise themselves with the men serving under them. As Second Lieutenant Peel wrote to his wife Gwendolen:

> *It's like having a family of 50 children, with the Platoon Sergeant as their mother. You have to, or ought to, know everything about every single man – his capacity, his training, his shooting, the size of his boots, how many shirts & socks he has, whether he washes his feet, who his particular friends are, to see that he gets clothes, letters, boots, equipment, ammunition, to tend him when he's sick, to curse and bless him at the proper time.*

It wasn't always easy for the junior officers, or subalterns as they were known at the time, since the rank and file often viewed them as little more than public schoolboys in uniform. At just 19, Peel was younger than many of the men he commanded, but his dedication to them soon earned their respect. When he was transferred from one company to another, several men told him they would miss him – and his faithful servant, Rifleman Bob Manning, insisted that he would follow wherever his master was sent.

Despite the loyalty he inspired among his men, Peel was not always the easiest man to work for, as Manning was well aware. One day, when he served up some fried mutton, his master was furious – 'Remove this rubbish!' Peel shouted. Winning his men's respect was one thing, but they had to earn his as well – and as far as he was concerned, frying mutton was beyond the pale.

But despite the occasional angry outburst, generally speaking a position as an officer's servant, or 'batman', was considered to be a pretty cushy one. Peel's fellow platoon commander Lieutenant Croysdale had a servant by the name of Pat Patterson, who had eagerly volunteered for the job not long after he arrived at Abbots Langley. A postman based at Mount Pleasant Parcel Depot, Pat had already spent four years in the Post Office Rifles as a younger man and had returned to the unit in September 1914 as soon as his supervisors allowed him to. In recognition of his previous service, he had been offered a promotion to lance corporal, which would have made him a non-commissioned officer or NCO. But Pat had turned down the NCO's stripe – as he put it, he had no intention of 'lording it over' men he had served with before.

When Pat heard that an officer's servant was required, however, he put his name down immediately. He knew from his earlier time in the Post Office Rifles that this was one way to escape many of the less desirable aspects of Army life.

Pat was chosen for the role, and told to report to the Manor House, where Lieutenant Croysdale was billeted. His plan worked like a charm. From that day on he was exempted from almost all parades – and on top of that he was given a pay rise.

The extra work Pat performed was far from onerous, his main responsibility being to wake Croysdale up in the morning and help him get dressed. And even this task brought with it a number of perks: the servants at the Manor House treated Pat as a gentleman's valet, often inviting him down to the cellar to share a jug of ale, and always addressing him – in the tradition of the British aristocracy – by his master's name, as 'Mr Croysdale'. War was supposed to be a tough business, but the way Pat saw it, he was now 'one of the lucky ones'.

After all the new drafts and reorganisations, at last the First Battalion of the Post Office Rifles was complete, and ready to be sent off for foreign service. By now, the unit comprised four companies of up to 200 men each, a signal section, a band, a machine-gun section (boasting two Maxim guns) and a transport section with 50 horses, as well as the grooms to take care of them. There was also a medical officer (Captain Faulkner), a priest, a butcher, several cooks, a couple of farmers, and a number of regimental policemen.

Soon the Post Office Rifles even had their own civilian blacksmith, a local man who had been persuaded to train one of the battalion's drivers in the art of shoeing horses. The driver had successfully mastered the trade but not before Lieutenant Deverell, the battalion's transport officer, had talked the smithy into joining them himself, and kitted him out with a khaki uniform and a rifle.

As Territorial troops, the Post Office Rifles were not actually obliged to perform foreign service, and they had to be asked to volunteer for it. But for any stray souls who chose a transfer to a post on the home front instead, there were plenty of willing recruits ready to take their place. All over the country, Lord Kitchener's appeal continued to draw men by their thousands. In fact, by December 1914 there were so many New Army recruits that there wasn't enough khaki to dress them in – ironically, many volunteers disdained the blue serge outfits they were offered instead, complaining that they made them look like postmen.

Now all the Post Office Rifles were waiting for were orders to set off, and yet stubbornly the Army refused to give them. In December, a rumour went round about imminent departure for Egypt – it was said that the Sixth and Seventh Londons had already been informed of the plans. But the days and weeks went by and the rumour came to nothing. 'We have had no real exercise for a long time, & are getting horribly soft & flabby,' Second Lieutenant Peel complained in a letter to his wife Gwendolen.

Before long, Christmas was approaching. As the soldiers on the Western Front exchanged presents with their German counterparts, and buried their animosity with carol singing and games of football in no man's land, the Post Office Rifles were still holed up in Leavesden Asylum. 'I shall be rushing around from morning to night & most of the night Xmas day and Boxing day,' Peel wrote to Gwendolen. 'Altogether the whole thing is going to be intolerable.'

Peel was helping to organise a party for the NCOs in his company and had volunteered to help write the battalion's Christmas Day revue – a very 'scrappy business', as he put it. The show climaxed with a song written by Peel and another officer, and everyone stayed up celebrating until two in the morning.

The Army, however, obviously had a sadistic sense of timing, because two hours later, at 4am on Boxing Day morning, the entire battalion was roused from their beds and sent on a nine-mile march through driving rain and hail, before being turned around to march right back again. The spirit of festive goodwill was being pushed to the limit, but the men were well-trained soldiers now, and they all knew better than to complain.

The New Year brought renewed frustrations as the men continued to wait anxiously for orders. On 10 March the British Army on the Western Front attacked at Neuve Chapelle, and successfully took the town. More than ever, the Post Office Rifles were itching to get going. No one wanted the war to be over before they had even made it to the front.

At last, the orders they had been waiting for arrived, and the men were told to ready themselves for departure, although they were still given no clue as to where they were going. There was a final medical inspection, and then at 2.30am on 17 March, they set off on the five-mile trek to Watford, from where they could catch a train to Southampton. Much to Pat Patterson's delight, Lieutenant Croysdale had been put in charge of the 'entraining' operation, so instead of marching with the rest of the men, Pat shared a taxi to the station with his master.

On its way through London, the train happened to go right past the home of Bill ('Tich') Howell, the messenger boy who had snuck into the Army despite his diminutive height. Craning his neck out of the window, Bill saw his mother in the backyard taking out the rubbish, accompanied by the family dog Bones.

'Hello mum!' Bill yelled out to her, remembering the moment he had first come home in Army uniform and his poor mother had fainted from the shock.

But Mrs Howell was oblivious to her son's cries and didn't respond.

Soon all the other men on the train were joining in, shouting 'Hello, mum!' in an effort to get Bill's mother's attention.

Mrs Howell looked up and gazed at the train full of soldiers, on their way to death or glory in a foreign land. She waved at them weakly, feeling it was only polite, but never thought for a moment that her son might be among them. For a second time, she had failed to recognise him in uniform.

The dog, though, was rather more perceptive. It heard Bill's cries at once, and didn't stop barking until the train had passed well out of sight.

CHAPTER 2

A FORTNIGHT IN FRANCE

—

Dear Flo. We arrived safely here at 4 o'clock in the morning. Slept all the journey. This is a photo of the boat that brought us here. Will write later. Ernie.

Postcard sent home by one of the Post Office Rifles

AT 3.30AM ON THURSDAY 18 March 1915, the SS *Empress Queen* docked in Le Havre. It had been an uneventful journey, across an inky black sea that barely rippled. Those men who had never been aboard ship before were relieved that the seasickness they had feared never came to pass. Some spent the night trying to sleep on the overcrowded paddle steamer, while others stayed up all night gambling.

At Le Havre, the boat was held in harbour for four hours, before the men from the Post Office were allowed to disembark and begin the six-mile march to a rest camp up on a hill overlooking the town. The climb was arduous, especially for a group of men who had barely slept the previous two evenings and were carrying the assorted paraphernalia of war on their backs.

When the Post Office Rifles arrived at the camp, they found that it was still under construction and consisted of little more than a few tents. It was a cold, bleak place, with a sharp wind blasting through it from the east, and all that night the men shivered under their blankets.

On Friday morning some brave souls decided to try shaving in the inhospitable conditions – which meant finding a bucket of water and breaking the ice. But in the harsh wind the water froze on their faces, and their friends teased them for their foolhardiness.

The next stage of the journey to the front lines was made by cattle train. That afternoon, the men from the Post Office piled into a long line of rickety wooden carriages, which were marked 'Hommes 40, Chevaux 8'. The trains were a familiar sight to all Tommies sent to France, and the labelling always drew wry remarks. As a private in Wilfred Owen's battalion, the Artists' Rifles, joked, there was 'an uncomfortable feeling of suspense as to whether it meant "40 men or 8 horses" or "40 men and 8 horses". After 39 other people were duly packed into my truck I was more than ever anxious about the "Chevaux 8" business.'

As it turned out, the Post Office Rifles were relatively lucky, as they averaged a couple of men under the maximum of 40 per carriage, but even so the train was uncomfortably cramped. There wasn't enough room for everybody to lie down properly, so the only chance of getting any sleep was for the men to lie across each other, one man using another's chest as a pillow. Frequently, a rifleman would be woken in the night to find one of his comrades' boots in his face.

The train was cold and draughty, thanks to cracks in the floor and in the side panels, and for much of the journey it travelled at little more than a walking pace. When it stopped – which happened frequently – the men would dash out of their compartments and run up to the driver with empty biscuit tins, begging for a little hot water to brew up some tea.

Finally, at 2pm on Saturday afternoon, the train arrived at the small town of Berguette, a few miles outside Béthune. The 200-mile journey had taken well over 20 hours.

The men were exhausted and shaken up by the constant stopping and starting, which had made the train carriages crash together. They had little enthusiasm for the next stage of their journey: a three-hour march to the French mining town of Auchel. But at least they had survived the experience of French troop transport. Not all on board had been as lucky – one of the transport section's old draught horses, which went by the improbable name of Nick Carter, had died during the journey.

A handful of men had actually got off the train early. Rifleman Jim Coleman had been ordered to disembark at the seaside town of Boulogne, where he spent a fortnight working in the docks. One day, Jim was surprised to see a group of soldiers standing around an empty railway truck and he asked what they were doing. He learned that they were on punishment detail, having been court-martialled for a variety of offences ranging from cowardice in the face of the enemy to rape. As penance, they were sorting through the uniforms of men killed in action and collecting their personal belongings to return to their families at home. The terms of their punishment stipulated that they were forbidden to sit down, even when there was nothing left to sort, hence much of the time they just stood around waiting. The aimless soldier criminals were a peculiar sight, but for Jim, who had yet to see any front-line action of his own, the thought of the piles of bloodstained uniforms was more disquieting.

Meanwhile, the rest of the battalion was settling into billets in Auchel, where once again Lieutenant Croysdale's batman Pat Patterson found that being an officer's servant had its advantages. Pat had been billeted in a cowshed, along with the rest of the rank and file in his company. But when his 'guv'nor' found out, he was horrified. 'A cowshed?' Croysdale exclaimed in dismay. 'Pat, *you* cannot sleep in a cowshed!'

The lieutenant told Patterson to bring his kit along to the house where he himself was billeted, and asked its French owner if she could find a spare room for 'mon valet'. The woman was happy to oblige, and Patterson soon found himself sleeping on a comfortable bed between clean sheets, while the rest of the men shivered in the barn.

Such rustic billets could lead to problems, as a sergeant in No. 1 Company discovered when he was sent out late one evening to give the men their orders for the following day. In the pitch-black night, it was hard to tell one barn from another, but he managed to find his way to what he thought was the right building, and hearing a rustling in the straw deduced that the men must still be awake. 'Silence!' he demanded, as he barged through the open doorway.

The sergeant went through the plans for the next morning, detailing certain riflemen for guard duty and giving the particulars of the parade. But, receiving no response, he began to grow anxious, and after a long silence started fumbling for a light switch. As the bulbs above his head flickered on, the sergeant realised he had picked the wrong building and had been addressing a barn full of pigs.

On 22 March, the Post Office Rifles paraded in the streets of Auchel for inspection by Sir John French, the Commander-in-Chief of the British Armies in France and Flanders. But the general kept them waiting for four hours, and when he did arrive he was evidently unimpressed. 'They look like boys!' he blustered.

The men were immediately ordered to begin growing moustaches, although the results were often less than satisfactory. As Sergeant Archie Dunn wrote in a letter to his wife, 'You should have seen some of the efforts, especially the fair Anglo-Saxon ones – hardly discernible, and would far from frighten the wildest of Germans.'

Not that the Post Office Rifles had come near any Germans yet, aside from a handful of prisoners glimpsed briefly as they got off the boat at Le Havre.

Auchel was only 15 miles from the firing line, and the guns could be heard faintly in the distance, but the mood among the men was still less than warlike. On 22 March, Second Lieutenant Peel told his wife Gwendolen, 'So far the whole thing is like a huge picnic. Everything is so quiet and peaceful here that it is hard to realise what is going on a few miles off.'

Soon the battalion was on the move again, and getting closer and closer to the line. After a 10-mile march along greasy paved roads, they arrived at Béthune, where they were billeted in the local *École de Jeunes Filles*. The men were amused at the choice of location, which hardly seemed appropriate for the military (although all the *filles* had long since been evacuated). In its favour, though, the school did boast a playground that could be used for parades and football matches.

Béthune was just behind the line, and was actually within range of German artillery, although so far the town had escaped any shelling. According to local rumour, there was some kind of unofficial gentlemen's agreement between the two sides: as long as the British left alone La Bassée, on the German side of the line, the Germans would do the same for Béthune.

The time had come for the Post Office Rifles to complete the final stage of their training – learning the ropes in a genuine front-line trench. Their instructors were to be Lord Cavan's Irish Guards, who were holding a nearby stretch of the front running from Festubert down to the La Bassée canal. Soon the men from the Post Office were winding their way through the elaborate maze of communication trenches that led up to the front, to find out what trench life was really like.

My darling,

I'm really not quite sure what the date is, but I believe the day is Sunday. I am writing in a dug-out. I brought my platoon into the trenches yesterday afternoon for 24 hours & go out again in a few hours. I am not allowed to say the place of course, nor really to give any information as to what exactly we are doing or who we are with – But already we are getting quite accustomed to the sound of bursting shells & continuous rifle fire. The day before yesterday we were out digging in a place where shells were bursting within 100 yards & stray rifle bullets were actually coming over. Gore Browne (Captain, D Company) was hit very slightly in the left arm coming up to the trenches the first day – pure luck, a stray rifle bullet.

We had quite an exciting night last night, expecting an attack which didn't come off ... Sniping & occasional shells all day & night with from time to time heavy bursts of both artillery & rifles. I have had no casualties yet, nor any real chance of one, except the danger of stray bullets when we were digging & coming up to the trenches. Aeroplanes of both sides overhead with shrapnel shells bursting round them.

Brilliantly sunny but very cold. Heavy frost last night. I'm fearfully fit & thoroughly 'enjoying' it so far. But at present we are really no further than the instructional stage. My boys are in the highest spirits.

Letter from Second Lieutenant Home Peel
to his wife Gwendolen, 28 March 1915

Thanks to the Irish Guards, the Post Office Rifles were introduced to life in the trenches, each soldier personally instructed by a counterpart of equivalent rank, until everyone was clear about what was expected of them. Among the innumerable hints and tips passed on by the Guards, the Post Office men were told to blacken their silver cap badges, which could draw enemy fire, and to be careful when lighting cigarettes after dark not to show any light to the Germans.

Once everyone was up to speed, the Irish Guards were relieved and the Post Office men were left in charge of the trench. Fortunately for them, the sector was relatively quiet at the time – but there were signs that it hadn't always been so. Over the top in no man's land the corpses of a large number of Gurkhas were rotting away from a previous attack, and the cloying smell of death was inescapable.

For many of the former Post Office workers, the dead and decomposing bodies came as a shock, despite all their training for war. Sergeant Archie Dunn wrote to his wife, 'Out here, what a sheer waste of men's lives, just to gain some few hundred yards of ground.

As time goes by, I expect to become callous to death around me, but right now, I am much disturbed in mind, being a beginner as it were.'

For some, though, the dead bodies were a source of fascination as much as horror. One rifleman decided to jump up from the fire step (a raised ledge that ran along the front wall of the trench) so that he could see properly over the top and get a good look at the dead Gurkhas. His friends told him not to be a fool, but the man would hear no argument.

The moment his head was above the parapet, a German sniper took a shot at him. The British soldier was incredibly lucky that the bullet didn't quite hit its mark. It came very close, though, knocking the Post Office Rifles badge right out of his cloth cap. 'That was b-b-b-bloody near!' he exclaimed as he climbed back down into the trench. He had survived his first brush with death in the trenches, but the stutter remained with him for the rest of his life.

Before long, the Germans were doing more than just sniping. Manning the periscopes that allowed them to see over the top across no man's land, one of the Post Office men noticed a sign had gone up in the enemy trench. Someone over there obviously spoke English, because in large clear letters they had written:

WE WILL BE OVER IN THE NIGHT

The sign sent chills down the spines of the men from the Post Office, and they spent the rest of the day in a state of anxious anticipation. Night fell with no sign of an attack, and by midnight they were beginning to hope that the threat had been a hollow one. But in the early hours of the morning the alarm sounded, calling the men to 'stand to' on the fire step. The Germans had proved as good as their word.

'Blimey,' shouted one of the Post Office men, transfixed by the sight of an enemy patrol rushing across no man's land, the moonlight glinting off the spikes on their pointy black helmets. 'There they are, like bloody great coppers!'

The Post Office Rifles had been trained in rapid fire, and began unleashing a volley of bullets. Fortunately, it was enough to deter the enemy, and the German attack was called off before any of them reached the British front line.

Enemy raids were not the only problem the Post Office men had to contend with in the front lines. After less than a fortnight in France, many of them were suffering from a complaint familiar to Brits abroad: 'traveller's tummy'. Since it wasn't always possible to make it to the latrine in time, they were forced to improvise – and discovered that an empty sandbag kept close at hand made an excellent emergency potty.

As the men grew used to the paraphernalia of trench life, they began to improvise more and more with the humble hessian sacks. Rifleman James Harvey, formerly a postman in Erith, found a sandbag was invaluable when he decided to make a jam roly-poly, one of his mother's specialities.

The front-line version was a little adapted from Mrs Harvey's recipe. First, James took some hardtack biscuits and bashed them around until they had crumbled into a powder, then he added water and kneaded the mixture into a dough. He then rolled it up with some Army-issue plum-and-apple jam and folded the whole lot into the sandbag. Once he had cooked it for a couple of hours, submerged in a petrol tin of water over a 'tommy cooker', James did indeed have his very own roly-poly. It might not have rivalled his mother's in appearance or taste, but for James it was a reminder of home.

The Post Office men's first spell in the trenches passed relatively quickly, and without any serious incidents. Before long they had settled into a regular routine, alternating between two days in the front line and two days of rest in Béthune. In their time behind the lines, they got to know the French town well and began to find ways to enjoy themselves.

For the officers this meant riding out on horseback and marvelling at the beautiful French countryside. Home Peel wrote blissfully to his wife about a 'wood carpeted with anemones, butterflies flitting about and everything very springlike and nice'. The effect the scenery had on him was profound. 'It's too ridiculous that people should want to fight one another,' he commented wistfully.

Meanwhile, the rank and file were more likely to find their pleasures in the town. On 28 March, they received their first pay packet in France – the princely sum of 10 francs, which they could spend as they wished. Although for some payday meant a search for the nearest brothel, most found a slap-up meal and a night on the town more appealing.

There was little need to try genuine French food, since everywhere served egg and chips for the Tommies, but they did get to sample the local booze. Rifleman Selley, a former Post Office clerk, wrote in his diary:

> *Tasted French beer for the first time. It is called 'Bock' and is 5% per litre. Not bad. Very light. Went to bed at 4 o'clock (not as a result of the Bock but through not having any sleep worth the name for three nights).*

Wherever they went in France, the Tommies invariably spent much of their time in the local *estaminets*, small cafes that generally stayed open late and sold beer and wine as well as coffee. Some of the men, however, took a while to cotton on to the unfamiliar French word. One of the Post Office men exclaimed to his friends, 'Blimey, don't this bloke Estaminet own a lot of caffs!'

The language barrier was a challenge, but the men did their best to make themselves understood – often in the time-worn manner of Brits abroad, in other words shouting. The Post Office magazine *St Martin's Le Grand* published a series of letters from the front written by Second Lieutenant Gordon Stroud, whose father worked in the Central Telegraph Office. Stroud had probably been taught French at school, and his attitude towards his men in the York and Lancaster Regiment is rather condescending:

> *Yorkshiremen endeavouring to talk French are decidedly funny, they think if only they shout at the top of their voices, the peasants will understand anything. A few minutes ago a man strode up to the door and confronting my dear landlady, yelled, 'off-hits-her'. Don't laugh, he wanted me, and meant 'officer'.*

Some of the men made more effort than others, and tried to actually use the native language. Corporal Thomas May, a former telegraph messenger boy from Islington, carried a small pocket diary that contained within it such useful materials as a map of France and Flanders, a 1915 calendar and information on how to determine your orientation at night using the Pole Star. But most helpful of all was the page of French phrases, including not only words for food, drink and essential toiletries but also such useful emergency expressions as 'Je ne parle pas français,' 'Halt! Qui va là?' and 'Ami! Je suis anglais.'

Aside from eating and drinking, the most popular pastime for British Tommies when out of the front-line trenches was writing letters to their families back home, and the Post Office Rifles were no exception. The former postmen knew better than anyone the pleasure letters could bring to their recipients and devoted long hours to keeping up with their correspondence. At times the task could seem something of a chore – as Corporal Thomas May wrote in his diary:

> *Sunday. Rouse at 7 AM. Church Parade 9 AM. After church found a quiet spot and answered all my letters. Most boring job but had to be done.*

For the most part, though, the men seemed to enjoy the link with home, and were generous in the missives they sent back to family and friends. Many of them purchased beautiful embroidered silk postcards, which were all the rage in France at the time and never failed to impress mothers, wives and sweethearts back in England.

The amount of correspondence back and forth was prodigious, but thanks to the Royal Engineers Postal Section, which itself included many former Post Office employees, deliveries were fast and efficient. Over 500 people were now being employed full time at the REPS Home Depot in London, with 10 floors of the King Edward Building dedicated to parcels being sent out to the troops. Meanwhile, almost 10,000 registered letters a month passed through the hands of the Home Depot staff, reaching their recipients on the Western Front within only a couple of days of being sent.

On the Continental side, another huge depot in Le Havre sorted the mail so that it could be delivered by train to a series of smaller Army post offices set up ad hoc wherever the officials could find room – be that in a stable, a bowling alley or a bakery. From there, the post would be taken by lorry to the relevant brigade headquarters and then on by handcart, reaching a given unit in the evening along with the rations – it was said that however hungry the soldiers were, they would always read their letters before eating. Any post to be sent home was collected at the same time, and followed the same journey in reverse.

Aside from the large quantity of letters, the constant stream of parcels arriving at the front lines meant that the men were surprisingly well provided for, and the quick delivery times meant that even perishable items could be posted, including fresh fruit and homemade cakes. At the front it was common, among both officers and men, for what was sent to one soldier to be shared with his friends. 'My darling, very many thanks for the parcel,' Second Lieutenant Peel wrote appreciatively to his wife Gwendolen. 'We all love Oxford marmalade, & the figs are a most welcome addition. The mess praises and magnifies your name.'

A lot of the correspondence sent back to Blighty from the front was concerned with requests for things that could not be purchased in France. Among the list of items that Peel asked his wife and family to send him during his first few weeks at the front were writing paper and envelopes, two pairs of thick drawers, several pairs of calico drawers, tobacco, cigarettes, matches and socks, Euthymol toothpaste, a bottle of Tenax and a couple of pipes ('badly needed'). On top of all these, he received plenty of unexpected deliveries as well – chocolate and newspapers from his mother, a Harrods hamper from his in-laws and a handkerchief and several pairs of socks from his sisters Helen and Ruth.

But despite the constant stream of deliveries, Peel still found himself running out of provisions. In one letter he lamented his lack of tobacco:

> *I HAVE NO JOHN COTTON!!! & cannot get it here – cigarettes also getting low – I hope Helen has another couple of pairs of socks for me. The last lot were absolutely perfect but the ones of the very soft wool, though delightfully comfortable, won't stand the wear.*
>
> *I am very busy. Not at all unlike Private Secretary's work.*
>
> *So glad to hear my funny little family of Missus – Elizabeth – John & Mr Dog are flourishing.*
>
> *Very best love,*
>
> *Mister*

Of course, for the men at the front, the connection with those back in England was about more than just tobacco and toiletries. Letter-writing provided a means of escape from the reality of life in the trenches, and a reminder of family and friends at home – not to mention the country that they were fighting for. What in peacetime might have seemed trivial local gossip suddenly grew to be vitally important – proof that the world they had left behind still existed, and that they were not completely cut adrift. Captain Gore Browne, the commander of No. 3 Company, grew so used to the constant stream of letters from home that he struggled on days when none arrived. 'I do hate a day when there are no letters,' he wrote to his wife Imogen. 'I feel sort of injured when they do not come, which is very ridiculous of me.' Many of the Post Office Rifles were former postmen, but until now they had never quite appreciated just how precious a letter could be.

For most men at the front, the arrival of letters from home was seen as a blessing, and, like food parcels, new missives were often shared out among friends, so that everyone could enjoy the latest news from Blighty and the men could get to know each other's families. But for the junior officers, every letter their men wrote meant extra work, since it was their job to read and censor them, slashing out any militarily compromising information as well as sentiments that might be damaging to civilian morale. 'We spend hours every day censoring letters,' Peel complained to his wife. 'They are a perfect curse. I wish we had the spare time the men seem to have.' It was true that, for all the creature comforts the officers enjoyed, they often worked very long hours.

Peel wasn't the only one who found censorship distinctly trying. Second Lieutenant Gordon Stroud wrote to his father:

> *If you should come across a busybody who is dying to do something for the soldiers, ask her to send me parcels of 'Player's Weights' for my men. I have to censor all the correspondence of my platoon and I find that cigarettes are mostly what they require. The things I*

read in these letters are sometimes humorous, sometimes pathetic, but always, or nearly always, cheerful ... I get a deal of insight into their character and I read a deal of badly expressed sentimental nonsense.

Of course, as much as the censorship of letters was tedious for the officers, it was a source of great embarrassment to the men, knowing that their lieutenant had read their most private messages to their loved ones. But there was one way around this compromising situation, as Sergeant Archie Dunn explained to his wife:

This letter, you will note, is in a 'green envelope', known to us as the 'lovers' or 'married man's domestic troubles' envelope. We sign, on our honour, that they contain personal affairs only, and of course they are not censored.

The green envelopes were strictly rationed, at the rate of one per month, although they often changed hands unofficially, as some men found themselves in need of a little extra privacy.

It wasn't really true that the special envelopes weren't censored – their contents would still be checked by someone further along the line. But they did at least provide some anonymity, since the author and the censor didn't know each other, and would never have to look each other in the eye.

Monday 29th March. Paraded again at 7 AM, and went to Givenchy to finish digging a communication trench, had a very warm time and while at dinner a shell fell 20 yards away killing five Herts territorials. For once had a good dinner, but was spoilt owing to the horrible sight. We all arrived home safe at 5.15pm.

Diary of Corporal Thomas May

By Easter 1915, the Post Office Rifles had been in France for a fortnight and had witnessed their fair share of horrors. But so far they had been lucky and had escaped with only the most minor of injuries.

The men had settled into life in the trenches, and fears for their own survival no longer took up every waking minute. They had even grown used to the presence of the enemy only a few hundred yards away across no man's land. On Good Friday morning, when a German voice bellowed 'Have the Post Office Rifles got their hot cross buns?' they were able to laugh at it.

Some were even beginning to see war as something of a game. As Peel put it in a letter to his wife:

It's rather fun in the trenches when you are close up. You can hear the blighters singing and shouting the other side, and we and they put up caps and sticks and so on – you get a bullet plump through it at once.

There was little to enjoy about the Easter weekend, however. It was a miserable one, with almost 48 hours of rainfall. Pat Patterson was struggling with his responsibilities as an officer's servant, finding that trench life brought many additional challenges. Frequently he would get up early to prepare Lieutenant Croysdale's breakfast, only to find that Peel's servant Manning had already taken all the utensils.

Although as a batman Pat spent much of his time with his lieutenant in No. 4 Company, he had a close friend in No. 1 Company, which was holding a section of trench a little further along the line. Percy Weston had been a postman at Fulham Sorting Office and was engaged to marry Pat's youngest sister. The two had been mates for many years now, and Percy had followed Pat into the Post Office Rifles hoping that they would be able to serve together.

On Easter Saturday, while Pat was worrying about how to fix Lieutenant Croysdale's breakfast, Percy was on sentry duty at the fire step. Another rifleman was sitting by his feet, cleaning out the barrel of his gun. But the man had forgotten to take the load out of the breech before he cleaned it, and as his finger brushed the trigger, the rifle went off in his hand. The bullet went upwards and straight into Percy's head.

By the time Pat heard what had happened, it was already too late for Percy, the first casualty of the Post Office Rifles in France – not slain in a heroic battle with the enemy, but killed by one of his own friends in a horrific accident.

In the early evening of Easter Sunday, the riflemen were relieved and began the journey back to Béthune. But by now they had a little less spring in their step.

CHAPTER 3

FESTUBERT

—

Just a line in a violent hurry, darling, to say all is well.
We are in the trenches still, with a pretty stiffish battle
going on. This is the second day of it. We are in
support, and have come in for some heavy shelling, but
have been fortunate and not had a great many casualties
… It's beastly wet and I am up to the neck in mud, and
very dirty as water is much too precious to be used for
washing. Have at last seen many Germans, but only so
far as prisoners, wounded and dead. Am becoming
acclimatised to the horrors, which do not bear thinking
about. No need whatever for you to worry at all.

Letter from Second Lieutenant Home Peel
to his wife Gwendolen, 18 May 1915

AS THE DAYS GREW LONGER, and the wintry
weather began to subside, the French and British
generals began to plan for a new spring offensive.
Although the men from the Post Office weren't
privy to the detailed battle plans, it was obvious
that something was in the works. 'Events seem to
point to "something doing" shortly,' Sergeant
Archie Dunn wrote to his wife. 'It's all "spit and shine"

once again ... Parades, drills and inspections from generals downwards.'

Since they had arrived in France almost two months before, the Post Office men had spent plenty of time in the front line, but the situation had always been static, with no real prospect of advance. Now they began training for an assault, practising on a set of mock trenches that had been built behind the lines.

Allied and German trenches were constructed on the same basic pattern. Although on a map of the front they looked like reasonably straight lines, they were actually made up of a series of zigzags or crenellations. This not only reduced the potential impact of a shell exploding in a given section, but made it impossible for the enemy to use a captured machine gun to 'enfilade' a large number of men by firing down a trench in a straight line.

The art of 'trench-clearing' was to deal with one section of the zigzag at a time. First bombers would hurl hand grenades to take out as many of the enemy as possible, then their colleagues would rush in and shoot or bayonet the survivors. The process could then be repeated for the next section, and so on – until the attackers ran out of bombs, or out of bombers.

It didn't take long for the men from the Post Office to master the technique, although to begin with the new offensive went ahead without them. On 9 May, British forces went over the top at Aubers Ridge, in support of a French assault further south at Vimy. The attack was a disaster, with more than 11,000 casualties, and within a day the battle had been called off.

The failure was due in large part to the artillery bombardment of the German trenches that preceded the advance, which had delivered only a fifth the intensity of shellfire seen at the Battle of Neuve Chapelle three months earlier. According to *The Times*' war correspondent Charles Repington, who sent a telegram from the front soon after the battle, the cause was a dangerous shortage of high-explosive shells.

But despite the fiasco, the British were under pressure to keep trying, and were soon planning a second attack at Festubert. This was where the Post Office Rifles came in.

On 11 May, the Post Office men moved into a new section of the front lines, on a marshy plain a little further north than the positions they had occupied before. They passed by the ruined village of Festubert itself and gawped at the wholesale destruction. Houses were reduced to piles of rubble and the town's church had been almost totally obliterated, leaving only a crucifix standing in the middle of a bombsite.

The men from the Post Office advanced, under heavy German gunfire, to a position occupied by their old friends in the Shiny Seventh Londons. It was not technically a trench but a 'breastwork' – a wall of sandbags built up from the boggy ground, which was too wet to dig into safely. It was a foreboding place, and the riflemen didn't like the feel of it. Used to operating within the enclosed confines of a trench, it felt strange to be so exposed from behind. The men were widely dispersed along the length of the sandbag wall, and were anxious the Germans might see it as a weak spot. Corporal Thomas May and two other men spent the night walking up and down the breastwork, firing their rifles from different positions to give the impression of a larger fighting force.

But despite the men's misgivings, they were thrilled at the thought that they were actually going to advance. In a war that had long since become bogged down in trench warfare, any chance of movement was seen as an exciting opportunity. Home Peel's servant Manning had burned himself badly in a chip-fat fire and had been sent away for a fortnight to recover – but far from feeling relieved that he had escaped the front line at such a dangerous time, he was disappointed to miss out on the attack.

On Thursday 13 May, the men from the Post Office moved a little further down the line to a sector known as the Grouse Butts. Behind them, the British artillery began blasting the enemy positions opposite to prepare the way for the infantry – for two days, over 400 guns fired across a 5,000-yard front. The advance itself began at 11.30pm on Saturday evening, the first night attack of the war. It was initially very successful, with several stretches of German trench being taken, but once again the Post Office Rifles sat it out. Their job was to hold tight and wait for orders to move forward, while the Germans tried to blow them to smithereens.

The counter-bombardment unleashed by the enemy was devastating. Subjected to days on end of continuous shelling, the men from the Post Office suffered badly. As the shells rained down on them, churning up the soggy earth all around, the men and their equipment were spattered with heavy clumps of mud. They began to sustain losses at a rate unlike anything they had experienced before – within a week, a dozen had been killed, and many more seriously injured. As one of the men later wrote, 'Our casualties became very heavy and to see pals you have known and worked with for years wounded and killed, it nearly broke our hearts – especially when the dead had to be buried in a quickly dug hole.' Even for those not physically injured, the relentless bombardment had serious psychological effects – one rifleman lost his mind and ordered a tree to halt. When it didn't, he began firing wildly into the trunk.

Even men based far away from the front line were suffering from the effects of the bombardment. On the morning of Sunday 16 May, Pat Patterson was with his officer, Lieutenant Croysdale, billeted at an old brewery in what was left of Festubert itself. The building offered a good view of the landscape across no man's land, and had been commandeered as an artillery observation post.

That Sunday, Pat got up early to prepare Croysdale's breakfast. With him in the makeshift kitchen was Bert Storer, the batman to a tall and very nervy new officer, Lieutenant Cochrane. Pat was just starting on the cooking when he heard a colossal explosion as a shell burst just outside the building. A few moments later, it was followed by a second blast on the other side. Pat knew what that meant, but there was no time to run. Seconds later, the third shell arrived, bang on target, and the brewery took a direct hit.

Pat was briefly knocked unconscious and came round to find himself buried under a load of rubble. He had wounds to the thigh, hip and shoulder, but, finding that his legs still worked, he managed to wriggle out and begin the search for survivors. There was no sign of Bert or Lieutenant Croysdale, but he found the new officer, Lieutenant Cochrane, lying by a gap in the wall, barely conscious.

'For God's sake, get out of here, sir!' Pat shouted, pulling the lieutenant to his feet. Together they staggered out of the brewery and into the open, heading for a nearby dressing station. But, wounded and weak, they couldn't make it that far – Cochrane fell to the ground, and Pat collapsed on top of him.

The lieutenant's eye had been blown out of its socket, and there was blood streaming down his cheek. Pat fumbled in his breast pocket for some cotton gauze and pressed it down as hard as he could. He was vaguely aware of someone coming over to them from the dressing station and beginning to treat his wounds, and of being taken away to an ambulance. There was a figure on a stretcher beside him that he was sure was the lieutenant, and he heard a harsh snoring noise, followed by silence. That must be the death rattle, Pat thought to himself. He could hear the stretcher-bearers debating whether it was worth taking the other man further, given the danger they faced from continued shelling. But, in the end, they decided to press on.

Pat was taken to a Canadian general hospital at Le Tréport, arriving pretty battered and bruised – not to mention covered in dust from the shell-damaged brewery post. He was told that Lieutenant Croysdale had survived the shelling, as had Lieutenant Cochrane's servant Bert – both men were already on their way back to England.

Although Pat was pleased to hear that Croysdale had made it, he was sad that they would no longer be serving together. He had grown fond of his master and would miss him. But more disappointing was the fact that, with Croysdale out of the picture, Pat would lose his privileged status as a batman, and would have to be sent back to the ranks.

On Saturday last we were sent to take up a position in a trench which had been half captured ... so that the right of my company was up against the Germans in the same trench. Of course a barricade had been erected in the trench between us, but we were only 40 yards apart ... Naturally, they did not leave us in peace long.

Letter from Captain Wilfred Whitehead
to his father, 29 May 1915

While Pat was laid up recovering in a Canadian hospital, for the rest of the Post Office Rifles the hellish bombardment continued – and their real battle hadn't even started. After a week in the line they were ordered forward to relieve some Canadian troops who were occupying sections of a German trench, from which the enemy had withdrawn several days earlier. But just getting up to the new position was a terrifying prospect – normally, the forward lines on a battlefield were linked by communication trenches so men could move relatively safely between them, but the marshy ground around Festubert meant that a communication trench was impossible. Instead, the route up to the newly captured position was via something called the 'yellow road' – in reality, little more than a rough track with some canvas screens on either side so the enemy couldn't see when it was in use. The Post Office men went up in the dead of night, a single platoon at a time, doing their best not to attract the attention of the Germans. They were lucky to make it across in one piece.

Not that the position they were taking over was exactly a safe one. There were German strongpoints on two sides of them – one in front (in the direction of the enemy's second line) and one on their right-hand side, in a section of trench that hadn't yet been taken. This meant that they were actually sharing the old German front line with the enemy – although the section of trench between the Post Office men and the German troops had been blocked up.

It was an awful night. The Germans bombed them constantly from both strongpoints, and several times the men were ordered to stand to and perform rapid fire in anticipation of an enemy assault. But as if having enemy troops on two sides wasn't bad enough, they soon began receiving fire from British troops further back, who had evidently mistaken their position. Three runners were sent to tell them to stop and were killed on the way, before a fourth managed to get through and the firing ceased. But still the Post Office men were under constant bombardment from German bombers, and, having run low on bombs of their own, they were ill-equipped to retaliate.

Just before midnight, new supplies arrived from the reserve companies, including a batch of Battye bombs, primitive grenades containing an ammonal charge with a fuse sticking out of the top. The men began hurling them at the Germans. But before long the weather was adding to their troubles. A terrific storm broke and sheets of rain started pouring down on them, while forks of lightning lit up the sky. The roar of the thunder overwhelmed the explosions of the bombs and made the guns sound like little more than firecrackers. The men winced with every flash of lightning. Soon they were soaked through to the skin, and standing in several inches of water.

Those of a superstitious or spiritual bent began to wonder if they had brought the wrath of God down upon them. Others feared that their bayonets might be struck by the lightning and they would end up not blown to pieces but electrocuted. A feeling of panic began to grow.

As the remorseless exchange of bombs continued, the night seemed to drag on forever, and the drenched forces of the Post Office Rifles began to long for dawn. At last, when the sun finally broke across the horizon, the bombing slowly came to a halt. The storm had passed by as well, and the battlefield was eerily quiet.

It was Whit Sunday, 23 May, but there was little time for spiritual contemplation. The trench the Post Office men were occupying had been blasted badly out of shape, and there were wounded soldiers lying all around. The water filling the bottom of the trench had turned a muddy red.

The holy day went by relatively peacefully, but soon the Post Office men received new orders: the following morning an attack was to be made on the two German strongholds. While Canadian troops, assisted by some of the Post Office Rifles bombers, stormed the enemy position ahead of them, No. 2 Company, under Captain Wilfred Whitehead, would launch an assault on the stretch of trench to their right. Their job was to push on as far as the stronghold at the end of it, which contained an enemy machine gun that was preventing the Allied infantry from advancing further. It was exactly the sort of attack the men from the Post Office had trained for – working along an enemy trench, bombing and bayoneting their way through each section until they reached their objective. Now the time had come to put what they had learned into practice.

Between the Post Office Rifles and the German troops to their right was a 'double block', a pair of barricades with empty space between them, which created a sort of miniature no man's land that neither side normally dared enter. A little before 2am on Monday morning, the Post Office men scrambled over the first barricade, and then as quietly as they could, progressed along the empty trench towards the second, hoping that the Germans hadn't heard them.

When everyone was in position and ready for the attack, the bombers began hurling Battye bombs over the barricade. For a few seconds, they listened to the chaotic mix of explosions and screams of agony. Then it was time for them to meet the enemy face to face. 'Come on you pig-stickers!' called Lieutenant Basil Moon to his bayonet team, as he hauled himself up over the barricade.

Moon was a popular commander, well loved by the rank and file. On route marches back in England he had often ended up carrying two packs – his own and that of one of his men who was struggling. Now, with the same heroic selflessness, he led his men over and into an intense fight with the enemy.

The Germans put up heavy resistance, hurling their own bombs as they fell back, and the men from the Post Office began to sustain heavy casualties. But despite the stiff opposition, they continued to press on, clearing one section of trench and then moving straight on to the next.

As they pushed forward, the Post Office men saw the damage the British artillery – not to mention their own grenades – had done to the enemy. There were dead bodies everywhere. Some had been left leaning against the walls of the trench, their faces fixed in a deathly grimace, while others littered the floor, covered in hideous wounds. 'We found everything in a most loathsome state,' Captain Whitehead later wrote to his father. 'It was simply too horrible for words, walking along the trench over a floor of bodies, some of which had been there for weeks.'

But of more immediate concern than the German dead were the Post Office Rifles' own casualties. The further the men advanced, the more of them fell by the wayside, either killed outright or too badly injured to go on. Soon every yard gained meant another soldier down.

Most worrying, from a tactical point of view, was the loss of the bombers, without whom the attack could not continue. The bombing officer, Roy Hatsfield, was mortally wounded by a bullet to the groin, and it wasn't long before all but one of his men were out of action as well. Only Sergeant Charlie Tapsfield was left to hold off the Germans with his Battye bombs.

With just one bomber, it was clear the Post Office men could go no further. Captain Whitehead called a halt to the advance and ordered the survivors to start work on a new double block between themselves and the German forces. The conditions were far from ideal for construction work – as the men struggled to build the sandbag barricades, they were under constant attack from the enemy.

A message was sent back along the line: 'Send more bombs and bombers.' But by now it was daylight, and everyone knew it would be hard for any more men to get through. If something was to be done to hold off the Germans long enough for the men to complete the barrier, it was going to have to be here and now.

Impulsively, Lieutenant Moon grabbed a rifle from one of the men and hauled himself out of the trench up into the open. He began rushing along the parapet and picking off the German soldiers one by one. 'Number Five Platoon, out of the barricade,' he shouted. 'Follow me!' The men scrambled up after him, and they too began firing at the enemy for all they were worth.

Moon's brave attack bought his men some time, but it cost him dearly. While he was firing on the Germans, a bomb exploded in the air right in front of him, blasting off the lower part of his face. It was all his comrades could do to get him back into their section of the trench.

At last reinforcements arrived, in the shape of a trio of Canadian bombers who helped hold the Germans off a little while longer. It was enough for the men from the Post Office to finish building their barricades – they were safe from the Germans, for now. In the day's brutal fighting, the riflemen had advanced about 250 yards, but they hadn't yet managed to capture the machine gun. That would have to wait for a second attempt.

In the meantime, there were the wounded to deal with. One man had been set alight in the attack and had suffered horrific burns all over his body. He moaned and gasped on the floor of the trench as he waited for medical attention. Many others were in an equally serious state.

Despite the horrific injury he had sustained, Lieutenant Basil Moon was still clinging on to life, although no one – least of all the lieutenant himself – believed that he could do so indefinitely. Right up to the end, he was the model of a conscientious young officer. When he needed the toilet, he begged some of his men to carry him to the latrine as he couldn't bear the thought of soiling his uniform. That afternoon, with great effort, Moon managed to scrawl a short note for Captain Whitehead, apologising for being put 'out of action'. They were the last words he ever wrote, and he died not long afterwards.

The assault had left the company with over 20 dead and many more seriously wounded. But not all the deaths were readily explained. Rifleman Weaver had perished mysteriously, without a single mark visible on his body. Whether he had suffered a heart attack, or brain damage from the force of continuous bombing, nobody knew, but such cases had been heard of before – in time, the phenomenon would come to be known as 'fatal shell shock'. The following day, Sergeant Tapsfield, the bomber who bravely held out when all his fellows had been killed or wounded, was found dead in exactly the same way.

The Post Office men settled into their newly captured trench, determined to hold it until they were relieved, since taking it had cost them so dearly. But the Germans continued to hurl bombs at them from the other side of the double block, and they were reaching the end of their tether. To make matters worse, the supply of water had all but run out, and the sun was beating down on them mercilessly. Captain Whitehead wrote to his father:

We remained the whole day without food or water, for we had had to leave everything of that sort behind us, and it was impossible to get anything up to us during the day. Everything had to come about 300 yards across open country from our old first-line trench now the support trench. So we simply had to parch in the blazing sun and make the best of it, doing what we could, weary though we all were, to put the trench into decent order.

That afternoon, Whitehead received new orders: he was to push on again after nightfall and take the remaining 250 yards of trench leading up to the machine gun. But looking at the exhausted, shaken men around him, none of whom had received food or water all day long, he could see they were not up to the task. He wrote back at once requesting that fresh troops be sent forward to make the attack – his own men, dedicated and brave as they were, were not in any fit state to attempt it.

Fortunately, Colonel Harvey, the officer commanding the battalion, took Whitehead's words seriously and agreed to send one of the other companies to take their place.

It was gone midnight when No. 2 Company was finally relieved, after almost 48 hours in the thick of the action. While Whitehead and his men returned to the support line, via the alarming canvas-shielded 'yellow road', No. 1 Company took over in the German trench. Soon they were making their own attempt on the machine gun – and the result was pretty much the same as before. Again, some ground was gained, at a heavy cost, but the men were unable to make it all the way – they ran out of bombs before they had reached the stronghold and were forced to double block and consolidate.

The Post Office men were another hundred yards closer to the machine gun, but it was still out of range of their bombers. That evening, No. 1 Company tried its luck again with a fresh supply of bombs, and managed to push even further along the trench, but at midnight they were still 40 yards away from the stronghold when they were once again forced to halt and double block. By now the men of the new company were as shattered as their predecessors had been, and another 25 men were dead. Many more had been seriously wounded, while some were showing the early signs of shell shock.

The Post Office men back in the support line had their own problems to deal with. That evening, some nearby British and Canadian forces launched an assault on another stretch of the German front line. For the first time, the use of gas bombs had been authorised by the Allies, and the Canadians were carrying 200 of them to use on the German trenches.

The men from the Post Office had been trained for gas, although they had never put their training into practice. Their equipment was not exactly sophisticated – it consisted of a thick wad of cotton and some strips of fabric to tie it around the mouth and nose. In the event of a gas attack, the soldiers were to urinate on the wads before stuffing them into their mouths and tearing off a couple of plugs to put up their nostrils. Although it sounded both revolting and improbable, the scheme was scientifically sound – the ammonia in the urine neutralised the chlorine in the gas.

As the Canadians advanced, the gas alert was sounded, and the men began preparing their wads of cotton, lined up against the wall of the trench as if it were a public urinal. When the wads were duly soaked and stuffed into their mouths and noses, they waited for the gas to pass over.

Soon they heard the sound of the all-clear, and in relief they returned the cotton wads to their breast pockets. But 15 minutes later the alert was sounded again. For a second time, the men whipped out their wads and attempted the necessary preparations. But for many the previous effort had left them with nothing more to offer. As they anxiously willed their bladders to oblige, some men began to start whistling, hoping that this would help move things along –but given the crippling stress they were under, they found it didn't make any difference.

The situation was looking increasingly dire. Was it possible that men might really die just because they weren't able to pee on command? And, caught as they were in the midst of such a personal act, what kind of tableau would they present to anyone who stumbled across their bodies?

Fortunately, no one ever had to find out. After several increasingly anxious minutes of stressing and straining, the wind changed and the poison gas was blown in another direction. Once again, the men put away their wads of cotton – not to mention the rest of their 'equipment' – and breathed a hearty sigh of relief.

That night, Captain Whitehead's company was ordered back into the German trench to make another attempt on the machine gun. Brigade headquarters had given express instructions on how they were to capture their objective: 100 men would leap out of the trench in the dead of night and charge across open ground until they reached the stronghold, where they would engage the enemy and attempt to gain control of the gun. There would be no more trench-clearing, section by section, with teams of bombers and bayoneting – just a short, sharp dash across no man's land.

How the men of the Post Office Rifles would have welcomed another thunderstorm then, with cloudy skies and peals of thunder to disguise the noise of an attack. As it was, the night was perfectly clear, with a shining crescent moon casting a clear blue glow over everything. 'We'll be mown down in a minute out there,' muttered one rifleman to another.

Captain Whitehead was of the same opinion:

I went along and had a good look at the place from both sides, and came to the conclusion that to storm it with 100 men (which was all I was to have – 70 of my own and 30 from another company) in the

*bright moonlight would have been mere suicide – we
should every one of us have been wiped out by the
machine guns.*

Anxiously, Whitehead sent a message to his superiors,
requesting for a second time in as many days that they
modify their battle plans. But as zero hour for the
attack approached, his company had received no
reply. Unless the original order was officially
countermanded, they would have no option but to do
as they had been told and hope for the best.

At a quarter to one in the morning, the riflemen
gathered for the assault, the points of their bayonets
covered with handkerchiefs to prevent them from
glinting in the moonlight. They crept up to the edge
of the parapet and waited for the order to attack,
hoping against hope that it would never come.

Meanwhile, Colonel Harvey, who commanded the
battalion, was also waiting anxiously. He had passed
on Captain Whitehead's urgent request to brigade
headquarters, but so far he had heard nothing
back from them, and zero hour was getting closer by
the minute.

Seeing a messenger heading his way, Harvey sent
his adjutant, Tom Morris, out to meet him. The news
was just what everyone had been hoping for: the attack
was to be postponed until 8am the following morning,
and would follow a major artillery bombardment.
Breathlessly, Tom raced back to Colonel Harvey with
the new instructions, and a runner was dispatched to
the German trench to countermand the attack.

Many of the riflemen gathered for the assault that night had been telegraph boys before the war, but never in their lives had so much depended on a message getting through. As the minute hands on their watches crept closer to the hour, the chance of a reprieve was growing increasingly slim. They were beginning to make peace with the situation and readying themselves for the dash across no man's land, when – only a few moments before zero – the runner arrived in the trench, panting heavily.

The men rejoiced when they heard the news he had brought, scarcely able to believe that it was true – they knew just how close they had come to oblivion. As Corporal Thomas May wrote in his diary the following day, 'If this messenger had been two minutes later we would certainly have rushed to our doom.'

But the men from the Post Office were not quite out of the woods yet. With the attack rescheduled for 8 o'clock in the morning, the artillery bombardment was supposed to begin at 7.30. But, for some reason, the guns never did start firing. By 7.55 the men were once again in a state of abject panic. It seemed like they were destined for a suicidal assault after all.

This time their reprieve came not from their superiors, but from an even more surprising source: the enemy. A few moments before the attack was due to commence, the Post Office sentries began reporting a development that they were struggling to believe was really happening. On closer inspection, though, it turned out to be perfectly true: there was a white flag flying above the German stronghold.

As it turned out, the Germans had spent the night withdrawing most of their forces – along with the much-feared machine gun – leaving just a small crew, with orders to defend the position. But the 37 German soldiers, including one officer, who gave themselves up to Captain Whitehead had no interest in dying a glorious death. As far as they were concerned, they had already held out long enough.

Accounts of the surrender soon began to vary wildly. Whitehead himself claimed, in a letter to his father that was subsequently published in *The Times*, that he had personally stood upon the German parapet and demanded the enemy lay down their weapons. Most of his men remembered the event rather less heroically. Lieutenant Colonel Derviche-Jones, who wrote the battalion's first official history in 1919, believed that the Germans had actually surrendered in error, mistaking some British movement elsewhere along the line for the second prong of a massive combined assault.

At the time, though, the whys and wherefores scarcely mattered compared with the relief the men felt at knowing that the stronghold had finally been taken. The Post Office Rifles had won their first real victory in combat.

The men of the battalion were jubilant, and began scouring the captured positions for trophies to send home. Among the most popular souvenirs were the distinctive pointy helmets worn by the Germans. Bill Howell sent a particularly fine specimen to his mother in Willesden, packed carefully in an old biscuit tin.

While their trenches were plundered for relics, the German soldiers taken prisoner by the Post Office men had to put up with a certain amount of verbal abuse, not to mention a few obscene gestures. But not all of their countrymen were lucky enough to be taken alive. As Lieutenant Colonel Derviche-Jones put it in his account of the battle, 'Some enemy who were seen to be retiring provided interesting and useful target practice.'

My darling,

Just a line to say I am going strong and to thank you for your letter ... We are now reduced to about 500 men and only 11 officers all told. Maclehose, West, MacCabe, Moon, Hatfield, Russell, Noll all killed; Micky, Percy, Cochrane, Vince, Alexander, Gore Browne wounded; Brockman, Cook, returned with nerves gone, Davie sick, Guy at home, Mike and Powell still here but groggy. We really want to get away for a bit and have a complete reorganisation and re-fitting ... I have been highly mentioned by Maxwell for the last show, and he tells me to-day that I am to be mentioned in despatches. Not that I did much. But it was touch and go while it lasted – and by God! It was a little Hell on earth for a time.

Letter from Second Lieutenant Home Peel
to his wife Gwendolen, 30 May 1915

At long last, the Battle of Festubert was over. The men from the Post Office spent a final night in the German trench – the rank and file were so exhausted that the officers and NCOs performed the sentry duties so that they could get a few hours' sleep – before they were relieved by their old friends in the Civil Service Rifles and began to make their way out of the line.

Since the Post Office men had entered the front line two weeks earlier, 64 of them had been killed, and in the following days another six died from their wounds. To their colleagues in the reserve line, the men returning from the German stretch of trench seemed a shadow of their former selves. 'It was heartbreaking,' Corporal Thomas May wrote in his diary. 'The boys were knocked to the wide, and platoons who once numbered about 61 men have only about 14 left in some cases. The one consolation we have got is the PORs had earned a good name ... but this was done with a heavy cost.'

Every man of the battalion was shattered, from the top down. As Captain Whitehead explained to his father:

> *Several times I have not had time even to close my eyes for 56 hours, and once for 72 hours on end; so you must not blame me if, when I do get a few minutes quiet, I prefer to snatch a little sleep rather than write letters. In fact I can't help myself; if I sit down for a moment, I drop off to sleep at once, whether I want to or not.*

But despite their exhaustion, many did find the time and energy to write a quick note to their loved ones back home in Britain. Home Peel wasted no time in jotting off a letter to his wife Gwendolen to let her know that he was alright:

27.5.15

Darling,

No time for much. We are just out of the trenches after a pretty fair Hell of a time … The boys did very well in their first real trial. I was leading and was lucky. We had no sleep & practically nothing to eat & water as precious as diamonds. I'm fearfully fit, but deafened by a bomb which burst near me. Have just had a long sleep & wash & shave. Maxwell & I are all the officers left in our Coy. now. Such is war! … Bless you, darling – Don't worry about me. I'm all right. We are hoping for a real rest now. If we get it, I will write a better letter.

Your loving Mister

On 9 June, the men were able to wash themselves properly for the first time in over a month, when they were given a cold-water bath and a set of clean underwear. Many of them were lice-ridden, having worn the same clothes for six weeks. In the trenches, the only remedy for such an infestation was to run a candle along the seams of your clothing, listening out for the gentle popping sound as the insects were burned to a crisp. But however often the men performed this procedure, the lice always seemed to come back.

Once all the men were clean and free of vermin, it was time to take stock of what they had achieved. 'I can't say how well everyone did,' wrote the battalion's commanding officer Colonel Harvey. 'There are innumerable heroes under most trying and exhausting conditions.'

Some heroics were soon rewarded. Thomas May was promoted to sergeant, and Home Peel was made a full lieutenant, as well as receiving the Military Cross. His citation in *The London Gazette* praised him for being 'conspicuous for his coolness and ability' throughout the final two days of the battle.

Distinguished Service Medals were awarded to three men: Sergeant Heather, a former clerk at GPO headquarters, Rifleman Mills, a postman in the City, and Sergeant Major Peat, a parcel deliveryman at Victoria. All three were highly praised in a breathless article published in the *Daily Express* – 'Fearless Fighters win three DCMs at Festubert' – with Peat in particular coming in for high commendation: 'Sgt Maj Peat led a bombing party against the Germans, apparently delivering his bombs with the dispatch and precision he had formerly displayed in his parcel work.' The paper also lauded Basil Moon, who it said had 'covered himself with glory' before his death.

Overall, the Battle of Festubert had been a success, if a fairly insignificant one. The Germans had been nudged a little further east, but the advance had achieved no real strategic advantage. The cost to the Allied forces had been more than 16,500 casualties. Meanwhile, in the larger battle at Vimy Ridge, the French had lost seven times that number.

The battle had also confirmed fears on the home front that the munitions crisis was costing soldiers' lives. Compared with the efficient industrial production of Germany, Britain simply couldn't produce the number of shells the artillery needed for its bombardments, meaning that advancing infantry were placed under unacceptable risk. Sir John French, the British Commander-in-Chief, felt so strongly about it that he had begun leaking information to *The Times*.

On 25 May, as the Battle of Festubert was reaching its final moments, the munitions crisis came to a head as well. The result was the collapse of Herbert Asquith's Liberal government, which was replaced by a new three-party coalition. Asquith made his greatest rival within his own party, David Lloyd George, the first ever Minister of Munitions.

The battle brought lasting repercussions for the Post Office Rifles too. They were no longer raw recruits, inexperienced in battle, or 'Saturday soldiers' filling in for the regular Army. The men from the Post Office had proved themselves in war and had suffered badly for it. For them, the Battle of Festubert was a watershed that would never be forgotten.

CHAPTER 4

I REGRET
TO INFORM YOU ...

—

I have never realised how valuable life is, and how thin the thread that connects it up with death. While living in a safe, luxurious life at home, in England, I had regarded death much in the same way as a knighthood or measles – occasionally someone I knew had it bestowed upon them – but I'd never been in close acquaintance with it ... But now death doesn't seem a stranger: we've got to know each other well, and the more we meet the less we fear each other, though one always hopes the other will pass by. I've seen men full of life, and health, and happiness, and half an hour afterwards lying dead upon a stretcher; I've checked a man for being unshaven at a given time, and 8 hours afterwards have seen him put below 6 feet of clay muddy soil – and every time I knew that I might just as well have been the victim.

Letter from 2nd Lt Gordon Stroud to his father, published in *St Martin's Le Grand* – by the time the magazine came out, he had been killed in action

LIEUTENANT PEEL HAD COMPLAINED bitterly about censoring his men's letters, but it was far from the most onerous bit of paperwork for which a company's officers were responsible. Much more depressing was having to write the condolence letters that went out to a dead soldier's family at home, reassuring them that he had died heroically and without suffering, when often neither was the case.

To the Post Office men in the trenches, it was becoming increasingly clear that the fatal blow could fall at any time – and often at the most inopportune moment. Corporal Ernie Fulford was killed by a Minenwerfer mortar bomb in the act of tying up his boots – his friends found his body in two pieces, with the shoelaces still gripped in his hands. Even worse was the death of Lance Corporal Wally Kidman, a company bugler, who was sitting on the toilet when a shell landed in his lap and exploded. Clearly, death had little respect for human dignity.

In most instances, the news of a soldier's death would be broken to his family by a telegram, followed by the Army Form B 104-82, which provided a few extra details including the time and cause of death. So the purpose of the officer's letter was not really to 'inform' an unsuspecting relative – although they frequently began 'I regret to inform you' – but to try to find a way of softening the blow of bereavement. It was a difficult job, especially in the aftermath of an engagement like the Battle of Festubert, when each officer had to write dozens at a time.

The Post Office Rifles were more familiar than most units with the correspondence that surrounded a death. The former postmen had delivered their fair share of condolence letters, while every messenger boy had at times carried telegrams bringing news of a death in the family. Now, just as wives and parents up and down Britain had learned to fear the tread of a messenger's boot on their doorstep, men at the front who had brothers serving in other units had grown to dread the same devastating news.

In the front lines, the news of a family member's death in action was often delivered personally. Rifleman William Hill was passing through a communication trench with a group of Post Office men when he heard a sergeant from another regiment call, 'Anyone know Bill Hill in this mob?' When Bill identified himself he learned the reason for the sergeant's visit – his brother John had recently been killed in action. The sergeant had come to take Bill to where John's comrades had buried him, so that he could pay his respects.

At least Bill was near enough to where his brother had been serving for him to be able to visit the graveside. For Lieutenant Alfred Brooke, who joined the Post Office Rifles at the tail end of the fighting at Festubert, there was no such opportunity. Two thousand miles separated him from the Greek island of Skyros where his brother Rupert had been buried, having died on a boat in the Aegean Sea while he was on his way to Gallipoli.

To make matters worse, since Rupert was a famous poet, Alfred received the news of his death not through the Army's official channels but from the front page of *The Times*, which ran a glowing obituary penned by the First Lord of the Admiralty, Winston Churchill. Alfred was in Le Havre at the time, waiting for a troop train that would take him south to join the Post Office Rifles. Although his mother had attempted to warn him of the news before it went public, her message had failed to get through.

The two brothers had not always had the easiest relationship, ever since Rupert had bullied Alfred as a child. The younger sibling by three years, Alfred had grown up in Rupert's shadow, and even in adulthood his brother always referred to him by his slightly dismissive nickname, 'Podge'. When Alfred followed Rupert up to King's College, Cambridge in 1909, he found his brother was already a local celebrity, admired and indulged both for his outspoken politics and for his flamboyant performances in the theatre. For a quiet, thoughtful man like Alfred, it was an impossible act to live up to.

Growing up together, the two brothers had been close despite their differences. Their only other siblings were a much older brother, Richard, who had died when they were teenagers, and a sister, Edith, who hadn't survived beyond infancy. In adult life they had begun to drift apart, although Rupert had tried to persuade Alfred to transfer to the Royal Naval Division so that they could serve together. Rupert had remained fond of his younger brother, even if he never quite saw Alfred as an equal.

Alfred was a conscientious young man, and as soon as he heard that his brother had died his first thought was to write to their mother. Mrs Brooke knew that her two sons had never quite seen eye to eye, but Alfred was determined to dispel any anxieties she might have that there had been bad blood between them. From Le Havre he wrote:

> *The news came to me this afternoon like a nightmare, but I want to say this. In the past five years no family could have been happier than ours: no two brothers could have been better friends. Since this war I think I saw more of Rupert than I had before, & whenever we were at the same time in London we always lunched or we dined together. We never quarrelled in any way about anything & I, at least, always looked forward to seeing him in a way that I looked forward to seeing no one else. I can say no more except that I am proud to have had him as a brother – as you must be proud.*
>
> *We must, mother, look forward now & not backwards.*
>
> *With deepest love. ALFRED*

Alfred's letter was one of many that Mrs Brooke received in the wake of Rupert's death. Her son was the first real celebrity to be killed in the war and the great and the good of the literary world were soon queuing up to pay tribute, with everyone from Henry James to D.H. Lawrence publicly expressing their sorrow. The story of the young warrior-poet tragically slain before his time had a powerful ring to it, but for those who knew Rupert, the heroic Adonis celebrated by a nation in mourning felt far removed from the flesh-and-blood man they had known and loved, despite his many flaws.

Although his commitment to the Post Office Rifles meant that Alfred couldn't be with his mother in person, in his letters home he did everything he could to console her. 'It is as well that Rupert died before reaching the Dardanelles,' he wrote to her on 28 May. 'That landing must have been terrible and frightening ... not an experience to be desired on anybody.' In a way, Rupert had written his own kind of condolence letter too, in the form of his most famous poem, 'The Soldier' – a sonnet that had already offered solace to many families mourning a lost serviceman:

> *If I should die, think only this of me:*
>   *That there's some corner of a foreign field*
> *That is forever England. There shall be*
>   *In that rich earth a richer dust concealed;*
> *A dust whom England bore, shaped, made aware,*
>   *Gave, once, her flowers to love, her ways to roam,*
> *A body of England's, breathing English air,*
>   *Washed by the rivers, blest by the suns of home.*
> *And think, this heart, all evil shed away,*

A pulse in the eternal mind, no less
  Gives somewhere back the thoughts by England given;
Her sights and sounds; dreams happy as her day;
And laughter, learnt of friends; and gentleness,
  In hearts at peace, under an English heaven.

In France, Alfred had received a letter from his godfather Robert Whitelaw. 'I shall always think of you and Rupert together – a living pair not to be sundered,' Whitelaw wrote. Now sundered the two brothers were, although it wasn't for long. Eight weeks to the day after Rupert had died, a Post Office messenger boy, in his traditional blue-and-red uniform, was once again treading the gravel path up to Mrs Brooke's house in Rugby. In his hand the young lad held a telegram:

Regret to inform you that 2nd lieu W.A.C. Brooke 8 London Regt was killed on 14 June. Lord Kitchener expresses his sympathy.

Alfred, too, had died unexpectedly, blown to pieces by a German shell while he was sleeping.

The loss of the last of her four children sent Mrs Brooke into a spiral of grief. Once again, of course, she was deluged with letters of condolence. 'I pray you may find comfort in the splendour of your sacrifice,' wrote one of Rupert's fellow poets, Lascelles Abercrombie. 'There is nothing nobler in England today than your sorrow.' Meanwhile, a friend of the boys from university, Steuart

Wilson, wrote with sympathy from himself and his half-brother Hugh:

> *Cambridge & Kings particularly are full of ghosts for me, & I fear they will soon be so full that I shall feel more at home among the ghosts than I do among the living. You know how much Hugh loved and admired your sons, and I can say for both of us that no two brothers' deaths could hurt us as much as Rupert & Alfred.*

But perhaps the most touching letter of condolence that Mrs Brooke received came not from an old friend or a family member, but from someone who had barely had a chance to know Alfred at all – Jim Webster, a fellow officer in the Post Office Rifles. The day after Alfred died, Webster wrote:

> *Dear Mrs Brooke,*
>
> *It is with deepest regret that I have to inform you of the death of your son Alfred, who was killed yesterday in the trenches in front of Vermelles. He had gone up to the trenches with a view to being instructed in the use of the machine gun, and he was lying down under cover (it is supposed he was asleep) when a shell came over killing him instantaneously. Our machine gun officer, who was with him, was badly bruised and shaken and is suffering from a severe shock.*
>
> *I wish on behalf of my brother officers and myself to express to you our deep and respectful sympathy with you in the great affliction which has now befallen you for a second time in the space of a few months. In so*

great a sorrow it would be presumptuous on the part of a stranger to offer any words of consolation; but I think it may be a source of some little gladness to you in after days to know how much your son was liked by all the officers in the battalion. When he came to us at Abbots Langley for a few days before the battalion moved abroad his charm immediately won all hearts, and when he rejoined us out here, there was a struggle on the part of every company officer to secure him for his company. We were all very glad in No. 3 Company when he was assigned to us, but to our great regret he was a few days ago taken from the Company to be reserve machine gun officer, and in that capacity met his death … We buried him this afternoon in the little cemetery behind the trenches which has been used by the brigade. Tomorrow evening my Company goes into billets close by, and we shall see that the flowers which have been planted on his grave are watered and that the grave itself is properly cared for.

With deepest sympathy from all of us,

Yours sincerely,

J. A. Webster

Lieut.

CHAPTER 5

KILLING TIME

—

This trench warfare is very mysterious. The two sides sit in two holes. Both work hard at their respective holes. We make no attempt to stop them making their hole stronger and they do not try to stop us. But – this is what puzzles me – why should we who want to push them back let them go peacefully making it much more difficult for us to do so?

Letter from Captain Eric Gore Browne
to his wife Imogen, 4 August 1915

BY THE LATE SUMMER OF 1915, the Post Office Rifles had settled into a new routine in the Maroc sector, not far from the mining town of Loos-en-Gohelle. After the ordeal of Festubert, it was a period of relative calm, and the men were concerned mostly with trench digging. Every night after darkness fell, working parties were sent out to connect up saps (small, temporary trenches) dug by the French, construct new communication trenches and provide jumping-off points for a future Allied advance. Unfortunately, the ground in the area was very chalky and the walls of the trenches had a tendency to cave in while the men were digging them – so by the end of each night their hair would be white with chalk dust.

Loos was a coal-mining community and the paraphernalia of the local industry was visible all around. The Germans, who held the town itself, were also in possession of its most striking manmade landmark – a pair of twin pylons with a walkway between them, which the Tommies had christened 'Tower Bridge'. To the southwest of Loos, meanwhile, stood the imposing black forms of two giant slag heaps. From studying French maps of the area, the officers knew them as the 'double crassier'. By the time the name reached the men it had been bastardised to 'the cressies', while one rifleman was so impressed by the giant structures that he insisted on referring to them as 'the pyramids'.

In fact, the whole area around Loos was dotted with smaller slag heaps, which made a tempting target for the artillery on both sides – although such strikes achieved no military objective, the sight of a billowing cloud of coal dust was enormously satisfying. It was a quiet time – a lull between major battles – and many soldiers felt at a loose end. Scoring a direct hit on one of the slag heaps kept the gunners entertained.

The Allied generals had actually agreed an attack plan as early as 27 July, and it was pretty obvious – both to the British troops and to the Germans – that something was in the works, given the amount of digging that was going on in no man's land. But so far the Post Office Rifles had received no definite orders. In the meantime, the men existed in a kind of suspended animation, waiting and trying not to worry.

For some of the men, the free time offered an opportunity to settle old scores. Bill ('Tich') Howell was one of many riflemen nursing a grudge against their platoon sergeant, George Ward, a man who hailed from the southernmost tip of Cornwall but lacked the good nature for which his countrymen were famed. Ward was a tyrant, and he had it in for Bill, never missing an opportunity to pull him up on the flimsiest pretext. The men of the platoon hated Ward, and he wasn't much more popular among his fellow NCOs either. Corporal Chilmaid, a former postal sorter from Canning Town in East London, loathed him even more than Bill did.

It was Chilmaid who saw the opportunity for the men to get their revenge on Ward. The sergeant was a heavy drinker, and was often found propping up the bar in a local *estaminet* long into the small hours. One night after a battalion concert, Bill had retired to bed along with the rest of the company, when they were woken by the arrival of Corporal Chilmaid. In a whisper, the corporal told the men that he had seen Ward at an *estaminet* not far away, already much the worse for wear.

Under Chilmaid's instructions, the men got up and dressed hurriedly, following him to a grassy bank by the side of a cesspool, which was just across the road from the *estaminet*. They armed themselves with sodden clumps of earth and waited.

'Sergeant Ward, you are wanted in the orderly room!' Chilmaid bellowed, doing his best to disguise his voice.

A few moments later, the door to the *estaminet* swung open, and Ward was silhouetted in front of them, tottering slightly on his feet. The men of his platoon let him have it, pelting the drunken figure with their sodden clumps of earth. As he struggled to recover himself, they dashed back to their billets, and were in their beds 'asleep' within minutes.

The sozzled sergeant went storming off in search of the culprits, but instead found an innocent victim – a man by the name of Truelove who had got up to use the latrine. Truelove knew nothing of his comrades' act of vengeance, but before he could protest his innocence Ward had sent his glasses flying off his face.

The incident evidently left a lasting impression on Ward, since from then on he began treating the men differently. But Bill Howell hadn't finished with him yet. One day Bill was out in the front lines when he pulled on what he thought was a clump of grass on the lip of a shell hole. It turned out to be the hair of a dead French soldier, and Bill was shocked when a whole head came away in his hand. But he felt much better once he had decided what to do with it. 'I thought you might like a look at this, sir,' he commented chirpily, shoving the head into Ward's hands.

It took a moment for the sergeant to realise what he was holding. But as he stared dumbfounded at the blackened skin and lanky dark hair, the expression of sheer horror on his face was one that Bill would never forget.

We have just got five new officers – not from either the 2nd or 3rd Batt'n but from a Kitchener (4th Army) Battalion of the London Fusiliers. God knows why except that I suppose they have got such an enormous stock of officers that they have to be distributed somewhere.

Letter from Lieutenant Home Peel
to his wife Gwendolen, 25 August 1915

After the substantial losses at Festubert, the Post Office Rifles was well under strength, and new men had begun to be drafted from the Second Battalion in Sussex. But plans were now afoot to deploy the Second Battalion to the front lines en masse, so a Third Battalion was being formed to take over the training of new recruits. In the meantime, a large number of new junior officers had joined the Post Office Rifles from other units, and some of them were not entirely welcome.

At the time there was a lot of suspicion, both in the regular Army and in the Territorials, about Lord Kitchener's New Army volunteers. Their training had been very short by traditional Army standards and they were untested in battle – many believed them to be little more than amateurs. It didn't help that the New Army's 'Pals' Battalions, made up of men who knew each other in civilian life, were not always formed on a basis that inspired confidence. A unit of professional footballers was one thing, but a group of stockbrokers in uniform somehow didn't sound as impressive.

It was perhaps a little rich for the Post Office Rifles to hold such prejudices, since their own shared background was not exactly one to inspire terror, but they were far from alone in feeling sceptical about the quality of the new volunteers. Sir John French, the British Commander-in-Chief, was wary of committing the New Army units to the battlefield, although everyone knew that sooner or later they would have to be ordered to fight.

Thankfully, the rank-and-file recruits in the most recent draft of men were all genuine Post Office Rifles. Among them was Rifleman Walter Shewry, a boy of just 16. His elder brother Leonard had been with the battalion when war broke out, and Walter had been desperate to follow him, despite being underage. On his second attempt, in December 1914, he had managed to convince a recruiting sergeant to let him in, and had been sent to train with the Second Battalion in Cuckfield.

Where young recruits were concerned, the Territorial Army was a little more relaxed than the regular forces – boys could join at 17 rather than 18, although it was still against the rules for any young man to be sent abroad before his 19th birthday, apart from in exceptional circumstances. But Walter was far from unique in signing up underage. Up and down the country, keen young men were lying to recruiting sergeants about their ages, and the sergeants – whether out of sympathy for the boys' patriotic dreams or tempted by the two shillings and sixpence they received for every recruit they signed up – were waving them through. Contemporary estimates by the National Service League suggested that up to 15 per cent of volunteers were underage, some of them as young as 14.

Although some boys went to extreme lengths to fool the officials – producing the birth certificate of an elder brother or even fabricating a fake identity – it was rare that such measures were necessary. Boys were not generally required to prove their age in order to sign up, and for those who struggled with lying there was a neat workaround: they would write the number '18' on a piece of paper and slip it into their shoe. Then when they were asked if they were over 18, they could honestly answer, 'Yes, sir!'

Some families waved young sons off to war reasonably willingly – in a country where most children left school at 14 it didn't seem so strange that a boy of that age should want to join the Army. Others protested, but there was little they could do – since new recruits were rarely expected to prove who they were, a boy turned away from one unit on his parents' instructions could apply to another with a whole new identity, and if anything did happen to him on the battlefield, his family would never find out.

Walter Shewry's parents, like many others, expressed their disapproval at his decision, but they didn't do anything to try to stop him. He had signed up for the Post Office Rifles in the grip of patriotic fervour – as he put it, 'full of romantic ideas of charging the enemy with bugles blowing and Union Jack flying' – but what he found on the Western Front soon dampened his enthusiasm. The sight of enormous shell holes left by an enemy artillery barrage turned his blood cold as he realised just how easily he could be obliterated. On his first trip up to the line he was horrified at the sight of corpses littering the ground, their bodies contorted into grotesque shapes and their faces pale as ghosts. The men he was joining had long since grown used to such horrors and barely noticed them, but the sensitive young 16-year-old struggled to shake what he had seen from his mind.

Although Walter had maintained a pretence about his age throughout his training in Sussex, there was one man in the battalion who he couldn't fool when he arrived for active service in France: his brother Leonard. 'You bloody fool!' Leonard exclaimed angrily when Walter tipped up at the mining town of Noeux-les-Mines, only a few miles behind the front line. They were the only words that passed between the two brothers that day.

Walter had hoped that serving with his elder brother would bring the two of them closer, but it didn't work out that way. Leonard was attached to the signals section, so they rarely saw each other, and when he did come to pay Walter a visit there always seemed to be a gulf between them. Neither brother was able to express how he was feeling – Walter couldn't bring himself to share his horror at the realities of trench life, and Leonard's fears for his little brother's safety were beginning to drive him to distraction. The time they spent together was utterly miserable.

One night, after laying wires in the pouring rain, Leonard contracted rheumatic fever and was sent home to a London hospital to recover. The illness was a blessing in disguise – back in England he was able to persuade his parents to write to the War Office and request that Walter be removed from the front lines. The younger Shewry soon found himself working as a runner and general dogsbody at brigade headquarters. There was nothing he could do about the transfer – and secretly he felt rather relieved. His brother had saved him from a terrible mistake that he should never have been allowed to make in the first place.

This morning we did battalion drill in a stubble field and I drilled the battalion from my chestnut steed while Morris and the C.O. stood by criticising. I enjoyed it very much. Jim Webster was sternly critical afterwards. We call him the Field Marshal. He asserted

that I gave several unheard of commands, to which I indignantly replied. I really love old Jim – he is the worst soldier God ever made, but an unending source of humour to me.

Letter from Captain Eric Gore Browne
to his wife Imogen, 19 August 1915

Another recent arrival in France was Captain Eric Gore Browne, a 29-year-old former barrister who had been with the Post Office Rifles since 1914 but was relatively new to the front lines. On his first visit to the trenches in the spring he had been injured by a stray German bullet, and when the wound turned nasty he had been sent back to England to recover. As a result, he had missed out on the Battle of Festubert, and was only now getting to grips with life at the front.

Gore Browne was a very sociable man and lost no time in getting to know everyone. He enjoyed the cheerful banter of the officers' mess, and soon found himself included in the gentle ribbing that went on between the captains and lieutenants. His fellow officers enjoyed nothing more than winding each other up – and no target was more popular than their immediate superior, Major Maxwell. One day, Gore Browne found Maxwell 'quivering with rage' because he had been allocated an inferior billet, despite his seniority in rank. The story, as he related it to his wife Imogen, amused him enormously:

It has happened that Maxwell finds himself billeted on a lady of evil repute who has a very dirty house and is herself both dishonest and unattractive. The Battalion has been here before and Maxwell's view was that he had every claim to the best billets always in spite of the fact that on their last visit here, other people had to put up with the place he is in ... What a man! Jim and Vince shrieked with laughter behind me – while I tried to comfort him. They had been the victims on the last occasion and rejoiced to think of the major landed properly this time!

Captain Gore Browne had not been at the front long before he was transferred to Lieutenant Peel's company. They clashed almost immediately. While Gore Browne was outgoing and jovial, still brimming with raw enthusiasm for the war, Peel was a thoughtful, solitary man, a pessimist with a sardonic sense of humour. 'I do not find him easy,' was Gore Browne's initial assessment, and closer acquaintance did nothing to improve matters.

In almost every respect, the two men were chalk and cheese. Peel had worked as a civil servant before the war, and although he got on well with his men, he felt most at home pondering logistics from behind a desk – in the parlance of the time, he wasn't 'clubbable'. Gore Browne, on the other hand, had been a junior barrister and was naturally gregarious. He took every opportunity he could find to go out horse-riding with his fellow officers, and share with them his hopes for the future – his dream was to buy a cottage in the countryside where his family could live after the war. 'All the young married men (except Peel!) go off quietly together to talk about their wives and homes,' Gore Browne told Imogen in one letter.

Peel was a devoted family man as well, as is clear from his letters to his wife Gwendolen. But he was also very private, and preferred not to mix business and pleasure. To Gore Browne, he seemed aloof and unapproachable. 'Peel is capable, there is no doubt of that,' he explained to Imogen, 'but he is unlovable – I think that sums him up for me and you know the sort of men I like.'

It was little surprise that the two officers soon began rubbing each other up the wrong way – and by 10 August, things had come to a head. 'Home Peel and I decided yesterday that we could not bear each other or Maxwell any longer and should dine out,' Gore Browne told Imogen. He asked one of the other officers, George Alexander, if he could come and dine with him instead that evening. But the plan was not exactly a success. 'When I got there I found Peel had done the same thing!' Gore Browne explained. 'And there we were again.'

It didn't help that Peel and Gore Browne were soon in the running for the same job. The gaps left by the high number of officer casualties at Festubert meant that there were plenty of opportunities for promotion – and equally for bitterness and resentment when men didn't get what they were hoping for. Amid the life-

and-death drama of the war, such jostling for position might seem rather petty and blinkered, but potential changes to the chain of command always weighed heavily on the officers' minds.

At the time, vacancies were trickling down all the way from the top. The First Battalion's second in command, Major Hood, had been promoted to lieutenant colonel, with a view to taking over command of the Second Battalion in England. Maxwell was earmarked for Hood's old role, but the question of who would take over Maxwell's No. 4 Company was a vexed one. Maxwell himself had told Peel that he wanted him to have it, while Colonel Harvey had given Gore Browne the impression that the company was his.

The cogs of the Army hierarchy turned slowly, and a hitch at one level could lead to delays for everyone below. It transpired that Hood's promotion hadn't gone through in time for him to command the Second Battalion after all, since another officer, Lieutenant Colonel Preece, had slipped in just before him. Understandably annoyed, Hood travelled back to England to discuss the situation with the head of the Territorial Force Association, and was offered the new Third Battalion instead. But the delay had only served to make the officers further down the chain of command even more impatient to find out about their own positions. Maxwell was fed up of waiting for his transfer to battalion headquarters to come through, and Gore Browne and Peel were anxious to know who was going to get his job when he left.

The situation was further complicated by the fact that Tom Morris, who had served as the Post Office Rifles adjutant since before the war, was beginning to get itchy feet himself. Gore Browne was sympathetic – 'he feels so much the fact that nearly all his friends and contemporaries in the Rifle Brigade are high up on the staff or commanding battalions,' he told his wife Imogen. So, added to the mix was the possibility that Morris's job at battalion headquarters would soon be up for grabs as well – a prospect much more tempting than No. 4 Company.

Eventually, the situation was resolved. Maxwell departed for headquarters as expected, Gore Browne was given No. 4 Company, and while Tom Morris stayed put for the time being, Peel was offered the job of assistant adjutant, with a view to taking over from Morris at some point in the near future. The solution was a tidy one, and it suited Peel to a tee – as a former civil servant, taking charge of the battalion's admin was something for which he was extremely well qualified. But it did little to improve relations between Peel and his fellow officers, since both Eric Gore Browne and Guy Portman, the current assistant adjutant, were distinctly put out. 'There has been a good deal of heart-bashing,' Peel explained to his wife Gwendolen:

> *Gore Browne really has no case, as he got No. 4 Coy, & ought to be jolly glad to have such a fine Coy. Guy on the other hand had acted as Asst. Adjutant for some time, and was not particularly tactfully handled, so has*

been very sick. Both of them are perfectly all right to me about it, but it has been a little inclement for a bit.

With the issue of the promotion behind them, the officers tried to enjoy the period of relative calm as best they could. For Gore Browne that meant plenty of horse-riding, dinner with fellow officers, and enjoying the small luxuries he received in the post from home. He told his wife Imogen contentedly, 'I am writing this letter in my little sitting-room with the sun streaming in at the window and Purnell has just brought me tea – your delicious China tea – bread and butter and strawberry jam and cake. So I am doing very well.'

Peel's letters to his wife Gwendolen, meanwhile, were beginning to include increasingly complex requests. Where once he had asked for little more than tobacco, socks and stationery, now he demanded obscure reading material: 'Do you think you could get me Richard Garnett's *The Twilight of the Gods?*' he asked her in one letter. In another, he sent her out shopping for a refill for his Drilux lamp. 'It comes from a man called Stewart next door to Charing Cross Post Office,' he informed her helpfully. And the chores didn't end at shopping, either – Peel also begged his wife to visit some of his men who were convalescing in London, among them Sergeant Major Peat, the bomber and former postie whose delivery of explosives to the enemy trench had been praised in the *Daily Express.* 'You might look in especially on Peat, who is a splendid fellow,' Peel told Gwendolen. 'Give him all my best messages, & also to any of our other chaps – with some tobacco, papers, cigarettes, etc. or whatever they would like.' For poor Gwendolen, keeping up with her husband's errands must have seemed like a full-time job, but she evidently completed the tasks with diligence.

Such was the efficiency of communication between England and the Western Front that there was no need for a soldier to feel cut off from his responsibilities at home, as long as a willing family member could act as a proxy. But even so, Peel seemed unusually concerned with matters back in England, especially given the demands of his job in the Army. In another letter, he barely gave any news of himself at all, but requested an even more involved favour:

My darling,

I have no time for a real letter. This is just on a point of business. One of the women in your district is MRS COTTON, 109 FENHAM ROAD, PECKHAM. She is the wife of Maxwell's servant, who also does all our cooking and runs our company mess – Old Cotton is one of the very best and I would do anything I could for him. Mrs Cotton is paralysed and has a son who apparently has some tubercular trouble. He is about 11 years old, I think. He has now become so bad that the doctor won't let him go to school and has said he should go to the country. He also has to have beef tea, milk, brandy etc. and to live out of doors. Cotton is writing to tell his wife to take the boy to the country. But the trouble is about money – she draws through the War Office

Cotton's Post Office pay, 23 shillings a week, and she says that the W.O. won't pay it unless she goes for it herself each week. Otherwise you have to leave it till you can fetch it. She can't get in without having the money weekly. So the problem is to see if it is true that the W.O. won't allow some arrangement to be made in a case like hers for somebody to draw the money on her behalf. I should think they would – otherwise I would gladly advance the money till she comes back from the country and can claim it. Could you please see to this as soon as you can? I'm very sorry for them, and he's such a good chap. We are just out of the trenches, and in Brigade Reserve and I've had a gorgeous wash. Will write properly to-morrow.

Best love to you all,

Your loving Home.

If anyone was to help out the Cotton family, one might expect it to have been Major Maxwell, given that Cotton was his servant, not Peel's. But for whatever reason, it was Peel who had taken up the cause. Less than 24 hours later, he wrote to his wife again about Mrs Cotton's predicament. 'I hope you will be able to manage it all right,' he told her anxiously. 'I've told old Cotton that everything possible will be done, and anyhow that I will advance the money if there is any difficulty. So, if there's any hitch, will you please let Mrs C. have the money.' However cold and aloof Peel may have seemed to Gore Browne – and however frustrating to his devoted wife Gwendolen – his desire to help others ran deep.

Gore Browne was focused on good deeds of a different kind, and his attention was very much with the men at the front. He began to throw himself into organising entertainment for them, beginning with a cricket match between the Post Office men and their old friends the Civil Service Rifles. A few days later the battalion played a nearby French regiment at football and won 1–0. The French didn't seem too disappointed – after the match, two of their lieutenants, who had insisted on playing in full uniform, invited Gore Browne back to their billet, where they polished off three bottles of champagne. 'I knew not how to gulp mine down and I did feel very dizzy when I came out,' the captain later confessed. High on the intoxicating bubbles, the French soldiers told him that they were certain the forthcoming battle would be a great success, and for the time being Gore Browne was inclined to agree with them.

And yet still, after so many weeks of digging, the promised battle hadn't come to pass. At times it was almost possible to forget that there was a war on after all, or to hope that the peaceful lull might last forever. In one letter to his wife Imogen, Gore Browne wrote:

> *We dug till 1 AM, a lovely starlit night. A very big fire behind the German lines lit up everything. The ruined houses in no man's land, the German trenches and ours. It was a very wonderful sight with the star-spangled sky above and occasionally a shell bursting in a ball of flame. I lay on the parapets beside the trench we were digging in perfect safety and looked at it all and*

*wondered over the mystery of war. It was too good a
night to fight and war has a great deal of beauty in it.
I looked at the stars and liked to think that you could see
them from your window at Gracedien.*

On 15 September, the battalion enjoyed an open-air
concert, with a piano dragged out into a nearby field
and a small stage set up for ragtime dancing. It was
a beautiful late summer's evening, and the songs
included such popular favourites as 'Why Did I
Join the Army?' and 'MacNamara's Band', while a
French soldier gave a rousing rendition of the
Marseillaise. One of the riflemen performed a
brilliant impersonation of a particularly unpopular
brigadier, and the evening was rounded off with 'God
Save the King'.

To the men of the Post Office Rifles, life seemed
good. But they knew it couldn't stay that way forever.
Before long, they would once again be called on
to fight.

CHAPTER 6

LOOS

—

I want you to understand as much as I may tell you of what is going to happen. There are going to be great doings here and hereabouts and it will probably happen that for 3 or 4 days we shall not be able to get any letters off or to receive them unless we are very lucky. Our part in the business is a very tiny one but it is a great thing for us even to take a share in it. I'm not going to ask you not to be anxious because I know you will be – as I shall be too.

I am happy in my own mind about it all and it will be a very great privilege to have taken part in what I hope we are going to do successfully.

Letter from Captain Eric Gore Browne
to his wife Imogen, 20 September 1915

THE BATTLE OF LOOS was set to be the largest Allied offensive of the war so far, and the planning and preparation were meticulous. On a railway embankment near the village of Haillicourt, several miles behind the lines, the distance between the British and German trenches had been taped out, so that the men could practise running across it. They were also encouraged to familiarise themselves with the geography of the ground they would soon be taking, thanks to a detailed scale model large enough for whole companies to walk across it. Every feature of the landscape was represented in miniature – bricks for houses, a sprinkling of chalk to show the trench lines, and small piles of coal to denote the slag heaps. As the men walked up and down, intently inspecting all the details, they looked disconcertingly like visitors at that most twee of English attractions – the model village.

The plan of attack was divided into two stages, and it was the first of these that concerned the men from the Post Office. On the morning of 25 September, there would be a two-pronged assault on the German trenches in and around Loos. The 141st Brigade would attempt to take the town itself, while the 140th (of which the Post Office Rifles made up a quarter) would attack the trenches to the southwest, as well as the vast double crassier, and allow the British line to pivot round eastwards. The advance in the Post Office men's sector would begin with an assault by the Cast Iron Sixth and Shiny Seventh Londons, and they would follow them over the top a few hours later.

Assuming all went well on Day One, Day Two would see new units pushing through the captured lines in an attempt to make further gains. Among them were battalions from Kitchener's New Army, about to make their debut in battle, under the command of General Douglas Haig.

The British Field Marshal, Sir John French, was far from sanguine about the role the New Army units were to play. But despite his misgivings, he agreed that, as long as all went well on Day One, and the German lines were sufficiently weakened, he would release the new men to Haig's command on Day Two so that they could participate in the second phase of the offensive.

There were high hopes riding on the battle. The idea was that a major push at Loos, coupled with a French offensive in the Champagne region, would break through the stalemate on the Western Front, forcing the Germans back out of their trenches and kick-starting a return to a war of movement. Captain Gore Browne was optimistic, and impatient:

> *I hope that things are really coming to a climax this time. In all our previous shows there seems to have been one weak link that has broken the whole chain and I wonder if all our past experience and failures will make our staff so provident that there is no opportunity for failure. I hope we shall soon stamp on the Hun but I am sure we are right to go very slow and not move till we have all the men and munitions that can be possibly wanted.*

This was actually quite a tall order, since munitions were still a major problem for the Army. On 21 September, the preliminary bombardment began, with 500 guns firing a quarter of a million shells. The figures sounded encouraging, but because the front was so broad – the largest in the British Army's history to date – the ratio of shells to yards of German trench was actually lower than it had been at Neuve Chapelle six months earlier.

From the position of the British soldiers, however, the bombardment was extremely impressive, and it provided a powerful boost to morale. Gore Browne marvelled at the heavy guns he passed on his way back from a visit to the trenches:

> We walked right through two of our batteries in action, an 18lb battery and some howitzers. I had never been so close to guns in action before. They are so concealed that from a few yards away you would never know of their existence, then a sudden burst of flame and the roar of the departing shell and a noise that goes right through your ears while the air for 20 yards around seems to collect in a heavy mass and bang you in the chest. It was very interesting indeed and sometimes I think I should like to have been a gunner. There is more romance about the other branches, but it is the one that wins battles in the end I think.

The bombardment at Loos was unlikely to win the battle, but fortunately the Army had another trick up its sleeve – something referred to enigmatically as 'The Accessory'. It was actually chlorine gas, and for the first time ever it would play a major role in the British preparation for an advance. Five thousand cylinders of gas had been produced, along with a series of 10-foot pipes that would be thrown out of the trenches to distribute it. As long as the wind cooperated on the day – the prevailing wind in the area blew towards the Germans – it would provide a substantial advantage.

By now, the British troops were well prepared for gas warfare, and were equipped with the latest technology. In place of the urine-soaked cotton wad was a brand-new gas mask known as the Phenate Helmet, which was distinctly sinister in appearance. It looked like a hessian sack draped over the head, with two round glass eyepieces and an exhaust valve coming out of the mouth, which attached to a bag made of rubber. A soldier wearing the mask bore an uncanny resemblance to the figure in Edvard Munch's *The Scream*.

Not everyone was convinced by the new gas masks. Captain Gore Browne declared them 'excellent', but Sergeant Archie Dunn was more sceptical. In a letter to his wife, he described the Phenate Helmet as:

> *a flannelette contrivance soaked in a repulsive solution, which we completely placed over our heads and tucked into the necks of our tunics; we breathed out through a mouthpiece flap, which made rude noises, there were two eye-pieces and we resembled the Ku Klux Klan.*

The new gas masks weren't the only piece of extra kit that had arrived in time for the battle. Some of the Post Office Rifles – among them Bill ('Tich') Howell – had been provided with the latest telescopic sights for their rifles, as part of their training as snipers.

Sniping – or 'sharpshooting' as it was known at the time – was a new concept in the British Army. The

Germans had been doing it since the start of the war, generally employing former hunters and gamekeepers who had proven their skills in civilian life, but the British had taken a while to cotton on. To begin with, they had assumed that men shot dead from a great distance were the victims of random 'stray bullets'. It was only as the war became more static and entrenched that they realised the shots must be deliberate. But sniping was a hard concept for the British Army to get its head around – although the upper-class officers often had plenty of hunting experience, they tended to feel instinctively that using modified weapons wasn't playing fair.

It was not until May 1915, around the time that the men from the Post Office entered the line at Festubert, that the British War Office tendered the first contract to produce a telescopic sight for the Mark III Lee-Enfield rifle. A few months later the new equipment began to trickle down to the troops at the front line, and the sights were handed out to men who were known to be particularly good shots. Training was pretty much ad hoc, but the men soon began to master the basics, learning how to breathe in such a way that the rifle didn't move, and to estimate distance and wind speed in their heads. Some of the tips they were given were rather ghoulish – for example, rather than aim for the forehead, and risk a bullet whizzing over the target's head, they were trained to shoot for the teeth. That way, a small error either up or down wouldn't reduce the chance of a kill.

At just five foot one, 'Tich' Howell was scarcely an imposing warrior, but as a sniper he had found his forte, and he was personally credited with 30 kills. But despite his talent for taking out the enemy, he found his comrades were not always pleased to see him with his telescopic rifle in his hand. In the trenches, snipers moved freely from section to section, often waiting patiently for hours in a given position until they were absolutely sure of a target, and then suddenly firing on him. As soon as they saw their victim go down, they would leave the area as quickly as possible, before the enemy had a chance to retaliate – the shelling that ensued would invariably miss the sniper, but the men holding that section of trench would suffer. As a result, resentment grew towards the snipers, and for some the stream of abuse they received from the regular infantrymen was more than they could handle. After a brief stint as a sharpshooter, Jim Coleman begged to be transferred to another duty, and was delighted to be offered a job in the cookhouse instead. He found he made a lot more friends frying bacon than he had killing Germans.

The advance at Loos had been planned for the morning of Saturday 25 September, and the days leading up to it were filled with last-minute preparations. Weapons and shoes were inspected, while burial registration books were handed out to chaplains in preparation for the anticipated casualties. There were more dinners and concerts in the companies, with singing and moonlit card games continuing late into the night.

Gore Browne had been back and forth to the trenches again and again, making sure everything was ready for the attack. He had even marked out with little noticeboards the areas where the four platoons in his company were to gather, to help them find their way in the dark. On Tuesday evening, the captain made one last visit to the trenches to see that everything was in order:

> *It was a lovely moonlit night, the same strange lifeless scene that I know so well now, the dim lines of the Hun trenches and behind them the terra incognita which perhaps we shall know one day as well as we know these parts. Everything was ready and in good order and all arrangements made for our coming.*

With the fateful day approaching, the men from the Post Office began writing letters for their loved ones at home, well aware that they could be their last. Some took advantage of the popular green envelopes to make their messages that little bit more personal, while others expressed their hopes for the battle. Gore Browne attempted to reassure his wife Imogen. 'Everything possible has been done to make this thing a huge success,' he told her. 'I am going up tomorrow happy and hopeful that at last we as an army are going to show what we are made of.'

Once the battle began, the only form of communication the men would be able to send home was the field postcard – a kind of multiple-choice form on which a soldier could strike through whichever options didn't relate to him, from 'I am quite well' and 'I have been admitted to hospital' to the rather more frosty 'I have received no letter from you lately'. All the men were allowed to add to the printed text was a signature and date – if any personal message was included, the postcard would be destroyed. Sergeant Archie Dunn explained apologetically to his wife:

> We are not allowed to take letters, or any correspondence into the trenches, and we make much use of the Field post-card. So far, I am glad I am still able to strike through all thereon except: 'I am quite well'. I know you like to receive them, but naturally you prefer letters.

The postcards travelled faster than regular troop mail, and would normally reach their intended recipient within a day or two – and sometimes in as little as 12 hours. At Loos, Captain Gore Browne took a packet of them forward to provide regular reassurance to his wife Imogen that nothing awful had happened to him. Although impersonal, the cards brought great comfort, proving that – at least until recently – the sender was still alive. As Agatha Christie remarked on receiving one from her husband Archie, 'for all its meagre information ... it was a good omen.'

Before leaving for the front line, some of the Post Office men clambered up a slag heap in the town of Noeux-les-Mines to get a better view of the spectacular artillery bombardment. Others, meanwhile, witnessed rather less edifying sights. Rifleman Jim Coleman looked on sadly as the civilian population of North Maroc was forcibly evacuated. Although the move was for the people's own protection, the sight of women and children laden with all the worldly possessions they could carry was a depressing one.

Over the preceding months, the battle had been planned to the letter, but, as it turned out, the Army thought nothing of introducing a few last-minute changes. On Friday morning, less than 24 hours before the attack, Captain Gore Browne received an order that two of his officers, Second Lieutenant Maitin and Second Lieutenant Bounin, were to be left behind when the rest of the men advanced. There was sound reasoning behind the decision – keeping a handful of officers in reserve made it easier to rebuild a company in the event of truly catastrophic casualties. But neither the captain nor the young officers took the news well:

> *Maitin had tears in his eyes when I told him he was not to come – poor boy it is very hard on him. He has worked hard on our line and knows it backwards and his men like him, he is a great loss to me. The order to reduce came from high authority, and the CO, whom I dashed off to see, can do nothing to help. But did you ever hear such a thing? ... Ye gods! – I should like to have five minutes with the man who is responsible, and give him a bit of my mind.*

On Friday evening, the battalion gathered for an address by their commanding officer, Colonel Harvey, who told them sombrely, 'I know I can count on you all.' That night, they began the long march up to their starting positions for the battle – a five-hour trudge through white chalk trenches, the walls of which were already covered with graffiti. Among the scrawled names and the occasional cartoon was an inscription:

BERLIN 500 MILES →

But the men from the Post Office were not in the mood for humour. It was an unpleasant journey, through narrow and uneven trenches, and they soon began to grow tired of the trek.

A couple of hours in, the British artillery let rip with a terrific bombardment, followed soon after by the German reply. Lumps of metal whizzed over the heads of the men, and several of them sustained injuries. One man began to lose his grip on reality and started digging himself into the wall of the trench with his bare hands. A corporal gave him a slap around the face, which was enough to bring him back to his senses.

Finally, the Post Office Rifles reached their destination – the old front-line trench of the Allied forces. The Sixth and Seventh Londons, who were to go over the top in the battle's first wave, were already in place further forward, in one of the new trenches that the Post Office men had helped dig in no man's land.

Captain Gore Browne made some coffee on a little stove, and as dawn began to break, the rum ration was passed round to those who wanted it. Some young men who had never tried it neat before spluttered as they attempted to swig it down. But in the cold, misty morning they were glad of the extra warmth. Not every soldier preparing for battle was as lucky – a little further up the line, Colonel Sandilands, the abstemious commander of the Seventh Cameron Highlanders, ordered his sergeants to pour their battalion's rum away, declaring, 'If my men are going to meet their maker, they will meet Him sober!'

The gas brigades were already in the front-line trenches, making their final preparations. The previous night, General Haig had barely slept for worrying about the strength and direction of the wind. He took advice from the Met Office's finest operatives, who were collating information from over 50 sites. At three o'clock in the morning, they had recommended that the gas should be released as soon as possible.

It was 5.50am before the gas supply was finally turned on, with the infantry advance scheduled for 6.30. Many hopes had been pinned on the new weapon, but already it was looking unlikely that the gas would live up to expectations, since, as with the high-explosive shells previously, now there was a shortfall of chlorine. The German gas masks were known to last for only about half an hour, so 40 minutes of continuous exposure would be sure to wipe out the enemy, but the amount of gas on hand wasn't sufficient for such a prolonged release. Instead, it would have to be let off in intervals, rationed to twelve-minute bursts interspersed with six minutes of smoke.

To begin with, the gas seemed to behave itself, gently drifting over to the German lines. But soon the wind began to drop, and by 6.20am, before the German gas masks had quite lost their efficiency, it was blowing back in places, smothering the British trenches instead. The cylinders were immediately switched off, but not before more than 2,500 British soldiers had become casualties.

Almost as soon as the gas was released, the Germans unleashed a fearsome artillery barrage. 'Rifles, guns and shells of all kinds seemed to pour down all this time,' Gore Browne later wrote to his wife. 'Our guns were going all out too, and the noise was awful. I sat in the trench feeling very frightened.'

Soon the Post Office men began to suffer casualties: two men were killed and another's leg was shattered. Bill Howell felt a piece of shrapnel strike him in the left arm. Once he had got over the initial shock, he was overwhelmed with a feeling of relief. 'This is it,' he thought to himself, 'a Blighty wound.' Taken from an Indian word for England, the 'Blighty' was an injury that, while not life-threatening, was severe enough to require treatment back home, and hence offered a ticket out of the trenches.

But Bill was to be disappointed. A fellow soldier cut the sleeve of his tunic open and carefully removed the piece of burning metal – it had scorched his skin a little but hadn't broken it. Bill would be going over the top with his company after all.

At half past six the great advance began, and the Post Office Rifles had front-row seats. The smoky waste of no man's land was suddenly filled with figures, rushing towards the enemy lines. As the German machine guns rattled away, some of them began to drop to the ground.

But more of the men were getting through. In the distance to their left, the men from the Post Office could see the Scots heading straight for the town of Loos, while right in front of them, the Sixth and Seventh Londons were converging on gaps in the enemy wire. A few moments later, they had broken through and were pouring into the German trenches.

It was a spectacular sight, despite the horror of the frequent bloody casualties. All the planning and preparation of many weeks and months had reached a climax in this one critical moment.

With the Sixth and Seventh Londons now hard at work on the battlefield, the trenches they had departed from lay empty, and the Post Office Rifles were ordered forward to take up their friends' old positions. It was a distinctly uncomfortable advance, thanks largely to the number of dead and wounded in the communication trenches, but soon the men were ready and waiting for their own orders to proceed over the top. Ahead of them loomed the twin peaks of the two giant slag heaps, each the height of a five-storey building. Around their lower reaches, the smoke and gas were still swirling.

The Post Office men waited anxiously for orders to attack, but in the meantime they were told to hold their positions. Then, after what seemed like a lifetime, some good news began to trickle back to them. The Sixth and Seventh Londons were making good progress in the enemy trenches and had captured over a hundred German prisoners.

Soon the Sixth and Seventh Londons had taken the first German line, and had begun to move on to the second. But the two giant slag heaps remained in German hands. Finally, the Post Office Rifles received their orders: while Gore Browne's No. 4 Company remained to hold the British trench, Companies 1, 2 and 3 were to prepare to move forward and attack. It was the moment the men had been waiting for: at last they were going over the top.

Zero hour was set for 11am, giving the men enough time to smoke one last cigarette, shake the hands of their comrades for what they knew might be the final time, and prepare themselves mentally for the assault.

Ladders were fixed along the line to enable the men to get up quickly. Then, at 10 minutes to 11, the order came to fix bayonets. The men from the Post Office stood patiently, waiting for the whistle to blow. Many had grown superstitious and had pockets stuffed with the kind of objects often credited with stopping a bullet: bibles, shaving mirrors, cigarette cases and so on. The entrenching tools that were supposed to hang down behind their haversacks were nudged round to the front to protect their private parts.

Those last few minutes felt like an eternity. Some men prayed, while others' thoughts turned to family and friends back home. As Rifleman Jim Coleman explained:

It is hard to describe your feelings before zero hour. The bottom of your stomach has left you, you are cold all over, you pray, the whistle goes and your mind becomes a blank. All this time we are shelling the enemy lines and they are shelling ours, machine guns are rattling, dealing out death, and all hell is let loose. Thoughts are only for your own safety. Why is it happening to you? Indeed why are you here at all? I don't think King and Country entered my mind.

At long last, the appointed moment came. As soon as they heard the sharp shrill call of the whistle, the Post Office Rifles began to rush over the parapet. Immediately, the enemy opened fire from the slag heaps and the men began falling to the ground. There were plenty of screams and curses, and one man yelled, 'Bugger charging!'

But the men from the Post Office pressed on. They advanced in stops and starts, one platoon offering covering fire while another dashed a hundred yards forward, before dropping down to the ground. It was like a relay race, but the further along the course the men progressed, the fewer of them went forward in the next burst.

To help the British gunners avoid shelling their own men, certain soldiers had been given large yellow discs to carry, rather like a lollipop lady's sign. But while these were very helpful to the artillery, their bearers were an obvious target for German snipers. Bill Howell was extremely alarmed to find himself alongside one of the disc-carriers, and did his best to get away from the man. But every time he looked, the poor fellow was by his side again. 'Blimey George, can't you go with someone else for a while?' Bill asked him anxiously.

As it turned out, Bill was right to be worried. Not long after, the disc-carrier was shot through the neck and fell down dead. It was a very near miss for Bill too – the bullet shaved one of his eyebrows clean off, and left him with a thundering headache. But he was able to keep moving and soon got as far as the German wire, which by now was strewn with the corpses of men from the Seventh Londons who had got tangled up in it.

Bill leapt into the German trench and landed on a pair of dead bodies. One was a Seventh Londoner, whose head had been almost severed from his body. The other was one of the German soldiers.

The enemy trench was littered with corpses, but it was nonetheless a very impressive sight. Compared with the British lines it was deep and spacious, with the walls supported by a kind of latticework. Duckboards had been laid across the floor to keep it dry and wooden stands placed along the walls to hold rifles when they weren't in use.

Before long, the rest of the Post Office men had reached the German trench as well, and were heading for the base of the slag heaps. They managed to take the first one fairly easily, but the Germans on the second proved more tenacious and began hurling bombs at them.

To start off with, the men from the Post Office were able to retaliate, but their own supply of bombs soon ran out, and the Germans were beginning to drive them back again. In desperation they reached down to their feet for lumps of coal and began throwing them at the enemy.

Meanwhile, a Post Office signaller was waving his flags wildly, doing his best to summon reinforcements. A bombing team from the Civil Service Rifles saw the message and began dashing across no man's land to assist, but they were mown down by a German machine gun before they could reach the Post Office men.

Captain Gore Browne and his company were still in the old British front line, waiting for orders to move forward. At around midday the message came through that bombers were needed up ahead. Without hesitation, Gore Browne sent all 10 of his bombing specialists, with six boxes of bombs between them, and a machine-gunner.

They arrived in the nick of time. The bombers stormed the second slag heap, chasing the Germans up to the peak. As well as grenades, they were carrying large coshes, and a number of the enemy soon succumbed to blows to the head. Meanwhile, the machine-gunner had taken over a gun captured by the Seventh Londons and turned it on the Germans who remained on the crassier.

The battle continued for several hours, but now the Germans were on the back foot. Bill Howell made his way up to the edge of the first slag heap and found a secluded position behind a coal truck. From there he had a good view of the battlefield and was able to put his sniper's training to good use, picking off any remaining German soldiers one by one.

For the Post Office Rifles, the first day of the Battle of Loos had been a triumph – and their success was echoed further up the line. That afternoon, news arrived that the 141st Brigade had successfully taken Loos itself.

For the men from the Post Office, the priority was now to defend the slag heaps against a potential German counterattack. At last, Gore Browne and his company were ordered forward to join their comrades in the German trench. It was getting dark and the former no man's land was secure, so they were able to walk across safely. But what they found on the battlefield was enough to turn their stomachs. As the captain later wrote to his wife:

> *I cannot describe that walk to you. It will be a dreadful memory forever. I went right through the battlefield with all its dreadful relics – it was my nearest touch to war, though I had had men killed and wounded by me in the early stages – but on this walk, I went right through it all. The profusion of dead and wounded makes one's heart stand still.*

In the German trench, Gore Browne found Major Maxwell, the battalion's new second in command. No. 4 Company was ordered to hold the slag heaps overnight, in case the Germans attempted to retake them.

Gore Browne led his men to the base of the double crassier and they began to ascend to the top. But even without being fired upon, getting up the slag heaps wasn't easy. The ground shifted constantly under the men's feet, and by the time they reached the peak they were exhausted. To make matters worse, it was raining heavily by now, and as they slipped and fell on the dirty ground, they began to get blacker and blacker.

Gore Browne posted four sentries at the very top of the second peak, lying in the slag with a good view of the German trenches below them, and told the rest to remain just the other side of the crest, ready to come to their aid in the event of an attack. With his men all in position, the captain sat down in a shell hole and waited for the dawn.

Fortunately, the attack the men were waiting for that night never came. The Germans sent over a couple of shells, and fired periodically into the darkness, but the company on the slag heaps escaped injury. At 4.45am on Sunday morning, as the light began to seep across the horizon, they were ordered back to the old German trench.

No man's land was still littered with the dead and dying, and there were not enough stretcher-bearers to cope, so that morning Captain Gore Browne and Guy

Portman went out to assist in the search for casualties. Since the Germans' first and second lines were now in British hands, the nearest enemy soldiers were a thousand yards away. If any German snipers were in the area and could have taken a shot at that distance, they must have chosen to show mercy, for the men were not fired on once all morning.

By noon, the two officers were exhausted. They returned to the German trench to rest and share a bottle of beer. But although the Germans had left plenty of their own alcohol behind when they withdrew, the two Englishmen point-blank refused to drink it, so Gore Browne's batman Purnell was sent back to the British trenches to fetch their own supply.

The rest of the day was spent making the German trench as fit as possible for British habitation, moving the fire step from one side to the other so that it faced east instead of west. With the rain still pouring down, it was not a pleasant task, but the men soon accomplished it regardless.

Gore Browne made himself at home in the dugout of one of the German officers. He helped himself to a telescopic rifle, sent off one of the German postcards he found to his wife in England, and had a look through the man's diary and personal letters. But he didn't keep all the plunder for himself – he passed on several boxes of cigars to the men in his company, along with some German boots, vests and underpants.

The next few nights followed the same pattern as the previous one. With the trench secured, the main worry was an attack via the double crassier, since the Germans had held their positions at the other end of it. Every evening, one of the battalion's four companies would be sent out to spend the night on the slag heaps, generally in miserable and wet conditions, to keep a lookout for German patrols.

Clambering about on black coal slag under a cloudy sky, the men were effectively working blind. Every so often a German star shell would light up the landscape, and they would drop to the ground to avoid being seen. The rest of the time it was pitch-black all around them, and in the confusing, sliding terrain it was easy to get lost.

On one occasion, when a star shell provided a sudden burst of illumination, Lance Corporal Robinson realised that he was standing only feet away from a German soldier. He quickly whacked him round the head with the butt end of his rifle and the man collapsed onto the ground, unconscious. But it turned out that he hadn't been alone. A brief melee ensued between the Post Office men and a German patrol, neither side really able to see what they were doing, before the Germans retreated. The Post Office Rifles had suffered no fatalities, but 18 men were wounded, and their cuts were aggravated by the coal dust that by now covered every inch of their bodies.

In the pitch-black nights on the slag heaps, it could be hard to tell friend from foe, and after several nights of guard duty, often in driving rain, the men from the Post Office were exhausted. One night, a young rifleman fell asleep at his post, and when the rest of his platoon retreated in the dark, no one noticed that they had left him behind. Still in something of a daze, he ran into a corporal from another platoon, who immediately raised his gun and challenged him. In his sleepy state, the rifleman didn't know what to say, and before he had worked out what was happening the corporal had already pulled the trigger. By sheer good luck the gun failed to go off, and the rifleman was able to explain himself.

On night patrols, silence was paramount, since the men could never be sure how far they were from the enemy. But moving about on a slag heap without making a noise was difficult. As they climbed up the loose ground, it slid back beneath their feet with a loud rustle, and large clumps of coal frequently became dislodged, rolling down the hills and crashing into the ground at the bottom.

One night, a group of Post Office Rifles had reached the peak of the second crassier when they heard a rustling sound coming from up ahead. In the darkness, they couldn't see a thing, but they silently brought their rifles up in front of them. After a few moments of squinting in the gloom, they were just able to make out some human figures – an enemy platoon about 12 yards ahead and coming their way. Evidently, the Germans had no idea that the Post Office men were there.

The riflemen stood stock-still, aware that the slightest movement or sound could alert the enemy patrol to their presence. Step by step, the Germans came closer and closer, until their leader – a spry, quick-footed character – was only inches away from the barrel of Rifleman Fay's gun.

What it was that finally tipped the German off no one could say, but he suddenly let out a cry and rushed to draw his pistol. It was too late: Fay fired, and almost instantly the rest of the platoon followed suit. The German soldiers began to fall to the ground.

But not all of the enemy had been hit by the first volley. There was a burst of return fire and the riflemen heard the bullets whizzing by their heads, but by now they could do little more than continue firing into the darkness. The exchange of bullets continued for a few seconds, and then all of a sudden it ceased. What was left of the German patrol had retreated.

On Thursday night relief came in the shape of a French Colonial regiment, a little lieutenant with a very strong company of stalwart French men took over about 9 p.m. still in pouring rain and my weary mud-stained lot ploughed their way slowly out, done to the wide world most of us with five days beard and feeling as if we had never known what it was to sleep. It was a pitch dark night and we came back across the open from the western nose of the crassier. The new communication trench was blocked by incoming Frenchmen.

Letter from Captain Eric Gore Browne
to his wife Imogen, 4 October 1915

After the best part of a week on the slag heaps, the Post Office Rifles were relieved by a company of French Algerians and began the slow trudge back to the town of Philosophe. Their part in the Battle of Loos had come to an end, and they had fulfilled their role admirably. When they gathered before General Henry Rawlinson a few weeks later, he assured them that their success had not been bettered by any unit of the Territorial Army. Their casualties had been relatively light – with only a dozen killed and fewer than a hundred seriously injured – and they had achieved every one of their objectives.

Overall, though, the Battle of Loos had been a disaster. The first day's attack had gone better than anyone could have expected, but on the second day the Allied plan fell to pieces. When Sir John French finally released his two New Army divisions to Haig's command, it took over six hours for them to reach the front line, by which time the Germans were ready for them. The volunteer soldiers thought the enemy had been smashed by the artillery bombardment the day before and advanced slowly in columns, as if on parade. When the German machine guns opened fire they were massacred, with over 8,000 men killed or wounded. The battle dragged on for a further couple of weeks before it was called off. By that time, the British forces had sustained over 50,000 casualties, against German losses of around half that number. Among the British dead was Jack Kipling, the only son of the nation's favourite author, Rudyard Kipling.

Sir John French's position had become untenable, and when he resigned Lord Kitchener saw to it that General Haig took his job. For the British Army, Loos had proved the greatest failure of the war so far. And once again, all the bravery, devotion and suffering of the Post Office Rifles had been for nothing.

The Post Office men spent their first night out of the line in pretty grim conditions. When he had recovered from his exhaustion, Gore Browne wrote a letter to his wife Imogen:

> *To Maroc and thence a very slow and weary march to some ruined houses behind our trenches at Philosophe. We were in some sort of reserve here for the night. The filth and desolation of these houses passed everything, they were full of bits of equipment, bully beef, rifles, and the hundred and one things that get thrown about in a battle and the house I was in had no doors or windows. We found a mattress and Smith was asleep within 10 minutes of getting there. I made some coffee and Penny and I found a mattress and clasped literally in each other's arms we soon fell asleep, waking up occasionally to curse the cold.*

The next morning the men faced a further 12-mile march before they could properly relax in more comfortable billets. In the harsh light of day, the state they were in was even more shocking. 'A bigger looking lot of ruffians I never saw,' wrote Gore Browne. 'Guy Portman had a crimson beard and Tom Morris a neat little imperial – we were all unwashed and covered in mud from head to foot.'

On arrival at Les Brebis, the men were finally able to bathe properly – courtesy of a converted brewery, which could accommodate a dozen soldiers in each beer barrel. Some men were led aside to wash separately, and sat uncomfortably in smaller barrels, still in their Army shirts. Their clothes were so infested with lice, and they had been scratching so badly for so long, that the garments had become stuck to their raw skin. Eventually though, the fabric began to come away and in time every member of the battalion was clean again.

Despite his desire to get back to safety and comfort that morning, Gore Browne had lingered in Philosophe before leaving. He wanted to take one last look at the battlefield – a patch of land onto which he and his comrades had pinned such great hopes a week before.

It was a moment of deep contemplation. Afterwards he wrote to his wife Imogen:

No painting or poem or writing will ever give you a picture of the battlefield, either while it is actually on or afterwards. I am glad to have seen both. There is something very magnificent and unselfish about it, and death in many shapes and forms, some beautiful, some ugly, makes one feel less fearful about it all, and that there must be a hereafter where all these brave good fellows are going to meet again and have their reward.

G. R.

THE

POST OFFICE RIFLES.

8TH BATTALION CITY OF LONDON REGIMENT

Are in Urgent Need of Recruits to complete Establishment of the 3rd Battalion, and an earnest appeal is therefore made to all Officers of Military age who are desirous of assisting their colleagues now fighting in Flanders.

The Object of the 3rd Battalion is to supply drafts, after having received the necessary training.

1. HOW TO ENLIST.

(1) See your Postmaster and obtain official permission.

(2) Having obtained permission write to Officer Commanding POST OFFICE RIFLES, 130, Bunhill Row, London, E.C.

(3) You should not be less than 5ft. 2in. in height with an expanded chest measurement of 34in.

(4) **Age limits - 19 to 40.   19 to 45 ex Soldiers.**

2. TERMS OF SERVICE.

(1) Four years or duration of the War.

(2) Foreign Service Only.

(3) Free Discharge on termination of War or engagement.

3. Civil Posts will be kept open until return from Military Service, and such service will count for Civil Pension and for Increment of Civil Salary.

4. THE PAY OF A RIFLEMAN is equal to full Civil Pay in the case of all Established Officers. plus Free Kit, Rations and Quarters.

N.C.O's receive Extra Pay of their Rank supplemental to Civil Pay.

Un-established Officers receive Full Army Pay and Allowances, Free Kit, Rations and Quarters.

APPROVED BY THE
POSTMASTER-GENERAL.

(Signed) A.M.O.
27/5/15.

(Signed)

J. HARVEY,
Lieut.-Col. 1/8th Battalion City of London Regiment.
(British Expeditionary Force)

F. A. LABOUCHERE,
Lieut.-Col. 2/8th City of London Regiment.

F. OWEN,
Major 3/8th City of London Regiment.

GOD SAVE THE KING.

Post Office Rifles recruitment poster from 1915
© BPMA

Post Office Rifles at a pre-war training camp on Salisbury Plain, 1908
© BPMA

Postcard featuring Post Office Rifles, June 1916
© BPMA

Post Office Rifles on parade in London
© BPMA

Signals section of the Second Battalion training in Cuckfield, Sussex
© IWM

Captain Home Peel
© BPMA

Captain Eric Gore Browne
(courtesy of Fanny Hugill)

Lieutenant Colonel Harvey,
from 1916 Post Office Rifles
calendar © BPMA

Captain Tom Morris,
from 1916 Post Office Rifles
calendar © BPMA

Sergeant Alfred Knight (with pipe) and comrades
(courtesy of Anne Walsh)

Sergeant Alfred Knight
(courtesy of Anne Walsh)

Front-line Army postbox
© BPMA

Men sorting mail at the front
© BPMA

Men sorting mail at the front
© *BPMA*

Wartime mail delivery
© *BPMA*

Sketch of Lieutenant Colonel Harvey, from 1916 Post Office Rifles calendar © BPMA

Sketch of Captain Home Peel, from 1916 Post Office Rifles calendar © BPMA

Sketches from the 1916 Post Office Rifles calendar © BPMA

21/V/15 My darling, just a line to say I
am all right. We came out of the
trenches yesterday after 72 hours, most
of it under heavy shell fire. We were
distinctly lucky in the Company, only
losing 3 killed & about 15 wounded.
The boys behaved very well. We
are not far behind now & have to
be constantly ready. But slept like
a log last night, although not yet
able to take boots off. I cannot tell
you much now but will tell you all
about it afterwards. Very interesting
to hear about the proposed change
of Govt: & can imagine everybody
busy cabinet making. Please send this
on to Adrian. I have no time to write
more & they are anxious to have it.
Best love to you all
Pheler.

Letter from Home Peel to his wife Gwendolen, 21 May 1915
© IWM

NOTHING is to be written on this side except the date and signature of the sender. Sentences not required may be erased. If anything else is added the post card will be destroyed.

_____

I am quite well.

~~*I have been admitted into hospital*~~

{ ~~*sick*~~ } ~~*and am going on well.*~~
{ *wounded* } ~~*and hope to be discharged soon.*~~

~~*I am being sent down to the base.*~~

{ *letter dated* 16/7/16
I have received your { ~~*telegram*~~ „ _____
{ ~~*parcel*~~ „ _____

Letter follows at first opportunity.

~~*I have received no letter from you*~~
{ ~~*lately.*~~
{ ~~*for a long time.*~~

Signature only. *[signature]*

Date August 14th . 1916

[Postage must be prepaid on any letter or post card addressed to the sender of this card.]

(93871) Wt. W3497-293 4.500m. 7/16 J. J. K. & Co., Ltd.

Field service postcard sent by Duncan Barrett's great-great-uncle Eric Layton, 16 July 1916

Green 'honour' envelope used in 1915
© BPMA

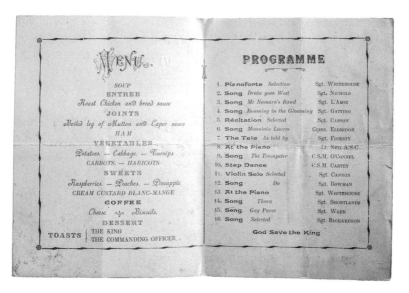

Programme for a Post Office Rifles dinner and concert held at the Theatre St-Cecile, Lillers on 7 December 1915. On the back, Eric Gore Browne scrawled the poem printed on page 13 (courtesy of Fanny Hugill)

Post Office Rifles examining captured German guns near Mallard Wood, August 1918 © IWM

Soldiers sleeping and writing letters in the trenches, April 1918 © IWM

Postwoman with bicycle
© *IWM*

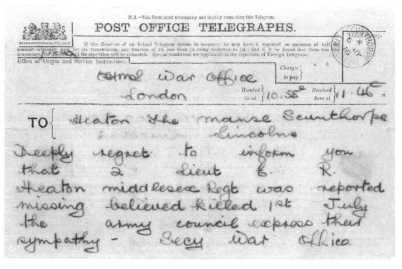

POST OFFICE TELEGRAPHS.

Deeply regret to inform you that 2 Lieut E. R. Heaton middlesex Regt was reported missing believed killed 1st July the army council express their sympathy – Secy War Office

Telegram from the War Office to Eric Heaton's parents following his disappearance on the first day of the Battle of the Somme © IWM

Warlencourt British Cemetery in 2013, with the Butte de Warlencourt visible in the distance © Duncan Barrett

CHAPTER 7

SEASON'S GREETINGS

—

*In order to remove certain misconceptions that have
arisen in connection with the Recruiting Appeal, the
Postmaster General thinks it well to state that,
generally speaking, it will not be possible to release
men from their Post Office duties till the Christmas
pressure is over. Exceptions to this will be made, where
possible, in the case of men who have special reasons for
joining units at once, but no man should enlist
for immediate service without the permission of his
superior officers.*

Post Office Circular No. 2261,
9 November 1915

IN OCTOBER 1915, the Postmaster General had
written a personal letter to every male Post Office
employee between the ages of 19 and 41, encouraging
them to volunteer for the Army. He was doing his best
to help the government with what was becoming a
major recruiting problem. The rush to the colours
that had occurred during the early months of the
war had begun to run out, thanks to growing
disillusionment. But the Postmaster's plea wasn't as

successful as he had hoped – less than half of those men he contacted responded by signing up, while over a thousand employees wrote back to tell him they had no intention of doing so.

The Postmaster General was disappointed, but as Christmas approached, with the prospect of delivering millions of parcels to the front in addition to the usual festive rush, his disappointment must have been mixed with relief. It was the one time of the year when the Post Office could absolutely not afford to be short-staffed.

For the Royal Engineers Postal Section, which was responsible for getting letters and parcels out to the troops at the front, the festive period presented new challenges. Special trains running from London to the coast were added to the regular service, along with extra boats running to Calais and Boulogne. In London, the Home Depot was moved into a single central office, a temporary 150,000-square-foot edifice built in Regent's Park, which was said to be the largest wooden building in the world. To help with the extra work, REPS began to take on extra staff, including a number of disabled soldiers as well as women. At its wartime height, the ranks of the Home Depot swelled to 3,000 people.

All the planning and preparation evidently worked. During the 1915 Christmas period, nine million letters and three million parcels were successfully delivered to the front.

Christmas Eve found the Post Office Rifles back in the trenches, occupying a notorious part of the line known as the Hohenzollern Redoubt. It had been captured from the Germans during the early days of the Battle of Loos, and had been hotly contested ever since. The redoubt's most alarming feature was a stretch known as the 'Hairpin' – two long parallel saps protruding from the British front line that connected it to a captured section of German trench. The men occupying this part of the line were only 40 yards away from the enemy, with not a single piece of barbed wire between them. In the cold, still nights, the two sides could hear each other cough.

Since the battalion's commanding officer, Colonel Harvey, had been sent home sick with a kidney infection and his second in command, Major Maxwell, was currently on leave, Captain Gore Browne was temporarily in charge. There had been other changes in the command hierarchy since Loos as well – Tom Morris had finally left the Post Office Rifles to take command of a battalion of the Rifle Brigade, and Lieutenant Peel had taken over his job as adjutant.

Meanwhile, 16 men who had joined the Post Office Rifles in the years before the war had come to the end of their four-year commitment to the Territorial Army. Captain Gore Browne did his best to persuade them to stay on, but he could hardly blame them when they refused – after nine months at the front, they had already had enough of war. They knew that with the prospect of conscription looming, they would be called back to the colours soon enough, but in the meantime they had every intention of hanging up their uniforms and going home.

Captain Gore Browne was not entirely happy with his own situation either. He had got over the disappointment of losing out on the adjutant's job to Peel, but was beginning to grow frustrated by the effect that temporary field promotions were having on the chain of command. Since many officers now had two different ranks, one 'substantive' and the other temporary, it was sometimes hard to be sure who outranked whom:

> *All TF [Territorial Force] promotions seem to be in the most desperate confusion, nobody being quite clear as to the exact difference between temporary and substantive ranks. In the meantime we out here are left with Jim the only alleged substantive captain, Vince and I temporaries (he is still a second lieutenant in the Army list) and no others. It is all rather baffling.*

The weather could do little to improve the captain's mood, for it was far from a traditional white Christmas. On the morning of Christmas Eve, the Post Office Rifles had left the relative comfort of Noeux-les-Mines, where Gore Browne had been billeted with a miner and his family, for a rain-soaked trudge up to the front lines. They had arrived to find a trench already two feet deep in water, and so muddy that their pumps got clogged up whenever they tried to clear it.

Fortunately, everyone had been provided with waders, although they still found their socks were soaked through within a matter of hours. Captain Gore Browne was sporting a hurricane smock sent out by his father-in-law, while one of the men had cut the bottom section off his greatcoat to keep it out of the water. His friends laughed at the sight of him in the roughly modified garment – he looked almost like a gentleman in evening dress, if you ignored the heavy coating of mud and the loose strands hanging down at the rear.

Keen to avoid a repeat of the Christmas Truce of 1914, in which Allied and German soldiers had met up in no man's land to sing carols, play football and exchange cigars, the Army expressly forbade the troops from any kind of 'fraternisation' with the enemy during the course of the festive period. On 21 December, Gore Browne received a message from the headquarters of the 47th London Division:

CONFIDENTIAL

140th Infantry Brigade

The G.O.C. directs me to remind you of the unauthorised truce which occurred on Christmas day at one or two places in the line last year, and to impress upon you that nothing of the kind is to be allowed on the divisional front this year.

Captain Lascelles at brigade headquarters had added: 'With reference to the above, the Brig wishes you to give the strictest orders to all ranks on the subject, and any man attempting to communicate either by signal or word-of-mouth or by any other means is to be seriously punished. All snipers and machine guns are to be in readiness to fire on any German showing above the parapet.'

But despite the ban on friendly interaction, the Post Office Rifles had been given some peculiar orders in relation to the enemy. The Bavarian troops in the trench only 40 yards away from them were from one of the units that had fought in the Battle of Loos. Many of their comrades were now languishing in British prisoner-of-war camps and the Army had a large stash of the prisoners' letters that needed delivering across no man's land. Who better to attempt such a task than a battalion of former postmen?

Of course, this was no straightforward delivery round. Even the bravest of posties wasn't about to risk being shot for delivering a letter, so the men decided that they would try to communicate their intentions first. Since no one was fluent in German, they took a large wooden board and wrote on it in capital letters:

DO YOU SPEAK ENGLISH?

Then they hung it on the butt of a rifle and gently nudged it up over the parapet.

Within moments, both the board and the rifle had been shot to splinters. If the enemy soldiers did understand the message, they evidently weren't interested in talking.

Perhaps they were aware of the British soldiers' predilection for playing pranks on their enemies. One account published in the Post Office magazine *St Martin's Le Grand* told of a foolhardy group of Tommies who had crept across no man's land in the middle of the night, tied a bell to a clothes line the Germans had put up just in front of their parapet, and by means of a string laid back to the British trench spent the rest of the day taunting them, ringing the bell and shouting, 'Ting-a-ling-a-ling, waiter! Ting-a-ling-a-ling!' The Germans had been so incensed they had spent most of the day firing at the British trench, but had been unable to stop the incessant bell-ringing until it got dark again and they could safely bring in their washing.

In any case, it was clear that the Bavarian soldiers across from the Hairpin were not going to accept their letters graciously, so the Post Office men would have to find another way to make the delivery. Bill Gibbs was one of the battalion's best sportsmen, and had distinguished himself in the summer's cricket match against the Civil Service Rifles, so he was selected as the most appropriate candidate to hurl them into the enemy trench.

The next problem was what to attach them to. By themselves, the letters weren't heavy enough to make it 40 yards through the air, but if the soldiers strapped them to the tin cans their food came in, they were liable to be mistaken for grenades.

Then someone hit on an inventive solution. The battalion had a stash of extremely large, and rather unappetising, French carrots that the cookhouse boys were more than willing to spare. By making an incision in the side of each carrot, the men were able to slip the letters inside them – almost as if they were posting them through a letterbox – and thanks to the tuft of greenery protruding from the top of each one, it was possible to work up a good swing. The Germans might be puzzled by an unexpected deluge of vegetables, but they were unlikely to mistake them for a real attack.

Once the carrots had been stuffed with the German letters, Bill Gibbs began his work. He grasped one of the oversized vegetables, feeling the weight of it in his hand. Then he drew his arm back and released it with the precision of a master bowler. The carrot soared through the air, before landing with a satisfying plop – bang on target in the German trench. The men from the Post Office did their best to stifle their sniggers.

Bill didn't wait to see if the Germans would respond. One by one, he hurled the remaining carrots across no man's land, until every one of the bright orange missiles had reached its intended destination. What the Bavarians made of the sudden downpour was never recorded – perhaps they feared that a new and mysterious form of warfare had been developed by the Allies, to rank alongside the invention of chlorine gas. In any case, the letters got through in one piece. After nine long months on the Western Front, the Post Office Rifles had finally lived up to their name.

The trenches here are a maze, every foot of which has been hotly contested and which changes hands very frequently. Then the lines are so close that there is an ever present fear of bombs and mines, both quite beastly. The line is badly made and wet – in fact I have very little use for it, and any change will be for the better say I.

Letter from Captain Eric Gore Browne
to his wife Imogen, 30 December 1915

The Hairpin's bad reputation turned out to be well deserved. For a start, it was one of the most uncomfortable positions to occupy on the entire Western Front. In many places, the trench walls were not built up high enough for the men to be able to stand safely, so they were forced to stoop. With much of the fire step under water, there was hardly anywhere to sit down and rest, so exhausted soldiers had to lean awkwardly against the muddy wall, their spines curved forward and their necks bent down to keep their heads safely below the parapet. As the hours wore on, it became increasingly hard to bear.

On Christmas Eve, two of the Post Office men, Rifleman Robinson and Lance Corporal Greenwood, were standing chatting in this uncomfortable position when, without thinking, Greenwood stretched a little, trying to get a crick out of his neck. It was all the opportunity that a German sniper opposite needed. The moment the crown of Greenwood's head showed above the parapet, the Bavarian put a bullet right through it.

Greenwood collapsed onto Rifleman Robinson, and was dead within a matter of moments. But he wasn't the last Post Office man to fall victim to the German sniper. Only a few minutes later, his good friend Rifleman Mills went the same way. Soon the water the men were wading in had turned red with blood.

Night fell on Christmas Eve, and despite the miserable conditions in the Hairpin, not everyone was immune to the spirit of the season. Standing on sentry duty at the fire step, Rifleman Broome found his mind wandering to Christmas Eves past, when he would walk into Leicester town centre and listen to the Salvation Army band. As he gazed out across no man's land on that cold, blustery night, he felt sure he could hear the band playing again.

The evening passed uneventfully, but at about 3am on Christmas morning the men in the trench began to notice a strange sound: a gentle tap-tap-tap that seemed to be coming from beneath them. They stood stock-still, listening anxiously until they were completely sure of what they were hearing. The regular tapping was unmistakable: a German mining team was operating in the area. The enemy had obviously decided that rather than try to capture the Hairpin, it would be preferable to blow it to pieces.

One of the men was dispatched to fetch Captain Gore Browne, who was understandably concerned at the new development. His battalion was quite literally sitting on a powder keg, but the captain's orders were to hold the Hairpin until the Post Office Rifles were relieved by another unit. If they abandoned the trenches now, the Germans would simply walk over and take them, giving the enemy a position dangerously close to the British front line.

The thought crossed Gore Browne's mind that, since the Hairpin was such a liability, its destruction might actually do the British a favour. But he certainly had no desire to be there when it went up in smoke.

For the men from the Post Office, the German mining operation put a serious dampener on the festive spirit, and Christmas Day was spent in a state of high anxiety. Another soldier, Rifleman William Beasley, had been killed in the night – the third victim of the Bavarian sniper opposite. As daylight dawned, the rain continued to fall in sheets, and the wind battered the parapets of the trench. The place felt uncanny somehow, and the men holding it began to grow superstitious.

Despite the strain of their situation, the Post Office men tried to make the best of Christmas Day. There was no grand feast, but they did manage a bit of cold turkey and plum pudding. The Christmas post provided an extra source of comfort. Thanks to the work of various Post Office committees back home, the men were well supplied with such necessaries as socks and candles, as well as magazines, footballs and boxing gloves – not to mention the most popular item, cigarettes.

Many soldiers were also opening their own mud-soaked parcels from home. One rifleman had received a special delivery from his grandparents, who were farmers. It contained a cooked chicken, which had sadly gone mouldy in transit, as well as a homemade pork pie. Sergeant Archie Dunn, meanwhile, had received a Christmas pudding made by his wife, and was sharing it out among the men in his section. 'They and I send our grateful thanks,' he wrote back to her. 'Those who got a silver 3d bit, I told them to keep for luck, and remember you.'

Coincidentally, another consignment from home had just arrived, and although not a Christmas present as such, it was certainly welcome: the Post Office Rifles' first shipment of the Army's new tin helmets. Up until this point, the men in the trenches had been equipped with no more than cloth caps for their heads, which offered little defence against shrapnel. The new Mark I, or Brodie, helmets provided a little more protection – although they soon drew the contempt of the Germans, who referred to them as *Salatschüssel* ('salad bowls').

Captain Gore Browne was not much more impressed with the design of the helmets than the enemy was. He wrote to his wife Imogen:

> *My steel helmet is the most appalling headgear that I ever struck – I cannot balance it on my enormous head and I look the most complete comic in it ... It is very*

heavy and most unbecoming – but they have saved millions of lives.

While the Post Office men busied themselves with their packages from home, the Germans, too, were celebrating, and their carols were heard loud and clear ringing out across no man's land. Mercifully, the Bavarian sniper seemed to have taken the day off, but the idea of fraternisation with the enemy was very far from anyone's thoughts.

That afternoon, Captain Gore Browne walked up and down the trenches, wishing the men a Happy Christmas. They did their best to respond enthusiastically, but he wasn't fooled. In such awful weather conditions, just keeping the trench in a state of repair was a full-time job, and many of the men had been up all night working on it. In any case, there wasn't really anywhere for them to sleep, although a few had tried to catch forty winks on the mud pile that passed for a fire step – that is, where it wasn't actually under water. But it was hard to relax knowing that at any moment they could be blown to pieces. The men were desperate to get out of the Hairpin as quickly as possible.

Boxing Day brought with it a small victory. Although the Post Office Rifles lost a fourth man, Rifleman Jack Kingdom, to the sniper in the German trench, at long last they got their revenge on him. One of their own sharpshooters caught a glimpse of the Bavarian through the tiny metal loophole that he had been using to target the Post Office men, and – in an act of breathtaking precision – managed to put a bullet right through it. The one-man campaign of terror was brought to a sudden, bloody end.

The brutal assassinations were over, but as Boxing Day wore on, the Post Office Rifles began losing men to an even more insidious foe: trench foot. They had been warned about the disease before they went into the Hairpin – in fact, a rather unsympathetic Army doctor had told them that anyone suffering from it would be held responsible and formally punished. Captain Gore Browne had set in train some elaborate preventative measures, with teams of stretcher-bearers rubbing whale oil into the men's feet and a constant supply of dry socks and hot drinks. But despite their commander's best efforts, after more than 48 hours of living in an icy swamp, many of the Post Office men had succumbed to the condition.

Some of their feet were so swollen that their boots had to be cut off them, the flesh flopping out like jelly as soon as it was released. With some effort, Rifleman Harvey managed to get his feet out of his boots without assistance, but what emerged looked more like a sponge than human flesh. When a medic came to examine him, pricking the skin carefully with a needle, it wasn't until he got above the knee that he found any sign of life.

The situation was so serious that 46 men had to be evacuated from the trenches. But for those who remained, the afflicted soldiers seemed like the lucky ones. The men left behind faced another sleepless night in the driving rain, and the constant threat of annihilation if the Germans decided to detonate their mine.

By the time the Post Office Rifles were relieved on the morning of 27 December, they felt as if they had been in the Hairpin for four months rather than four days. In a state of abject exhaustion, they staggered out of the line and back to billets in the village of Sailly-Labourse.

The following day, Captain Gore Browne wrote to his wife:

> *It was a sorry procession out, the main road dotted with little mud-caked parties and many limping along in great pain. I stayed outside my old billet at Noyelles-les-Vermelles and saw them all file past and collected the worst cases and got a hot drink at our old Quartermaster's stores, after which a well spent five francs sent them on here in a motor lorry ... I was done. I saw all the battalion in its billets, where we had fixed hot drinks and stews for them, and then I came to my own, very nice and clean, and took off all my clothes and lay on my bed but took a long time to get to sleep – it was just mental fatigue.*

Despite his exhaustion, Captain Gore Browne spent much of the rest of the day organising the men's entertainment for the following evening, which included a slap-up Christmas dinner. 'Some kind friend has sent us enough plum pudding for everybody and I have given each company a barrel of beer,' he told Imogen. 'I hope you will approve – it is English beer and I don't think we could have given them anything they would appreciate more.'

The dinner took place at a local *estaminet* on the evening of 28 December – three days late, but no less welcome for it. To the shattered, nerve-strained soldiers, it seemed like a feast laid on by the Ghost of Christmas Present himself. There was roast beef, pork and vegetables, Christmas pudding and mince pies, fruit and nuts, and plenty of beer, whisky and port. Captain Gore Browne made a speech praising the men of the battalion, and they all drank a toast to each other's health. It was a time to forget the traumas and distress of the last nine months, and to look forward optimistically to the New Year. Surely, the men hoped, 1916 would bring with it an end to the war.

The dinner was a huge success, and everyone enjoyed themselves greatly. One of the cooks drank so much in the course of the evening that he had to be carried home to his billet.

Two days later, the Post Office men received some fresh news from the Hairpin: the German miners had just blown it sky-high. If it weren't for the horrific casualties sustained by the battalion who were holding it, the news would have come as a relief. No one who had spent any time there was sad to see the end of that particular stretch of the front line.

CHAPTER 8

KEEP THE HOME FIRES BURNING

—

My darling,

Many thanks for your two letters of the 2nd & 6th & for the two postcards … We are back in the trenches again, after a short time out. It's beginning to get beastly cold. Harvey won't come back now – I'm afraid he is really seriously ill. Maxwell is now colonel. We go on much the same as usual. I am always very busy.

Afraid no chance of getting leave before 3 months from the last time – I'm fed up with this ridiculous life. A dreary round of monotony only relieved by moments of terror! I'm so glad the infants are going strong – How I should love to see them.

Letter from Lieutenant Home Peel
to his wife Gwendolen, 13 January 1916

BEFORE THE POST OFFICE RIFLES had even arrived at the Hairpin, their colleagues back home in London had been mourning the battalion's dead of 1915. In early December, a memorial service was held at Christ Church on Newgate Street. Colonel Harvey – still convalescing in the capital – read the lesson, and the battalion's chaplain, Canon E.H. Pearce, recited the names of the 119 men who had died during nine months of fighting at the front. Meanwhile, at the West Central Post Office, staff assembled at noon in the sorting office to remember their fallen colleagues and to sing the national anthem.

Despite its losses, the Post Office continued to function as one of the Army's staunchest recruiting sergeants. A month earlier, at the King Edward Building in London, the Postmaster General had made an impassioned speech calling for more volunteers, not just for the three battalions of the Post Office Rifles but for the many branches of the Army in which men from the Post Office served. 'There are some who think that each man who enlists is to be regarded as a doomed man,' he began. 'Out of 43,600, it is true, 1,500 have fallen. We deeply deplore their loss, but 42,100 have not fallen, and the vast majority of them will come home at the end of the war safe and sound.' There were cheers from the assembled masses of Post Office workers, before in a sombre voice he continued, 'However that may be, it is the custom of the British people to tread the path of honour and of duty, no matter what perils may surround it.'

Those who knew those perils at first hand were beginning to come home on leave. But adjusting to life back in Blighty – if only for a week or so – was not always easy for men who brought the mental scars of the war back with them. Bill Howell returned to his mother's house in Willesden, where he asked to see the spiked German helmet that he had posted home in an old biscuit tin. When Mrs Howell told him that it was in the garden shed he was disappointed – having seen its original owner shot dead at Festubert, Bill regarded it as a prized trophy. He went out and retrieved the helmet, cleaning and polishing it until it gleamed and then displaying it proudly in his bedroom. In the rim he found a name, written in indelible pencil: Private Hanches, Seventh Prussian Fusilier Regiment.

Bill had always been a very sound sleeper, and had got through plenty of nights in the trenches without once falling prey to a nightmare. But that first night back in his old bed again, he woke up in a cold sweat. He could hear a scratching noise at the bottom of the bedroom door, and was convinced that a creature with steel claws was trying to force its way into the room.

Frantically, Bill hurled one of his boots at the door, sending some fishing rods crashing to the floor and waking up the rest of the household. His mother and sister rushed into the room and flicked on the light switch. They found Bill gripped by terror. He insisted on inspecting the door for scratch marks, but of course there was nothing there.

When Bill told the two women about the noises he had heard, they soon grew terrified too, convinced that the ghost of the dead German soldier had come back for his helmet. They begged Bill to get rid of it as soon as possible. The next day, he took it to a local shop and offered it to them for their window display.

But even with the helmet out of the house, Bill didn't return to his own bed again. He spent the rest of his week's leave staying at a friend's place instead, and saw his family only in the daytime.

Not all Post Office men coming home on leave could claim to have brought a ghost back with them, but others turned up accompanied by even less appealing guests. When Rifleman Charles Miller arrived at his mother's house, she immediately rushed to embrace him, but he held up his hands to stop her, shouting, 'Don't come near me!' It seemed like the behaviour of a madman, but Miller wasn't shell-shocked or struggling, as many men did, to adjust to ordinary life at home after the horrors they had witnessed in the front lines. In fact, the reason was much more prosaic: he was lice-ridden, and he didn't want his mother to become infested.

Soldiers were supposed to be deloused at Boulogne before boarding ships to cross the Channel, but Miller knew that waiting at the rest camp for a bath and a change of clothes would eat into his time in England. His leave pass had a section on the back to be signed by a medical officer stating that he was louse-free, so when he spotted an Army doctor struggling with some heavy bags at the railhead, he rushed over and asked if he could carry them for him. The doctor gratefully accepted, and when Miller cheekily asked him, 'Would you mind doing something for me, sir?' he willingly scribbled his name on the back of the form. So it was that Miller arrived home a day early, but distinctly unprepared to greet friends and family.

Having explained the situation to his mother, he rushed along to the bathroom, tore off his Army uniform and threw it out of the window and into the garden. Then he hopped into the tub and enjoyed the most luxurious soak he had experienced for many long months. After the bath, Miller dressed in some of his old civilian clothes and went outside to inspect his uniform. The undergarments were infested beyond hope, and he set about burning them on a bonfire. Then he took a spade and began digging. He buried the rest of his uniform a couple of feet down and left it there for the remainder of the week.

The plan worked remarkably well. Miller spent the rest of his leave in mufti, and when he came to dig up his uniform again, shortly before he returned to the Western Front, he found it was entirely louse-free – if a little earthy.

How the soldiers chose to spend their leave varied from person to person. Some spent the time with their families or caught up with old friends from home. Others went out and painted the town red, making the most of opportunities that might not come again for many months – if ever. Rifleman Selley treated himself to a slap-up meal at the Strand Corner House in the West End, followed by a performance of *Faust* at the Shaftesbury Theatre. But slotting back into ordinary civilian life was a challenge, and however much a soldier tried to enjoy his leave, it was hard to ignore the nagging thought at the back of his mind that it was only a temporary reprieve.

Many soldiers struggled when confronted with the fact that, on the home front, life seemed almost to be going on as normal – certainly compared with the Western Front, where civilisation had been ripped apart at the seams. For men who had spent months amid the horrific trauma of the trenches, the transition could be difficult. A gulf had opened up between them and their nearest and dearest, separating those who knew the war in Europe only from the newspapers and newsreels from those who had actually lived through it.

But if adjusting to life back in Blighty was difficult, going back to the front lines at the end of a spell of leave, now with full knowledge of what it was like there, was even harder – and for various reasons, plenty of men never did. In January 1916, Rifleman E.J. Robinson left the Post Office Rifles for a week's leave at home in London. When he said farewell to his friends in France he was in perfect health, but after a couple of days back in England he had developed a mysterious illness. Robinson's temperature skyrocketed and his limbs began shaking uncontrollably.

Robinson's mother called the family doctor, who had him moved to a military hospital. As the months went by he was moved from one facility to another, but after almost a year under observation he still hadn't fully recovered. Finally, an Army Medical Board decreed that he was no longer fit for active service and he was discharged with a disability pension.

It is hard to be certain of what exactly was wrong with Rifleman Robinson. He may have had a recurrent case of trench fever (a flu-like illness carried in the faeces of lice) or one of the many other diseases that at the time fell under the rather imprecise category of 'pyrexia of unknown origin' (PUO). But, equally, his sudden illness could have been a form of shell shock, symptoms of which had been known to include psychogenic fever and uncontrollable muscle spasms. Whatever the cause, the illness was serious enough to ensure that Robinson never went back to the front lines.

Of course, not all of the Post Office men who returned home to England during the war were on leave. Many had been injured in battle, sustaining 'Blighty wounds' that required periods of recuperation on the home front, or in some cases a permanent transfer to a non-combatant role. Rifleman Bertram Ralph had been at the front for only a fortnight when he was knocked unconscious on his first advance. His wounds were serious, although not life-threatening, and after assessment at Le Tréport hospital he was sent home to England for treatment. But his voyage on the hospital ship SS *Warilda* wasn't exactly good for his health. About 35 miles off the coast of Sussex, the vessel was struck by a torpedo – Bertram was woken by a terrific explosion, followed by the screaming of wounded men trapped below decks as the ship began to sink. He was too weak to get up, and as the water rushed into the ship, he began kicking at the end of his bed in an attempt to summon help. But the effort was too much for him, and he soon lost consciousness.

Bertram came to a few minutes later to find that he was being dragged up the stairs to the deck by another wounded soldier. Men who could swim were already leaping overboard, but that wasn't an option for Bertram – instead, he was handed from one sailor to another until they managed to get him onto another boat that had pulled up alongside to help. He was drifting in and out of consciousness, but remained awake long enough to see the SS *Warilda* break in two and then slide below the waves. It took 123 men down with it to the bottom of the ocean.

Bertram was lucky to make it to Southampton in one piece, where he was put on a train to London. He shared a carriage with a German prisoner whose eyes had been gouged out by an English soldier's bayonet. Neither man could speak the other's language, but the encounter made a lasting impression on Bertram. Throughout his convalescence back in England, one thought kept returning to his mind: what if he and the German had been in each other's places, and he had been the one, blind and unable to communicate, held as a prisoner in the land of his enemies.

Like Rifleman Robinson, Bertram never returned to active service. After a few months in England he was discharged as unfit, and was given an Army pension.

Some men sent home to England to recuperate were able to work the system to their advantage and avoid having to return to the front lines – particularly, as Pat Patterson discovered, if they had friends in high places who were willing to help them. Although Pat's injuries from the shelling of the brewery post at

Festubert had got him only as far as Le Tréport hospital in northern France, not long after he returned to the Post Office Rifles he managed to break his ankle in a cricket match – and this time he was sent back to England for treatment.

After a spell at a Voluntary Aid Detachment hospital near Cromer in Norfolk, Pat was convalescing in London. He was still walking with a stick, but was required to report daily to Bunhill Row. One day, while on his way down Moorgate, he ran into his former master, Percy Croysdale, who had recently been promoted to captain.

The two men had not seen each other since the bombing of the brewery post, when Pat had dragged another officer, Lieutenant Cochrane, to safety. He had assumed that Cochrane had died on his way to hospital – in fact, he was sure that he had heard him breathe his last – but Croysdale reassured him that the lieutenant was alive and well. Although Cochrane had lost an eye in the attack, he had been fitted with a glass one to replace it, and other than that he was now as fit as a fiddle. 'I had lunch with him only yesterday,' Croysdale told Pat. 'I'm sure he would like to see you, for you undoubtedly saved his life.'

Pat replied that he had only done his duty. 'Someone would have found him,' he told the captain modestly.

But Croysdale would hear none of it. 'No, they wouldn't,' he replied. 'The next shell finished the place off!'

Captain Croysdale told Pat that he was about to take up a position with the Post Office Rifles Third

Battalion, which was based at Blackheath in London. 'How would you like to join me there?' he asked. 'I'll be in need of a good batman.'

Pat didn't think twice before agreeing – he knew there were few masters easier to get on with than Croysdale, and a chance to stay away from the Western Front was not to be sniffed at. As it turned out, the job was even cushier than it had been before. Since Captain Croysdale was often away on recruitment drives, Pat had plenty of time to himself.

It seemed like the perfect arrangement, but it didn't last long. While Pat's 'guv'nor' was in Scotland signing up new recruits, he was ordered to catch a boat to Le Havre and re-join the First Battalion in the trenches. His third period in France wasn't much more successful than the other two. He had already been hospitalised twice thanks to German shelling and sporting injuries, and this time it was trench fever that sent him back to Blighty again, after he awoke one morning unable to move, with a temperature of over 103 degrees Fahrenheit.

This time Pat was sent to a hospital in Whitstable. He recovered and was passed A1 by his doctors, before being sent to join the Third Battalion again. By now they were based at Fovant in Wiltshire, where they had made themselves busy carving the Post Office Rifles badge into the chalk of a nearby hill. Percy Croysdale was still with the battalion, only now he had been promoted to major. As soon as Pat arrived at the camp, he was summoned to see his old master.

'I would like to have you back with me again,' Croysdale told Pat kindly, 'but I'm afraid it just isn't possible.' He explained that under new Army regulations only men with low medical grades were allowed to perform the role of batman – Patterson's clean bill of health from the hospital meant that he was no longer eligible for the job.

But the major was determined that Pat should not be sent back to the trenches. 'We must see what can be done,' he told him gravely. 'You cannot take the risk of being sent back to the front for a third time.'

A few days later, Major Croysdale had come up with a plan. Once again Pat found himself summoned to his former master's quarters. 'Are you able to ride a bicycle?' Croysdale asked him.

'Yes, sir,' Pat replied, a little puzzled.

'Good,' the major replied. 'In that case I would like you to take a letter to a village called Hurdcott. It's about 14 miles away.'

'Yes, sir,' Pat repeated. It was a long time since he had delivered any letters, but he rather liked the sound of a ride along gently winding country lanes.

It was a pleasant day, and Pat enjoyed his role as the major's personal postman, despite the length of the journey. He took it easy and made the most of the opportunity to admire the beautiful scenery.

When Pat arrived back at the camp, he found Major Croysdale waiting for him. 'How do you feel?' the major asked, narrowing his eyes a little.

'I'm alright, sir,' Pat assured him breezily.

Croysdale lowered his voice. 'But didn't the hills affect you?' he asked pointedly.

Pat hesitated. 'Well, I felt a bit short-winded at times.'

'I thought so!' exclaimed the major, with palpable excitement. Soon Pat found himself recommended for a travelling medical board.

The day the board arrived at Fovant, Colonel Davey, who normally commanded the Third Battalion, was on leave, so Croysdale was temporarily in charge. As Pat walked up to be assessed in front of the Surgeon General, Sir Owen Lloyd, he distinctly heard the major whisper, 'This is the man I spoke to you about, sir.'

A couple of Army medics examined Pat, poking and prodding and measuring him for a few minutes. When they had finished, they scribbled a quick report and handed it over to Sir Owen. Pat was summoned to stand before the Surgeon General, who looked him up and down thoughtfully. Then Sir Owen turned to Major Croysdale and declared loudly, 'This man is not physically fit to walk around picking up paper! I do not consider it worthwhile keeping him in the service.'

'Well, sir,' the major replied innocently, 'if you will permit him to remain as my servant I promise he will not be overworked.'

'Very well,' the Surgeon General agreed. 'But it must be your responsibility if anything happens to him.'

With that, Pat's medical grade plunged from A1 to C3, meaning that he was no longer fit for foreign service. Once more, he was installed as Major Croysdale's batman, although in practice this meant little more than keeping him company, and occasionally caddying for him during a round of golf or beating the game when the major went out shooting.

But although Croysdale had got his servant – and, by now, his friend – permanently out of harm's way, ensuring that Pat could never again be sent back to fight on the Western Front, he wasn't able to hold on to him forever. There were staff shortages at REPS Home Depot, and Pat's Post Office background, coupled with his new medical status, made him an obvious choice to be drafted. Reluctantly, the two men said their farewells and Pat returned to London.

He reported for duty at the King Edward Building, where he was made a packet sorter and assigned to the 'N&O road' – meaning that he was responsible for parcels sent to regiments whose name began with one of those letters: the Nottinghamshire and Derbyshire Regiment, the Oxfordshire and Buckinghamshire Light Infantry, and so on. The job couldn't have been much more perfect – compared with the Army life Pat was used to, REPS offered a pleasant and relaxed environment, and the workers even stuck to normal office hours. If it weren't for the khaki uniforms everyone was wearing, he could almost have imagined that he was back at the regular Post Office, rather than still serving in the Army.

There was one area, however, in which REPS differed significantly from the Post Office that Pat remembered from his civilian years: now he was working alongside large numbers of women. At the King Edward Building, most of them were downstairs in the letters section, but a fair few worked up on Pat's floor dealing with the packets. However much Pat felt like he was back in Civvy Street, he was still obliged to follow Army regulations – and that meant an absolute ban on fraternising with the fairer sex. One day, he was wheeling his trolley of packets along the corridor when he accidentally brushed the heel of a young woman. 'I'm sorry,' Pat said instinctively, turning his head to look at her.

Within moments he found himself hauled into the office of a supervisor, another peacetime postal worker, who had been given the Army rank of sergeant major. The man was evidently enjoying his new military authority, and took his job extremely seriously. Pat was ordered to give an account of his behaviour, and the severity of the crime he had committed was explained to him in no uncertain terms.

In the end, Pat was lucky to escape with no more than a caution, but he wasn't trusted with parcel-sorting again. Instead, he was transferred to operate the heavy goods lift, where there was less chance of him disturbing the ladies.

CHAPTER 9

MAIL PRIVILEGE

—

'Men to trenches, women to benches'

Popular expression among
Post Office workers, circa 1915

PAT PATTERSON MIGHT HAVE been surprised to
find himself working alongside women, but on the
home front it was far from unusual for female workers
to take the place of men during the war. All over the
country, women were doing jobs once considered to
be for men only: driving trams, tilling the land and
even producing munitions for the artillery. It was
thanks to the army of female labour that the shell
crisis of 1915 was finally resolved, as munitions
production increased 20 times over. But working in
the arsenals and factories was far from safe, and many
women began to turn yellow from exposure to TNT.
They were known affectionately as 'canaries', but the
condition was no laughing matter – some were left
infertile as a result of the chemicals, while others died
of toxic jaundice. And long-term exposure to
hazardous substances wasn't the only worry – in
January 1917, over 20 munitionettes were killed in an

explosion at the Brunner Mond TNT factory in Silvertown, East London.

During the course of the war, more than one and a half million women joined the labour force, and the regular Post Office was no exception to the national trend, taking on more than 50,000 temporary female workers. There had been women working at Post Offices before, generally as telegraphists and clerks, but they had nearly always been kept in segregated departments, and until 1911 they weren't even allowed to leave the office at lunchtime for fear that they might fraternise with the men. The women had been far from equal partners in the Post Office hierarchy – they had earned less than half the rates paid to men in the same jobs and were forced to leave as soon as they got married. But with so many postal workers now leaving to go and fight in a foreign field, the old rules were beginning to be broken. In 1915, the marriage bar was lifted, and women were allowed to do 'men's work' – including outdoor jobs such as delivering the mail.

It was no progressive egalitarian gesture, however. The Postmaster General saw an increasingly female workforce as a necessary evil. He was in no doubt that employing women would have a negative impact on the standards for which the Post Office was famous. 'The employment of women has been largely increased and will be increased still further,' he told staff at the King Edward Building, 'but I do not hesitate to say, speaking with a full sense of the responsibility of the office I hold, that I regard it as of more importance to spare men and to beat the Germans than even to maintain the Post Office at the high standards of efficiency which it has already reached.'

Hiring women to carry letters was one thing, but the idea of putting them in managerial roles was almost unthinkable. Shortly before the war, a Parliamentary Select Committee had taken evidence from a female clerk who was demanding an end to sex discrimination. 'You contemplate a Lady Secretary to the Post Office?' the chairman asked her incredulously. 'Yes, certainly,' the clerk replied, 'and a Lady Postmaster General eventually.' The committee simply fell about laughing.

Given the strength of such attitudes, it is hardly surprising that the attempt, in April 1916, to appoint a female 'head postman' in Dorchester caused great consternation. The Dorchester Post Office had lost its original head postman to the Post Office Rifles, and his replacement had recently been released to join the Dorset Regiment. With the introduction of conscription in January, the pool of men eligible for the job was growing smaller. Two of the older postmen had been offered it already and turned it down. 'As I have no wish and also do not feel capable of performing this duty properly and in its entirety, I respectfully ask to be allowed to remain in my present section,' wrote one 44-year-old postman to the district postmaster. A week later, a 50-year-old postman was put on the job, and expressed the same misgivings:

Sir,

Having no knowledge of Bicycle or Tricycle I beg respectfully, to be relieved of Acting Head Postman's duties, feeling that I should not be able to carry the duty out satisfactorily ... I may point out sir, that I have always done delivery duties, rural or town, also sorting, for over thirty years. And I am willing to do any hard work still, and try to give every satisfaction.

In asking to be relieved altogether of this duty, I do so because I feel that I should be a failure in arranging duties as they should be done, having had no previous knowledge and the times being exceptional.

The district postmaster, Walter Drew, took a bold decision, writing to his superiors to request permission to offer the job to a female employee. He explained that of the four men remaining at the Post Office, two had already turned the position down and the other two – both in their fifties – were, in his opinion, 'not equal to the duty'. If he was allowed to consider female employees, there would be another nine candidates to choose from.

The obvious front runner for the job was a woman called Dorothy Baker, who had joined the Post Office in November the previous year and had immediately made a strong impression, thanks to both her formidable organisational skills and her confident, forthright personality. She was the perfect candidate for a managerial role and ought to have been a shoo-in, but Drew knew that obtaining his superiors' approval wouldn't be easy. Although a female postmistress wasn't unprecedented, generally women had only ever taken on such roles in small Post Offices serving very rural areas. The tiny village of Fringford where Flora Thompson had worked as a teenager – later immortalised in the *Lark Rise to Candleford* trilogy – was a world away from the busy market town of Dorchester.

Nonetheless, Drew was determined to try. 'I propose to place a woman on the duty,' he told his superiors boldly, 'one who is a cyclist and capable of carrying out the clerical work.' For a fortnight he waited anxiously to find out what they would make of his suggestion.

Eventually, Drew received a reply. It was curt, but to the point: 'Approved, as an experiment. Please report result in due course.'

Mrs Baker had the job – one of only five women in the country to be given such responsibility within the Post Office. She threw herself into it, proving that she was every bit the equal of the man who had performed the role before – in fact, few would dispute that she was the best head postman that Dorchester had seen in a long while. But it soon became apparent that the job itself was going to be the easy part – the much greater challenge was getting those higher up to treat her as they had her male predecessors.

It didn't take long for the first dispute to arise. When Walter Drew requested that Mrs Baker be given the standard head postman's allowance of five shillings per week on top of her wages, his superiors were deeply suspicious. 'Mr Drew, will you be so good as to say whether Mrs Baker performs the whole of the head postman's duties?' they asked sceptically. 'If not, please furnish a list showing the duties normally performed by the head postman, indicate those not performed by Mrs Baker, and state what proportion of the allowance should be paid to her.'

This time it was Drew's turn to offer a curt reply. 'Mrs Baker performs the whole of the head postman's duties,' he wrote back frostily.

But apparently that wasn't enough, and it was only after one of Drew's colleagues, Mr MacDonald, had listed in detail Mrs Baker's various responsibilities – checking overweight packages, examining bicycles, supervising postmen, performing street inspections, dealing with enquiries from the public, and so on and so on – that they agreed to a compromise allowance of four shillings.

Although Mrs Baker enjoyed the work at the Post Office, she was beginning to grow frustrated at the way she was being treated by those higher up. She was, as MacDonald put it, 'a woman of strong personality', and was not used to being taken advantage of, but it seemed fairly clear to her that the Post Office didn't value her abilities. Eventually, she wrote a letter of her own, demanding a raise:

I would point out that my duties are particularly responsible and varied – besides general supervision and street inspection I issue and keep records of uniform for 75 postmen of whom 40 are employed at sub-offices. Thus the uniform for these sub-offices has to be separately dispatched and involves a great deal of extra correspondence and labour. The same applies to the 50 bicycles attached to this office, all records of which are kept by me and I am responsible for examination and all repairs.

I may mention that women employed in some of the other government departments in Dorchester who are performing ordinary clerical work, with little or no responsibility, are in receipt of wages of 35 to 40 shillings a week – the work performed by me is, I consider, much superior.

I shall be grateful for an early reply.

Yours faithfully

Dorothy V. Baker

Mrs Baker got the raise she was hoping for, and was finally given the full supervisory payment of five shillings that her male equivalents were entitled to. But the battle with her superiors continued. When she went on annual leave, they seized the opportunity to dock her pay, arguing that the supervisory allowance was not part of her actual salary but a bonus attached to the job she was covering.

Mrs Baker was furious and threatened to resign – a prospect that sent those who worked with her into a panic. 'If Mrs Baker resigned there would be difficulty in replacing her,' Mr MacDonald wrote anxiously to the Secretary. 'Mrs Baker is known to be very dissatisfied with her present remuneration, and as she is an exceptionally competent woman she would, it is thought, have no difficulty in securing employment outside the Post Office.' Although the Secretary was well within his rights to dock Mrs Baker's supervision allowance, MacDonald begged him 'to see his way to modify the decision so far as this case is concerned and to agree to the allowance of five shillings being regarded as personal to Mrs Baker'.

Reluctantly, the Secretary backed down. Gritting his teeth, he wrote, 'In the circumstances ... the supervising allowance may be regarded as assigned to Mrs Baker personally & consequently payable during absence on annual or sick leave.' Mrs Baker had won another battle.

However, the Secretary's true feelings were revealed in an extra sentence that he had written and then crossed out before the letter was posted: 'No doubt the situation as regards attractiveness of employment elsewhere will be eased considerably in the near future.' He was well aware that once the war was over, and the men returned to the Post Office, Mrs Baker and other women like her would find themselves in a much weaker bargaining position.

Dear Sir,

We the undersigned wish to bring to your notice the fact that we have been employed for more than a month as Postwomen at Camp Hill Office & that although most of us have been measured for clothes to stand the inclement weather yet up to the present time no clothes have been supplied. There are some men's capes here but not sufficient to supply us all round & it follows that on days such as Saturday last women & letters are thoroughly soaked through. We trust you will give the matter your immediate attention so that we may be able to keep fit & do our duty efficiently.

Letter to the Birmingham postmaster signed
by 23 wartime postwomen, 6 December 1915

Not all female appointments in the Post Office were as controversial as Mrs Baker's, but the introduction of large numbers of women into traditionally male roles came with a whirlwind of confusion and anxiety. In the archives of the Post Office Museum in London is a large file of internal correspondence on the question of what the new female workers should wear. There was much discussion and debate before a uniform for postwomen and messenger girls was agreed on – consisting of a blue serge skirt, a matching jacket and a straw hat.

Although stylish, the new outfits were not universally popular, and the Post Office soon began receiving complaints from the women who had to wear them. In particular, they were unhappy with the bulky waterproof capes they were issued with when the weather turned nasty, which were just about suitable for sturdy postwomen but too heavy for the waiflike messenger girls. Then there were the straw hats, which the women claimed lost their shape in the rain and caused 'violent headaches' when they dried again. The Post Office was not very sympathetic to the latter complaint, responding that the loss of shape was caused by the women's hairstyles, and that they ought to look after their headgear better.

Most problematic of all, though, was the question of footwear. While messenger boys had always been provided with waterproof boots, girls were expected to work in their own shoes, which were not always suitable for wet weather. In December 1915, the Inspecting Officer for the South West District Office visited the girls at the Chelsea Branch Office and reported in horror, 'The messengers state that they cannot afford strong and durable boots. On Thursday last they had to take off their stockings and dry them at the fire.'

Male notions of propriety were easily offended where the new female staff were concerned. 'It would be a great advantage, in every way, if the pockets in the post-women's uniforms could be done away with,' another Post Office inspector, Mr F. Pullen, wrote. 'Apart from the dangerous practice of putting letters in the pockets, the large majority of the women present a very unsightly appearance from walking with both hands deep in their pockets at all times.'

Mr Pullen was given short shrift by his superiors, who were well aware that the pockets allowed the women to keep their hands warm during the winter months, and that removing them would be extremely unpopular. 'Mr Pullen, the Secretary is not disposed to pursue this question,' was the rather brief reply to his proposal.

Among the public, no group of female postal workers provoked such widespread concern as the 7,000 new teenaged messenger girls. But it wasn't their clothing that was at issue, it was their prospects. While messenger boys were forced to attend educational classes twice a week and were offered opportunities for advancement within the Post Office, the girls were not entitled to any such benefits. In December 1915, the Lanarkshire MP John Whitehouse asked a question in the House of Commons: could the Postmaster General say whether the messenger girls' interests were being safeguarded?

The Postmaster General provided a brief and straightforward reply: the employment of girls was intended as nothing more than a temporary war measure and would cease at the close of hostilities. As far as he was concerned, what happened to them after that was not the Post Office's concern.

Not everyone was willing to accept the Postmaster's position, however. Two days later, the issue was picked up by suffragette newspaper *The Common Cause*, which described the girls' work as a form of 'blind-alley employment'. For the Post Office, a can of worms had been opened, and one that would not easily be closed again. They soon found themselves bombarded with letters from committees on juvenile employment all over the country, requesting clarification on the prospects of the messenger girls. The response from the Post Office was the same one that had been given in Parliament: the girls were 'a war measure which will be discontinued when circumstances allow'.

Internally, correspondence on the issue was bullish. 'The question is largely one of demand and supply,' wrote one Post Office manager, while another commented, 'At present there is no difficulty in obtaining as many suitable girls as we require.' But in an attempt to deflect criticism, it was agreed that notices should be put up in Post Offices that employed large numbers of messenger girls, informing them that they were more than welcome to enter the usual 'competitions' for the jobs that had always been open to women, such as telephonists, telegraphists and typists. The suggestion was essentially disingenuous, since the Civil Service exams that provided entry to these positions were extraordinarily hard and the new recruits had little chance of making the grade.

An element of snobbery was almost certainly involved on the part of the Post Office managers. In a letter to the Undersecrctary for Ireland, who had taken an interest in the case, the Post Office Secretary's deputy, Edward Raven, wrote that 'comparatively few of these girls are likely to be of a sufficiently good type for appointment as telephonists'. What exactly defined a 'good type' he didn't say, but it's not hard to imagine accent and class having something to do with it. Candidly, Raven pointed out that to offer education to girls who didn't fit the right mould would not only 'raise false hopes' but would also be a waste of Post Office money 'in the payment of class-fees and travelling charges'.

Nonetheless, the pressure on the Post Office continued to build. The damning tone of a letter from the Brighton Juvenile Employment Sub-Committee was typical:

> *The committee having given careful consideration to the question of the employment of girls as P.O. messengers, is of the opinion that the conditions of such employment are highly undesirable in that no prospects of continued employment under the Post Office are offered, that no provision is made for the training of the girls, nor for fitting them for future employment elsewhere, and that from this point of view, the occupation must be therefore considered as not superior to that of any other kind of errand girl, admittedly one of the worst forms of blind-alley employment.*

As ever, the Postmaster General was unmoved and responded with his usual stock answer, stating that the employment of girls was only ever intended as a 'war measure'.

Part of the problem for the Post Office was the lack of positions for girls to move on to when they reached adulthood – while messenger boys could easily be converted into postmen, the role of 'postwoman' was another temporary one. As the assistant secretary general put it in a rather muddled letter to Lord Cavendish-Bentinck, who had raised the issue again in the House of Commons:

> *The normal outlet for Boy Messengers is to the Postmen's class, but ~~unfortunately~~ there is ~~nothing of the kind~~ no similar opening available for girls, ~~as Postwomen were purely a passing war product~~ the employment of Postwomen being merely a war expedient.*

The crossed-out words hint at the truth that the Post Office didn't wish to acknowledge: as far as the managers were concerned, the women they employed for the duration of the war – women who kept the organisation running despite the crippling lack of male labour – were not so much human employees as a 'product'.

Although the Post Office's female workforce enjoyed plenty of support among the public, not everyone was sympathetic to their cause. Women working across many industries faced hostility from skilled male workers who were concerned about what was known as 'dilution' – the simplification of jobs that had once required long apprenticeships, in order that women could learn them quickly during the war. Men who had worked hard to master their trades feared that their skills were in danger of becoming redundant.

At the Post Office, dilution brought significant changes, although often the effects were beneficial. For example, the modern system of alphanumeric London postal codes (N7, SE15 and so on) was introduced during the war to make mail-sorting easier without an encyclopaedic knowledge of the city. Many male postal workers felt resentful at the sight of women doing jobs for which, under the old system, they wouldn't have been qualified.

To the women workers, the men's complaints smacked of ingratitude. One temporary female sorter was infuriated by a letter published in the

Daily Post in which someone who signed himself 'A Mere Man' complained about the 'little bits of fluff' who were now working for the Post Office. The woman was so annoyed at the letter that she wrote to the paper herself. 'Is it chivalry,' she asked, 'which prompts men to criticise unmercifully those who have come forward to take men's places in the sorting office? We girls do not pretend to fill those places, but we are at least fired with the longing to "do our bit" and surely "mere man" might be less hasty in his judgement of us.' Her letter was signed 'one of the little bits of fluff'.

While most of the Post Office's new temporary female employees were filling in for men already serving in the Army, some found themselves supplanting workers who had no desire to leave their positions. Robert Nosworthy was a telegraph messenger boy from Fulham in southwest London whose father had worked for the Post Office all his life. He was a model employee, wearing his smart blue-and-red uniform with pride and willingly attending the classes laid on two mornings a week to provide for his educational needs.

It was a good job for a young lad who had recently left school, although the war placed a heavy burden on the shoulders of the messengers, since they were nearly always the ones charged with delivering the worst kind of news. Until the sealed envelope was opened there was no way of knowing for sure if a telegram brought good tidings or bad, but Robert soon learned that a message addressed to someone in one of London's poorer areas was almost certain to be the latter. He got used to anguished wives and mothers bursting into tears in front of him, or abruptly slamming the door in his face. There was no scope for rushing away from difficult situations, though, since messengers were obliged to wait until a telegram had been read by its recipient to see if there was any reply. Many postal workers actually quit their jobs during the war because they couldn't cope with bearing so much bad news.

But despite witnessing grief and suffering at such close quarters, Robert enjoyed his job at Fulham Post Office and got on well with the other boys working there. So he was more than a little put out when he found himself suddenly transferred to West Brompton, while a new cohort of messenger girls took over from him and his mates. Robert didn't think much of the idea of girls delivering telegrams, and he certainly didn't see why he should have to make way for them.

Despite his bitterness, Robert did his best to settle into the new work environment, but before long he was transferred again, this time to Earl's Court. For a second time he had been 'turfed out', as he saw it, by the girls.

The final straw came when the Army visited Robert's Post Office on a recruiting drive. A large crowd had gathered outside, and when he arrived to collect his telegrams for the day, a young woman marched right up to him and stuck a white feather through his buttonhole. The crowd erupted with laughter and jeering, and Robert felt utterly humiliated.

To the young messenger boy, that moment was a kind of epiphany. In an instant he was transformed, as he later described it, into 'a woman-hater'. With the exception of his mother, whom he loved dearly, Robert wanted nothing more to do with the female half of the population. He refused to talk to women unless it was absolutely necessary, and did his best to avoid even making eye contact with them.

For the next 20-odd years, Robert was a committed misogynist, and as the war went on and the casualties mounted, he was only confirmed in his hostility. He could never forgive those girls with the white feathers for sending thousands of men to their deaths.

After a while, however, Robert found a way to serve the Post Office that didn't involve any women at all. He resented the idea of being goaded into joining the Army by a girl, but in time Rifleman Robert Nosworthy was kitted out in a brand-new khaki uniform and set off to Blackdown Camp near Aldershot – where he joined the Third Battalion of the Post Office Rifles.

CHAPTER 10

THE SOMME

—

*Together with patience, the nation must be taught to
bear losses. No amount of skill on the part of the higher
commanders, no training, however good, on the part of
officers and men, no superiority, however great, of arms
and ammunition, will enable victories to be won without
the sacrifice of men's lives … The aim for which the
war is being waged is the destruction of German
militarism. Three years of war and the loss of one-
tenth of the manhood of the nation is not too great a
price to pay in so great a cause.*

Letter from General Douglas Haig to the editors
of several London newspapers, May 1916

IN THE GIANT WOODEN BUILDING that housed
REPS Home Depot in Regent's Park was a department
staffed almost entirely by women. The 'Returned
Letters Office' was responsible for processing mail
that had come back from the front marked 'Killed' or
'Missing', returning the letters to whoever had posted
them as soon as the official War Office telegram had
been dispatched.

Only married women were allowed to open the letters, and only then while under close supervision by a male superior – the higher-ups were terrified at the prospect of saucy photographs sent through the post being seen by innocent eyes. But while their modesty was carefully protected, the women did glimpse one dark and troubling aspect of the war. Well before news of the latest British engagement reached the newspapers, they would have a pretty clear idea of the number of casualties. How many letters were returned from the front on a given day was a barometer of the fortunes of the war.

The first of July 1916 saw the beginning of the Battle of the Somme. On a single day the department received over 30,000 letters. To the women of REPS it was obvious that something had gone terribly wrong.

The Somme was General Haig's great hope to win the war in a decisive 'big push', and although the specific details of the attack were top secret, everyone in Britain knew it was coming. Thanks to Kitchener's New Army battalions, the British forces had doubled in size, and for the first time in over a year there were plenty of shells, meaning that the preparatory artillery bombardment stood a much greater chance of success.

Haig was haunted by the Battle of Loos, in which the successful advance of the first day had been squandered by a slow start on the second. His plan for the Somme was to take the first German line and then press on immediately for the second. General Rawlinson, whose troops would be making the attack, favoured a more cautious strategy – a 'bite-and-hold' attack, taking things one step at a time. He feared that Haig's plan effectively meant halving the strength of the artillery barrage, since it would have to target two lines of trenches at once. But Rawlinson was overruled, and left in no doubt that his concerns were not appreciated. Haig was confident that the five-day bombardment, the longest the British Army had ever attempted, would be sufficient to ensure that there were no Germans left to resist.

On 24 June the artillery onslaught began, with zero hour set for the morning of the 29th. But even before the Allied advance began, it was clear that not everything was going according to plan. While the number of shells fired at the enemy was unprecedented, about a third of them turned out to be duds. German prisoners revealed that, while some parts of their line were badly damaged, others were still pretty much unscathed. But despite the alarming intelligence, calling off the attack was not an option. The British Army was under pressure from the French, who were bogged down in an increasingly bloody battle at Verdun, to take the heat off them.

Thanks to poor weather, the advance was delayed by two days, but at 7.30am on the bright, brilliant morning of 1 July 1916, 14 British divisions (around 120,000 men) began to go over the top. General Haig had predicted casualties at the rate of 10,000 per day, but his estimate proved wildly optimistic.

As soon as the British bombardment ceased and the men began swarming across no man's land, the German machine guns started to mow them down. It was the bloodiest day in the entire history of the British Army, with almost 20,000 men killed. But the Battle of the Somme was to continue for another four and a half months.

From: Central War Office, London

To: Heaton, the Manse, Scunthorpe, Lincoln

Deeply regret to inform you that 2 Lieut E.R. Heaton Middlesex Regt was reported missing believed killed 1st July. The Army Council expresses their sympathy.

Telegram received by Reverend Heaton,
6 July 1916

The Post Office Rifles were not involved in the initial stages of the Battle of the Somme, but that didn't mean they weren't affected by it. Among the officers training with the Second Battalion at Ipswich was Douglas Heaton, whose younger brother Eric was already out in France, serving with the 16th (Public Schools) Battalion of the Middlesex Regiment, one of the 'Pals' Battalions of Kitchener's New Army. As its name suggests, the Public Schools Battalion initially drew its membership exclusively from former public schoolboys – Eric had attended

Kingswood, a boarding school in Bath – although by summer 1916 it had begun to take on a more general mix of soldiers.

Eric had been expecting to go over the top at the Somme on 29 June, and when the attack was postponed by 48 hours, he took the opportunity to write a letter to his parents:

> *My dear Mother and Father,*
>
> *Thank you very much for the parcel just arrived, it will prove very useful. I also had letters from Doris + Douglas which I was very glad to get + also to read Wallace's letter. The weather here is improving after very heavy rains. We have just got an English paper & read that the guns can be heard in England, I don't doubt it! Well let us hope the Boche is done for this time, he will get it strong on all sides.*
>
> *We move soon now I believe – may it be to victory! Excuse more now, the best of love to you all.*
>
> *Ever your loving son*
>
> *Eric*

The cheerful tone of Eric's letter belied his true anxiety. He knew that it was touch and go whether he would make it through the forthcoming battle. As a junior officer, he had less chance of surviving than most – while the average fatality rate in the Army was 12 per cent, for the subalterns, whose job it was to lead their platoons over the top, the figure was more than double that. During the bloodiest periods of the war, the life expectancy of a junior officer at the front was just six weeks.

With this in mind, Eric had spent the previous evening writing another letter to his parents, one he hoped would never be posted. When it was finished, he handed it to the quartermaster for safekeeping.

My darling mother, father,

I am writing this on the eve of my first action. Tomorrow we go to the attack in the greatest battle the British Army has ever fought.

I cannot quite express my feelings on this night & I cannot tell if it is God's will that I shall come through – but if I fall in battle then I have no regrets save for my loved ones I leave behind. It is a great cause and I came out willingly to serve my King and Country. My greatest concern is that I may have the courage and determination necessary to lead my platoon well.

No one had such parents as you have been to me, giving me such splendid opportunities and always thinking of my welfare at great self-sacrifice to yourselves. My life has been full of faults but I have tried at all times to live as a man and thus to follow the example of my father.

This life abroad has taught me many things, chiefly the fine character of the British Race to put up with hardships with wonderful cheerfulness. How I have learnt to love my men. My great aim had been to win their respect, which I trust I have accomplished, and I hope that when the time comes I shall not fail them.

If I fall do not let things be black for you. Be cheerful and you will be living true always to my memory. I thank God for my brothers and sisters who have all been very much to me.

Well I cannot write more now. You are all in my thoughts as I enter this first battle. May God go with me. With all my love to you all.

Always your loving son,

Eric

On the morning of 1 July, Eric's battalion went over the top in the supporting wave of an attack at Beaumont Hamel. As a platoon leader, he was one of the first men out of the trench and into no man's land. He made it further than many, getting almost as far as the enemy front line before he was shot in the leg by a German gunner and fell to the ground, bleeding badly.

Eric's body was not recovered by his comrades, so he was listed as 'missing presumed killed'. Five days had passed by the time the Reverend and Mrs Heaton received a telegram from the War Office informing them of the news. But after that the word began to spread fast, and soon Eric's parents were inundated with letters of condolence from others who had suffered the same fate as a result of the events of 1 July. It was a day on which 20,000 young men had been taken in one fell swoop, and because of the 'Pals' system entire communities had been thrown into mourning together.

'I should like, as a fellow sufferer, to sympathise with you in your sorrow,' wrote one stranger in a letter to the Heatons. 'I had an exactly similar report from the War Office about my son, J. Kenneth, on same data. Same regiment, same battalion, and my son's last letter home was countersigned by your son.' Meanwhile, James Hanby, a friend of the family, wrote:

> *The thing we feared has befallen us all. I cannot tell you how distressed I am on your account but I pray you may be comforted by the thought of Eric's heroism and voluntary sacrifice. My eldest boy, so we are informed this morning, fell in the enemy's front trench & knowing what it means you will receive my words of sympathy as anything but empty words.*

The consolation of a noble sacrifice was something, but in the absence of an identified body, the Heatons had not yet given up hope that Eric might be found safe and sound. Two weeks after the attack, his brother Douglas, training with the Post Office Rifles in England, was still doing his best to encourage his parents that Eric might still be alive. 'I have looked in the papers and have been relieved that his name has not been mentioned,' he wrote. 'I cannot but think that he is perfectly safe, though perhaps wounded.'

On 12 July, almost a week after the Heatons had received their telegram from the War Office, a note arrived from a man in Eric's company called Wegg. Enclosed was the moving letter that Eric had entrusted to the quartermaster. 'I gather he gave it to him in case the worst should happen,' Wegg explained.

Clearly, Wegg believed that Eric was probably dead, but, nonetheless, he too encouraged the Heatons to keep hoping. 'You have no doubt by this time heard from the War Office that your son is reported "missing believed wounded",' he wrote, perhaps unconsciously putting 'wounded' instead of 'killed' because it was what everyone was hoping. 'That is at present all I know ... If I hear, as I hope I may, that he is wounded & a prisoner I will of course let you know.'

Meanwhile, the Heatons had been writing to Eric's comrades in the Public Schools Battalion, trying to find out what had happened to him, but it was a painfully slow process, despite the normally efficient Army post. A month and a half after Eric had disappeared, Mrs Heaton received a letter from another of his comrades, A.J. Bird. 'I regret I cannot give any direct information of Mr Heaton,' Bird wrote. 'But I can state that I saw him in no man's land not far from the German lines & at that time he was quite alright.' The message was encouraging, at least in so far as no news was good news. But like Wegg, Bird clearly felt the chances of Eric's survival were slim, as was clear from the tone in which he spoke of him. 'We can all understand your feelings in regards to Mr Heaton,' he wrote. 'He was loved and respected by every man in the Platoon and whatever might have been his fate we can all rest contented that he did his duty.' As much as Bird might hope that Eric was still alive, his message sounded like a condolence letter.

As well as writing to Eric's former comrades, some of whom were now in German prisoner-of-war camps, his parents had been in touch with the War Office, hoping to find out more about the circumstances surrounding his disappearance. On 6 September they received a letter containing a snatch of fresh testimony from the field:

> *The following report has been received from the Officer Commanding the 16th Battalion, Middlesex Regiment, respecting 2nd Lieutenant E.R. Heaton of that Battalion, previously reported 'missing believed killed':*
>
> *Pte. Henry saw this officer hit in the knee – in fact he says that the knee was almost blown off – 2/Lt. Heaton was bleeding very badly and Pte. Henry thinks he must have bled to death.*

It was hardly the news the family had hoped for – and yet it wasn't quite conclusive. Still nobody had actually come forward to say that they had seen Eric's body. The Heatons continued to press for more information, firing off letters to anyone they could think of who might shed some light on what had happened to their son.

Their insistence on getting to the truth was understandable – not least since other parents had sometimes been told incorrectly that their sons had died on the battlefield. One man from the Post Office Rifles was captured by a German patrol, but thanks to a case of mistaken identity, one of his comrades marked him down as killed in action. While the rifleman languished in a German military hospital, his parents received a devastating telegram from the War Office. They were overjoyed when they finally heard from him and realised that he was still alive, but even decades later, when he had long since returned from the war, they kept the telegram as a memento – to remind them of the tragedy that could so easily have befallen them, as it had so many others.

In November, the Heatons received word from the War Office that a private in Eric's battalion had come forward claiming to have seen their son's body. By now they were clutching at straws in their hope that Eric might suddenly reappear, and – struggling to accept what they were being told – they begged for the man to be questioned by a superior officer to confirm whether his testimony was true.

The War Office officials, despite their professional sympathy, were beginning to grow a little frustrated. To them, Eric was just one of 20,000 men killed on that warm summer's day in July, and, in the months since, more than 100,000 others had died on the same battlefield. Nevertheless, they agreed to pass on the family's request.

As the months went by, the waiting only got harder for Eric's parents. Their son had disappeared at the height of summer, and now winter was beginning to set in. The slow process of sending letters back and forth, often waiting weeks or months for a reply, was becoming unbearable.

Finally, on 2 January 1917 – almost six months to the day since Eric's disappearance – the Heatons received a letter from the War Office saying that his status had been officially changed from 'missing' to 'killed in action'. Enclosed was a signed statement from Private Earney, the man who said he had seen Eric's body:

> *2nd Lt. E.R. Heaton. 16th Mx. Regt. C. Coy. 9 Platoon.*
>
> *Was killed on the Sat of July 1st by shell, previously being hit by bullet, probably Machine Gun. We after the attack was in the Hamel Sector, Lancashire and Dublin Fusiliers took over our Sector, was taken in by either of Regts and the probable place of Burial is Auchonvillers or Engelbelmer near by.*
>
> *(Sd) Pte. H.H. Earney.*

The letter from the War Office concluded: 'There is no reason to believe that the statement by Private H.H. Earney, of which a copy is enclosed, is incorrect. The council are in consequence constrained to conclude that Second Lieutenant E.R. Heaton was killed in action on 1st July 1916, and I am to express their sympathy with you in your bereavement.' The talk was no longer of worrying or doubt – now the Heatons were officially bereaved. And as if the War Office's verdict wasn't final enough, soon it was given a royal seal when a telegram arrived from Buckingham Palace:

> *The King and Queen deeply regret to learn that it is now officially confirmed that your son who was previously reported as missing has fallen in the service of his country. Their majesties deplore the loss which*

you and the Army have sustained and truly sympathise
with you in your sorrow.

Eric's parents had held out as long as they could, desperately hoping for a miracle. But now at last it was time to accept what had happened. Their son had joined the ranks of the tens of thousands of young men who would never be returning to their families.

Several months passed before the Heatons heard from the War Office again. This time the officials wrote to say that they had finally located Eric's grave. He had been buried near Auchonvillers, as Private Earney had predicted, and at his head stood a sturdy wooden cross engraved with his name and rank. For half a year his parents had clung to the hope that Eric was still out there somewhere, and all along his last resting place had been clearly marked.

Eric's parents never did find out the full story of what happened to him on that fateful day in July 1916, but a year later, when Douglas Heaton was out in France himself, serving with the Post Office Rifles, he was at least able to visit Eric's last resting place, and to pay his own respects to his dear brother.

CHAPTER 11

FROM HELL'S VALLEY TO HIGH WOOD

—

My darling,

Just a line to tell you I'm all right. We've been through a pretty complete & thorough Hell, and have come out with the best part of the battalion scuppered – ι· · Hun with the most systematic & admirable thoroughness jι · blew our *line to bits with a four-hour bombardment of ι· ·edible intensity & then walked over into it. There was nobody to welcome him except dead men or men buried alive. He got two lines this way – we held onto the third ... We have lost all the Officers & practically all the men who were in the front line. Some of them I hope are prisoners. Guy was there, also Clark, Gormley, Ames, Wallace, Howell – these are all missing. Four others were killed & two wounded, including Maxwell who got a bit of shrapnel in the arm ... I haven't got the casualty list absolutely right yet – we must have lost over 400 men – of which there are still 250 I have no news of at all.*

Well, so long darling, I must get along. Best love to you all –

Your Loving Mister

Letter from Captain Home Peel
to his wife Gwendolen, 23 May 1916

WHILE THE POST OFFICE RIFLES were fortunate to miss out on the bloodbath of the first day of the Somme, that didn't mean they were having an easy time of it. On 21 May 1916 they had been caught in a box barrage at the foot of Vimy Ridge, an area they knew as Hell's Valley. The battalion's forward companies were occupying a line of craters when the five-hour bombardment began, a curtain of shells falling on three sides of them and cutting them off from any kind of support. With the Post Office men isolated, the Germans had attacked with a vengeance, and had taken the British front line from them. It was all that those further back could do to block their communication trenches and prevent the enemy from getting any further.

Even those who survived the assault were badly shaken by it. 'I got back to these headquarters about 4 AM this morning,' Captain Gore Browne told his wife Imogen. 'We have had a very bad time.' The captain was normally a keen letter-writer, and after Loos he had devoted pages and pages to describing every detail of the battle in his letters home, complete with diagrams. But now his ability to put what he had experienced into words – and, furthermore, words that would get past the censor – had deserted him. 'I cannot write about it and you will understand,' he explained apologetically. 'I am feeling horribly numbed but I am well and not hurt and my only trouble physically is a tummy full of the smell of gas shells and a great weariness ... It is very good to be where there are no shells again.'

Captain Gore Browne was not alone in feeling stunned by the events at Hell's Valley. In just one day almost a hundred men of the battalion had been killed, many more injured, and for the first time a large number had been taken prisoner – it was the worst day in the battalion's history, by a long shot. 'It is very sad taking stock of everybody,' Gore Browne wrote to his wife a few days later. 'I don't ever want to see a bombardment like that again.'

Fortunately for Gore Browne, his wish looked like it might soon be granted. He had been put up for a promotion to major, and had been spending the last couple of months at brigade headquarters, understudying one of the staff officers, or 'red tabs', with a view to taking a staff position himself in the near future. It was the kind of position he had been longing for ever since he had missed out to Peel as adjutant.

As it happened, Gore Browne and Peel, who had recently been promoted to captain, were getting on better than they ever had before. Witnessing the various staff officers going about their business – some fussy and particular, others frenzied and slapdash – Gore Browne had come to appreciate Peel's quiet, methodical approach. The two men shared a low opinion of the 'higher-ups' back home in England, although Peel's venomous disdain – he called them a 'shilly-shallying putrid invertebrate fat-headed self-seeking lot of swine' – went rather further than Gore Browne's mild frustration at their occasionally impractical orders.

Gore Browne was enjoying his time at brigade headquarters, despite the mountains of paperwork he had to deal with, but after the catastrophic losses at Hell's Valley, he was concerned about the battalion's morale. The following week he requested permission to go and spend some time with the men, and in an attempt to cheer them up began organising a day of entertainment for the weekend. There would be a picnic in some nearby woods, followed by a sports day and a concert by the Royal Army Medical Corps band. 'We had such a perfect spot on a hill,' he told his wife Imogen afterwards, 'our sports being held in a glade in the woods and our concert in a clearing with the men sitting in a big circle, I on a biscuit box with a shell to beat when I wanted "order".' Mercifully, the weather held out, and the event was a great success.

That night, Captain Gore Browne left the party in the best of spirits – not only had his day of activities gone down well with the men, but that morning he had received a wire from the War Office in London, requesting him to come for a six-week placement. It was just the sort of assignment that he wanted.

When he arrived back at his billet at 9pm that evening, Gore Browne found a telegram waiting for him. He was informed that 11 new officers would be joining the battalion – veterans of the Gallipoli campaign. By the time he awoke the next morning, the new men had already arrived.

Among them was a lieutenant by the name of Nathan, who had been given the temporary rank of major while out in Turkey. As soon as he met Gore Browne that morning, he began to commiserate with him for being 'passed over', clearly believing that as a temporary major he outranked him. Even worse, since the command of the battalion was up in the air following Maxwell's wounding at Hell's Valley, Nathan seemed to be under the impression that he was the obvious choice to take over.

Captain Gore Browne was furious. Nathan might be a temporary major, but his substantive rank was lower than Gore Browne's. As he saw it, the interloper was attempting to 'jump' him. Gore Browne was not about to see his battalion handed over to a man he didn't know from Adam, and nor was he willing for Nathan's captains to take precedence over long-serving Post Office Rifles, three of whom had been put forward for captaincies of their own. Well versed in the rulebook on substantive and temporary rank, he explained to Nathan that, while he might have been a major at Gallipoli, in France he would be expected to revert to lieutenant.

Nathan took the issue to the brigade commander, General Cuthbert, who confirmed that Gore Browne was in the right. But the new man had not given up yet. He now set his sights on jumping one of the other battalion officers, Captain Vince, who – like Gore Browne – had just been put up for promotion. Nathan demanded that the general put a stop to Vince's advancement until he had been promoted as well. But by this point Gore Browne was apoplectic. He told the general that if there was the slightest chance of

Nathan superseding Vince, and hence potentially commanding the battalion, he would turn down his offer from the War Office.

Fortunately, the general was able to smooth things over. Nathan reverted to lieutenant but was immediately put up for a promotion to captain, while Vince and Gore Browne's promotions to major went through as well. General Cuthbert reassured Gore Browne that there was no danger of Nathan taking over the battalion – if the job went to anyone, it would be Vince.

'I have been having a very agitated time but I think it is all smooth now,' Gore Browne wrote to his wife on 7 June. With the conflict resolved, he set off for his new position at the War Office. But he left a battalion that was still overflowing with officers, all of them in constant danger of ruffling each other's feathers. As he put it in a letter to Imogen, 'I never knew such a kettle of fish.'

My dear G B,

Your letter of the 24th reached me last night. We are on the move again so I write this on my knee. The Battalion after much longer rest than they thought they would ever have, went in strong and came out … well, as many another Battalion that has gone in strong has come out. The ordeal was doubly hard owing to the vile weather that set in the second day. We were a couple of days in bivouacs and shelters on the edge of the old front line, so everyone could see what those that had gone up before had done so magnificently. They were in fine fettle going up, and the last I saw of poor Mitchell was as he tried to catch the O.C.'s eye marching past the starting point with the one tall splendid piper (and pipes) that had come to No. 1 Company from Ireland, skirling for all he was worth at the head of the Company.

Letter from Ernest De Caux to
Major Eric Gore Browne, 30 September 1916

While the Post Office Rifles remained in the Vimy sector, less than 20 miles to the south the Battle of the Somme continued to rage on. By this point it had become largely a battle of attrition, in which periodically one side or the other would send its men over the top to be mown down by enemy machine guns, and there seemed little hope of a meaningful breakthrough. But General Haig still hadn't given up on his 'big push', and his confidence was bolstered by a new weapon that was on its way to the Continent. The 'Caterpillar Machine-Gun Destroyer', as the machine was officially known, was shrouded in secrecy. When 60 of the giant contraptions were shipped over to France, they were boxed up and labelled as 'Water Tanks' to avoid provoking too much interest. The pseudonym stuck, and soon the new vehicles had ditched their original name – from now on they were known simply as 'tanks'.

Haig hoped that the tanks would be what he needed to make a real breakthrough on the Western Front. Once again, he was under pressure from the French to launch an attack as soon as possible. The date he finally settled upon was 15 September, and this time the Post Office Rifles would be involved in the operation.

The plan was for an advance across a seven-mile front between Thiepval and Combles, and the brigade of which the Post Office Rifles made up a quarter (along with their old friends the Civil Service Rifles, the Cast Iron Sixth and the Shiny Seventh Londons) would have a key role in the attack. They were to take the German stronghold of High Wood, which sat upon the crest of Bazentin Ridge, much of which (including the nearby Delville Wood) had already fallen to the British. High Wood itself had long been the sticking point in the area, and the scene of much bloody fighting ever since the British had first tried to take it in mid-July. The current Allied front line cut through its southernmost tip, while the rest of the wood was in the hands of the Germans.

Although High Wood had at one point provided useful strategic cover, it now looked only marginally different from the rest of the blasted wilderness of no man's land. As one man described it, the place had become 'a wood only in name – ragged stumps sticking out of the churned-up Earth, poisoned with fumes of high explosives, the whole a mass of corruption'.

The proximity of the British and German positions in the wood meant that the usual artillery bombardment would carry an unacceptable risk to the British front line. Instead, the plan was to bombard the German lines further back, and use the new tanks to assault the front-line trenches.

The tanks were to start crossing the wood shortly before zero hour, so that they would reach the German trench a minute before the infantry went over the top. While the soldiers advanced, the tanks would distract the enemy and blow their machine-gun emplacements to smithereens.

Haig's plan did not enjoy much support among those charged with carrying it out. General Barter, who commanded the Post Office Rifles' Division, the 47th London, was worried that the new machines might struggle with the difficult terrain, littered as it was with tree stumps and shell holes, and the tank commanders themselves were equally sceptical. But General Haig was insistent – as with the disastrous attack on 1 July, once again his plan was not open to debate.

On 20 August, the Post Office Rifles began the three-day march to Franvillers, a town about 15 miles behind the front line. In the heat of the summer, it was an exhausting journey, but the men kept themselves in good spirits thanks to an array of marching songs, a mixture of old favourites they had learned during their training at the lunatic asylum in Abbots Langley and more recent additions to the repertoire. The songs ranged from the sentimental ('There's a Long Long Trail A-Winding', 'When I Leave the World Behind') to more risqué 'war vulgars' such as the popular 'Mademoiselle from Armentières'.

Mademoiselle from Armentières, parlez-vous,
Mademoiselle from Armentières, parlez-vous,
Mademoiselle from Armentières,
She hasn't been kissed for forty years,
Hinky-pinky parlez-vous.

According to Post Office legend, the 'mademoiselle' in the song was actually the daughter of an *estaminet* owner who had married a man from the South West District Office, 'Buster' Rogers, who was serving in the Royal Corps of Signals. Neither she nor her husband could have appreciated the increasingly saucy lyrics that the song accumulated as it became more and more popular:

Mademoiselle from Armentières, parlez-vous,
Mademoiselle from Armentières, parlez-vous,
She was true to me, she was true to you,
She was true to the whole damned army too,
Hinky-pinky parlez-vous.

Mademoiselle from Armentières, parlez-vous,
Mademoiselle from Armentières, parlez-vous,
She's the hardest working girl in town,
But she makes her living upside down,
Hinky-pinky parlez-vous.

Not all the Post Office men enjoyed the bawdy lyrics. As the riflemen belted out the latest verse, one of their company sergeant majors, Simeon George Chivers, made his disapproval abundantly clear. At 42, 'Chum' Chivers, as he was known to the men of his company, was one of the oldest members of the battalion, a long-standing Post Office employee who had worked his way up from postman to sorter at GPO headquarters in London. Chivers had proved himself in war as well as peace, and was respected by all in the battalion. Only a few days earlier, he had received the Military Cross for 'conspicuous gallantry' – his citation in *The London Gazette* noted that he had 'displayed great coolness under fire, and has set a fine example to his company'. Chivers was a kind, avuncular man and was well liked by everyone who served with him, but his taste in music made little impact on the men. Despite his constant tut-tutting, they sang louder than ever.

After three days of marching, the battalion arrived at Franvillers, where they began to train for the forthcoming battle. Wilfred Whitehead, now a colonel, was in command, with Vince as his deputy. Whitehead had spent many hours constructing a cardboard model of the territory that the men were expected to take. Meanwhile, the course had been taped out at a nearby training ground and they started daily rehearsals of the advance, at every hour of the day and night. Never had they been so well prepared for an attack.

Nonetheless, some of the men were growing twitchy. High Wood had a bad reputation among the Tommies, thanks to the large number of men who had already died there. It had acquired a sinister epithet that was known to every soldier on the Western Front: 'Ghastly by day, ghostly by night, the rottenest place on the Somme.' To make matters worse, the summer of 1916 had been a wet one, and although the sun was now beating down relentlessly, the men from the Post Office could imagine the state the ground must be in after so many weeks of heavy rain.

Aware that some soldiers were beginning to have second thoughts, the Army went to great pains to emphasise that the penalty for desertion – or indeed 'cowardice' – was death. It seemed almost daily that the Post Office Rifles were gathered together to hear the latest announcement solemnly read out. Years later, Rifleman Harfleet recalled the words that had seared his memory with disgust: 'At a field general court martial on 14 July, private [blank] of the [blank] regiment was found guilty of [desertion or cowardice] in the face of the enemy and sentenced to be shot at dawn. The sentence was duly carried out.' Over the course of the war, over 300 British soldiers were blindfolded, tied to a stake, and then shot dead by their own countrymen.

For those who had no intention of joining their ranks, there was only one real prospect of escape from the terrible lottery of the front lines: the Blighty wound. A man who sustained such an injury was generally considered to be lucky – through no dishonour or cowardice on his own part, he had bought a ticket home. But some soldiers felt that if the wounds weren't coming to find them, they would do their best to make their own luck. Whenever Rifleman Harvey opened a tin of bully beef for his dinner, he deliberately cut his fingertips on the sharp metal edge, and then dipped them in the dirtiest mud he could find, hoping that the wound would turn septic. But, to his frustration, the cuts always seemed to heal over. Meanwhile, another rifleman offered 20 francs during a football match to anyone who could put him out of action. Harvey obliged, kicking the man in the knee as hard as he could. It wasn't exactly playing by the rules, but, as he saw it, all was fair in love and war.

The more time the men spent preparing for the battle to come, the more fatalistic and superstitious some of them became. They wrote and witnessed wills, composed final letters to their loved ones back home, and gambled wildly at cards late into the night. If a man won big, he would be sure to blow his winnings quickly at the local *estaminet*, rather than tempt fate by holding on to them.

Some men became convinced that their number was about to come up. Also training at Franvillers were the Civil Service Rifles, among whose ranks was an underage private called Alec Reader. After five months in France, Alec had seen enough of the front lines, and – although he felt uncomfortable at the idea of running away – he had agreed to a transfer organised by his father. But as the day of the battle approached, Alec's papers hadn't come through yet, and it became clear that he would be going over the top after all.

With his chance of escape fading fast, Alec grew more and more resigned to the fate he felt sure lay ahead of him. On 3 September he wrote a letter to his family, which – for purposes of morale on the home front – was heavily censored by the War Office:

> *The reason I don't want parcels ... is that I stand to ------------------------ and my benevolence to the rest of the platoon does not exceed letter pads and socks. To give you an idea of how firm my conviction is, I may tell you that I shall ----------- within a fortnight. So why waste good stuff.*

At 3.15am on 12 September, the Post Office Rifles began the march up to the front lines. Just as dawn was beginning to break, they passed through the town of Albert, dominated by its giant red-brick basilica. The tower of the church was still standing, but the gilded statue of the Madonna and her child that had once stood proudly at its summit now tottered precariously at an angle of 90 degrees, the result of a shell strike in January 1915. In the early morning light, the men looked up at the statue contemplatively. The 'Golden Virgin', as she was known to the British Army in France, had already accrued a number of legends. Some said that the war would end on the day she finally fell, others that it would be lost by whichever side toppled her.

The Post Office men passed on in silence. By 8am they had reached a bivouac position just behind the lines, where they waited for another two days, playing endless rounds of cards and trying not to think too hard about what was coming.

On the afternoon of 14 September, the 900-odd men of the battalion gathered together in front of Colonel Whitehead, who was seated on his charger Buchanan. After a few words of encouragement, the colonel led them forward to their assembly trench at the edge of High Wood. It was well after midnight by the time they were all finally in position, but they had reached their jumping-off points with no casualties.

The plan for the battle was divided into three parts. While the tanks bombarded the German front line, the Civil Service Rifles would push forward and take a trench known as the Switch Line, which crossed through the far side of the wood. The Post Office Rifles would follow them over and then press on to what was known as the Starfish Line, 700 yards beyond. Finally, with the first two lines secured, the Cast Iron Sixth would move forward and take the third – the Flers Line.

As they waited quietly on that chill moonlit night, the men's thoughts turned again to the grim reputation of the wood – 'ghastly by day' and 'ghostly by night'. Looking out at the ravaged tree stumps and the corpse-strewn craters of the battlefield, you didn't have to be particularly superstitious to feel that there was something eerie about the place. What had once teemed with life was now a world of death and decay, a testament to war's power to annihilate everything good that got in its way.

By this point, the Post Office Rifles had grown accustomed to the presence of dead bodies. Arms and legs that protruded from the sides of a trench might be used to prop up a walking stick, and in one captured German position some skulls were even turned into candle-holders – that is, until a chaplain with an interest in craniology declared that they had belonged to allies rather than enemies. In a cramped trench full of dead bodies, men frequently found themselves stepping on the distended stomachs of their own former comrades. It was horrifying at first – and the smell was hard to forget – but in the end even the most squeamish got used to it.

High Wood, though, was unusually hideous, particularly in the sinister glow of moonlight. Many of the corpses there had been left unattended for two months, and, as one man put it, were 'returning to the state of the earth'. Their faces were almost pitch-black, leading some of the Post Office men to wonder whether they were native troops from the African colonies or Europeans who had turned that colour as a result of decay.

No soldier could afford to be too concerned about the fate of the corpses. While in the chalk pits of Hulluch the previous October, the Post Office men had witnessed a second lieutenant, temporarily attached to their battalion from the Royal Fusiliers, shot down in no man's land while attempting to retrieve the body of one of his comrades before it fell victim to the rats and hooded crows that swarmed over the battlefield. The lieutenant's corpse, at least, was easily retrieved, and he was given the dignified burial that he would have wanted. But his example was one that the rest of the men never forgot.

As long as there was no danger to their own safety, soldiers did usually take great pains to protect the bodies of the fallen, aware that some day their own mortal remains might be left to the care of their comrades. One of the eeriest jobs the men performed at the front was the Death Watch, in which a guard was posted to protect a dead body until it could be sent back behind the lines for burial. In some areas, a makeshift morgue was constructed out of corrugated iron, which the soldier on duty would beat periodically in an attempt to ward away vermin. Normally, the job was shared between several men, with each doing a two-hour shift and then handing on responsibility to someone else. But on some occasions a single sentry could be on duty all night long, alone in the pitch darkness with just his thoughts and his dead comrade for company.

While the men from the Post Office waited for the order to go over the top, fixing their bayonets and gulping down their rations of rum, they did their best to push their doubts to the back of their minds. They knew that their success was in large part tied to the Army's new weapon, the tanks – but as zero hour approached there was no sign of them. Finally, at around 6.20am the giant vehicles rumbled up to their starting positions. 'Look boys, what the hell's this?'

shouted one of the Post Office men enthusiastically. Just seeing the lumbering machines was enough to provide a boost to morale.

But the men's confidence in the new weapons didn't last long. As the tank commanders had predicted, the vehicles were entirely ill-suited to the difficult terrain. There were four allocated to the High Wood operation, and all of them soon lost their way – one driver actually had to stop and ask directions. And even when they knew where they were going, they had little success in getting there. Three of the tanks got stuck before they made it to the Germans, while the fourth reached the enemy front line just in time to burst into flames.

It was hardly the start to the battle that anyone had hoped for, but the infantry was under orders to advance nonetheless. At 6.30am, the Post Office Rifles watched anxiously as the Shiny Seventh and the Civil Service Rifles went over the top. With virtually no preliminary bombardment, predictably their casualties were heavy. The Post Office men watched in horror as one by one the men fell to the ground. Among the 300 dead was Alec Reader, the young lad who had been so certain that he wouldn't survive the attack. His premonition had turned out to be correct.

Meanwhile, the German artillery had begun bombarding British positions. Rifleman Bertie Whitehurst, a former mail-sorter, was rushing along the trench for a better view of the battlefield when he rounded a corner and stumbled across the body of one of his comrades – Alexander Rankin, a 21-year-old rifleman from Battersea. Rankin's corpse was slumped against the wall, his tin hat wonky and his breast gaping open where he had been hit by shrapnel. And Rankin wasn't the only man who didn't even make it over the top that morning. A little further along the trench was the corpse of Captain Mitchell, one of the company commanders, with a bloody bullet hole in his forehead.

Before long, it was zero hour for the Post Office men, and with a mighty yell they began heaving themselves up into no man's land. One of the company sergeant majors, Bill O'Connell, was among the first out of the trench, but he didn't even set foot onto the battlefield. The moment he rose above the parapet he was hit in the chest by a bullet, fell back into the trench and died.

But the Post Office Rifles kept going, swarming over the top and across no man's land. The German guns continued to fire, and soon men were falling left, right and centre. Their battle cries morphed into screams of agony.

There was no stopping to help a wounded comrade – the Post Office men had been warned in no uncertain terms that anyone doing so was liable to be shot for cowardice. 'Get on, damn you!' shouted one of the company officers, before he too was felled by a German bullet.

Within minutes, three of the four companies had lost their captains, and the platoon commanders started to take over. The men had got only 50 yards across no man's land, and already there seemed to be just a handful of them left, out of the 900-plus who had begun the advance. The smell of cordite hung in the air, mingling with the stench of blood, and the dawning sun was practically blotted out by the smoke from the German shells.

Under heavy fire from the enemy, most of the men who were not already dead or wounded were driven to ground. Only at the very fringes of the wood had some members of No. 2 and No. 3 Companies managed to press on for the Starfish Line. They had an awe-inspiring view of the battlefield beyond the wood itself, watching as tanks and infantry advanced together. Out in no man's land, an Army medic was rushing from shell hole to shell hole tending to the wounded, friend and foe alike. Every so often, he was shot at from a German emplacement, and each time he stood and shook his fist angrily. The riflemen were amazed at his bravery.

Within the wood itself, there was little chance of further progress, since the men there were under constant machine-gun fire. They took out their entrenching tools and began to dig themselves in. But however much earth they piled up in front of them, they were sitting ducks for enemy shelling.

The men's deliverance came a little after 9am when their brigade's eight trench mortars were turned on the German positions. The Post Office men watched in amazement as their friends in the Civil Service Rifles fired shell after shell over their heads, the giant cylinders passing through the air in almost unbroken lines – 'like a long row of single sausages', as one rifleman put it. Within minutes they had pounded the German trenches with over 750 shells. One by one, the machine guns fell silent.

Soon, the Germans who had been firing them emerged, standing with their hands above their heads in surrender. Some stepped forward, carrying wounded British soldiers on their backs. From behind, their own men began to fire on them, and several dropped down dead, but over 200 were successfully taken as prisoners.

The new captives were just grateful to be out of the fighting. As they passed by the Post Office men, one of them reached into his pocket and pushed something into Bertie Whitehurst's hand. Without thinking, Bertie accepted the present, but only after the enemy soldier had gone did he look down to see what he had given him: it was a snuffbox, of ornate European design. Bertie felt a little uncomfortable about what had just happened – he wasn't sure what the rules were about accepting gifts from the enemy – but he stuffed it into his pocket anyway.

The riflemen moved forward to the Starfish Line, where the men who had broken through earlier were waiting for them. Bertie and some of his pals started work on building a new fire step that faced towards the next German line. The Post Office men had attained their objective for the day, and High Wood was at last in British hands.

Not all of the battalion's survivors had made it to safety, however. Lance Corporal John McIntyre, a former messenger boy from Newcastle, had thrown himself into an abandoned stretch of trench to avoid a German stick bomb, slicing open his leg on a bayonet in the process. A pair of stretcher-bearers arrived shortly after dusk, but they were too weak to carry him and promised to come back later. McIntyre ended up spending the night in the German trench, with only enemy corpses for company. But the next day, there was still no sign of the stretcher-bearers – either they had forgotten all about him, or they too had been wounded or killed. It wasn't until the third day that McIntyre was finally rescued by a couple of New Zealanders, who took him back with them to their own base.

At the Starfish Line, the survivors of the Post Office Rifles continued to gather. A close friend of Bill Howell's called Jerry Hawkes had managed to crawl there with a bullet through his abdomen. After a quick examination, the medical officer told him that it had narrowly missed several vital organs. 'You must be the luckiest man alive,' he told the young man.

Jerry felt the truth of the doctor's words, for he had seen first-hand what his fate might have been. Crawling across the battlefield, he had come across 'Chum' Chivers, the avuncular sergeant major, lying in a shell hole with a horrific wound in his stomach. Chivers had been there for hours, with the hot sun beating down on him, and he begged Jerry desperately for water. But both men knew that to give food or drink to a man with a stomach injury was dangerous, and reluctantly Jerry had refused him.

Chivers was eventually found and sent off to hospital for treatment, but he never recovered from his injuries. He died a few days later at a base hospital in Rouen, leaving behind his wife Charlotte in Surbiton. The couple had never had children, but with Chivers' death the men of the Post Office Rifles felt as if they had lost a father.

The Post Office men settled into the Starfish Line, determined to hold it until they were relieved, but the final objective of the battle – the Flers Line – remained to be taken. On the morning of 17 September, Colonel Whitehead led a mixed assortment of Post Office Rifles, Cast Iron Sixth and Civil Service Rifles over the top in an attempt to finish the job. They advanced under driving rain, crossing ground so slippery that if they fell into a shell hole they knew they might never get out again. But somehow the men managed to make it the 300 yards across no man's land with hardly any casualties, and were able to take the Germans by surprise. They hacked their way through the barbed wire and began hurling bombs into the trench. Soon the Flers Line was in British hands, and the cost to the Post Office Rifles was only four men killed. All things considered, it could have been a lot worse.

Colonel Whitehead wrote to Major Gore Browne at the War Office in London to let him know how the battalion had fared in the battle. 'Everybody – Brigadier, Barter, Corps Commander – was delighted about it all,' he told him enthusiastically, 'but all the nice things they said were not half good enough for the men, who were simply grand.'

Not everyone took such a positive view, however. On 15 September alone, almost 5,000 British men had been killed, among them Grenadier Guardsman Raymond Asquith, the eldest son of the Prime Minister. Although all the objectives at High Wood had eventually been taken, Sir Douglas Haig did not view the battle as a success. The official verdict of the British High Command was 'lack of push', but Haig's personal diary entry was even more stark: 'The 47th Divn failed at High Wood.'

Haig felt that the losses sustained in the battle were out of proportion with the amount of ground taken, and he placed the blame for this squarely at the feet of the divisional commander, General Barter – despite the fact that Barter had done his best to change Haig's mind about using tanks in the wood in the first place, a strategy that had contributed to the heavy casualties. While Barter's opinion had been vindicated by what had happened, as far as his superiors were concerned he had blotted his copybook – and two weeks later he was relieved of his command.

The Post Office Rifles left High Wood on 20 September, and spent the night in billets in Albert. The following day they marched four miles to a camp at Hénencourt, where they gathered in the evening to take stock of their losses. Sitting outside at a table in the grounds of a grand chateau, Major Vince read the battalion roll by the light of a candle, and one by one Captain Peel marked the names off on a list.

The men from the Post Office stood around in a rough semicircle, their uniforms still encrusted with the mud of the battlefield. As each man's name was called, he answered, 'Yes, sir.' But time and again, Vince's voice rang out to silence from the ranks.

The battalion's French interpreter, Ernest De Caux, was struck by the simple poetry of the moment, as the list of names was called out one by one. A week later, he wrote a letter to Major Gore Browne in London:

I wish some great French Artist would paint a picture of the Roll Call in a British Regiment after one of these devastating yet splendidly victorious engagements on the Somme: a hollow square of jaded muddy figures standing in an orchard open on one side to the after glint of a sun that set red; mist begins to float up the valley, but the glint of light on some clouds high up has still the hardness of silver. A strong voice such as Vince's calls one name after another from a Roll lit by a fluttering candle shaded by the hand of the one remaining Sergeant Major. A dark mass of tall trees in the background.

There should never, never be anything but a brotherly feeling amongst Frenchmen for their English Comrades after this War. And you do it all so simply. On the eve of battle one would think you were preparing for a football match. Compared with earlier experiences of operations, what one meets with on every side here is admirable. It is hopeless to try and give any idea of it, and even the best dispatches in 'The Times' are weak. Wearing the uniform of any Army one feels a puppet, but here, one shrinks to the size of a grain of sand on a mighty beach, with about the same helplessness individually.

By the time the roll call was complete, the scale of the battalion's losses was clear. A total of 63 men were known to have been killed, and 185 had been wounded. A further 50 were missing, presumed dead – and for all but three of them, that presumption turned out to be correct. A week earlier the battalion had gone into battle with a strength of over 900 men. Now it could muster only two-thirds that number.

CHAPTER 12

THE BUTTE DE WARLENCOURT
—

Dear Elsie,

I am just writing a few lines to thank you for the papers which I received last night. They came in jolly handy as I have nothing to read. If you are sending them out each week (or fortnight or whatever it is) always wait until you receive a letter from me saying that I received the last lot before sending the next so as not to waste money in case I do not get them.

I hope you are quite well & have got over the vaccination. We are having a lively time at present, what with the noise of shells you cannot get to sleep. I suppose I shall get used to it soon.

It is very exciting to watch the anti-aircraft shells firing at the aeroplanes. We are having decent weather out here although it is very cold at night.

How are you getting on at the stores? I suppose you are quite used to the work now. Remember me to all I know, won't you?

My address is now 6527 Rfln F J Parker, 16 Platoon, 4 Coy, 1 / 8th Battalion City of London Regt, Post Office Rifles, BE7, France. Don't forget to drop me a line when you can will you as I always like to hear from you.

Well Elsie dear I think I have told you all and will close hoping all are quite well at home of course including yourself as this letter leaves me.

From your ever loving brother

Fred

Letter from Rifleman Fred Parker
to his sister Elsie, 30 September 1916

FRED PARKER WAS AMONG a draft from the East Surrey Regiment that helped bring the Post Office Rifles back up to strength after High Wood. He came from Tooting, and was devoted to his family there, in particular his 16-year-old sister Elsie. As well as sending her and his mother regular letters, he also posted several beautiful handmade silk postcards – luxuries that were as popular back home in England as they were ubiquitous in France. One card had been embroidered with the badge of the Post Office Rifles, while another featured a hummingbird and the words 'To my dear mother'. A third had a floral design, and incorporated a little flap that opened up to reveal a message on a pink slip of paper: 'Remember me'.

On the grey, misty afternoon of 7 October 1916, less than three weeks after they had been relieved at High Wood, the Post Office Rifles were in action again. In their sights this time was a trench system known as the Grid Line, about a mile or so ahead of the positions they had recently captured. The area around the German trenches was dominated by an ancient burial mound, the Butte de Warlencourt – a chalky lump, about 70 feet high, which was situated just off the old Roman road that ran from Albert to the town of Bapaume on the German side of the front lines. Set against the flat, open fields of the Somme, the Butte loomed like an ominous tumour on the landscape.

The plan was to advance under a creeping barrage – one that moved forward in stages, with the men following close behind – to take a section of the German line known as Diagonal Trench. Aerial reports suggested that they would meet little opposition in the attack, and gossip around the trenches was that the operation should be 'a piece of cake'. Some men joked that they might take the German line without even encountering the enemy.

How such rumours came about no one could say, but they turned out to be far from the truth. Unbeknownst to the Post Office Rifles, the burial ground was heavily fortified – it was surrounded by thick layers of barbed wire, and a network of tunnels dug into the chalk led to various mortar and machine-gun posts. To any Army that dared to approach it, the Butte de Warlencourt was a hornets' nest.

To make matters worse, the initial British barrage did not perform as planned, and the Post Office Rifles went over the top against an enemy that had barely been bruised. As soon as the first wave came within range of the German machine guns, the men began to fall to the ground. As one Post Office man put it, they 'just disappeared as though scythed down and moments later [there was] no one to be seen'.

The attack was a catastrophic failure and was rapidly called off – but not before 193 of the Post Office men had been killed. Among them was Rifleman Fred Parker.

At least Fred's family had his letters and beautiful silk postcards to remember him by. Sergeant Eric Eustace, a former assistant postman from Peckham, had written a farewell letter to his wife and handed it to a man called Dusty Miller who was serving with the Brigade Field Ambulance, to send on in the event that he didn't make it through the battle. When Dusty learned that Eric had been killed, his first thought was to make sure that his widow received his final message, but when he looked for the letter he couldn't find it anywhere. After hours of frantic searching, he was forced to accept that he had lost it. Dusty never forgave himself for his carelessness, and for the rest of his life he made a pilgrimage every year to Warlencourt British Cemetery, to lay a wreath on Sergeant Eustace's grave. It was the only penance he could think of to atone for such a terrible mistake.

The wholesale carnage at the Butte de Warlencourt made the stories of those who survived it even more remarkable. Bertie Whitehurst, the young postal sorter who had taken a snuffbox from a German prisoner at High Wood, went over the top with it in his tunic pocket. Alongside it was a copy of *Palgrave's Golden*

Treasury that had been given to him by his best friend, Johnny Hunt.

Bertie and Johnny had grown friendly during their time at the Post Office in London, and had signed up together for the Post Office Rifles. The two men were thick as thieves, and during their training together with the Third Battalion at Fovant had earned the nickname 'The Heavenly Twins'.

At Fovant, Johnny was found to have a heart condition and was classed unfit for foreign service. When Bertie was put forward for a draft out to France, his friend asked if there was anything he could give him. Bertie had long admired Johnny's copy of Palgrave's poetry collection and shyly asked if he could take it with him. Johnny agreed willingly, inscribing a blank page at the front of the book with Christina Rossetti's poem 'Remember'.

Within a few minutes of going over the top at Warlencourt, Bertie was struck by a German machine-gun bullet. He fell to the ground, along with the men on either side of him. But while others around him had been killed instantly, Bertie hit the earth astonished to realise that he was still alive. As the bullets continued to whizz past over his head, he hugged the ground as close as he could.

Before long, Bertie lost consciousness, and when he awoke a few hours later darkness had fallen. There were stretcher-bearers combing the battlefield, searching for survivors. One of the company first-aid men helped Bertie to his feet, and together they staggered back to the British lines. At a dressing station, he was given a cup of sweet tea and an anti-tetanus injection, before a man in a white coat arrived to examine his wound. It turned out to be more superficial than he had imagined – aside from a small piece of metal just beneath the skin, there was little to show for the bullet that had hit him.

When the medics turned out Bertie's pockets they soon found out why. The German snuffbox had been smashed to pieces, and the precious copy of Palgrave had suffered severe damage too. But Bertie was still able to open it and turn to the page Johnny had written on. In his friend's careful, elegant handwriting were Rossetti's lines:

> *Remember me when I am gone away,*
> *Gone far away into the silent land;*
> *When you can no more hold me by the hand,*
> *Nor I half turn to go yet turning stay.*
> *Remember me when no more day by day*
> *You tell me of our future that you planned:*
> *Only remember me; you understand*
> *It will be late to counsel then or pray.*
> *Yet if you should forget me for a while*
> *And afterwards remember, do not grieve:*
> *For if the darkness and corruption leave*
> *A vestige of the thoughts that once I had,*
> *Better by far you should forget and smile*
> *Than that you should remember and be sad.*

Bertie didn't forget his friend Johnny, but the two of them never were reunited. Despite his heart problem, in March 1918 Johnny was rushed out to France as part of an emergency draft to help stem the final German advance of the war. Within a month of his arrival he was dead.

Bertie Whitehurst wasn't the only Post Office man to cheat death at the Butte de Warlencourt – in fact, Bill Howell's tale of survival was even more astonishing. He went over the top that afternoon in good spirits, fortified by the customary tot of rum allocated to every soldier before battle. As he strode forward across no man's land, he was amazed at the sight of the men marching alongside him – it seemed almost as if the whole British Army was advancing together – and, in the distance, he was sure he could see Bapaume burning.

But before long, Bill's optimism faltered as the men around him started dropping to the ground. Bill watched as Rifleman William Boulton, a father of six from Chingford in Essex, went down in front of him, never to get up again.

Bill could see some Germans up ahead, firing from a half-dug trench. With a bit of assistance, he was sure that he could capture their position. He crouched down in some long grass, took a grenade out of his pocket and removed the safety pin, ready to lob it in the direction of the enemy as soon as the next wave of British soldiers came over.

What Bill didn't know, as he crouched there waiting for reinforcements, was that the attack had already been called off – there would be no second wave arriving to help him. He was just beginning to wonder what was taking them so long when a pair of bullets hit him in the abdomen. He was spun around and rolled down into a shell hole as the blood began to seep through his tunic.

Bill felt sure he was done for. One bullet wound to the stomach was generally fatal, and he had suffered two of them. He could feel the warm blood on his hands, and the bullets inside him felt like they were scorching his flesh.

Bill was beginning to feel weak and woozy when he realised that there was a more pressing problem than the stomach wounds – he had thrown away the safety pin of the grenade he was holding, so all that was keeping it from going off was the pressure of his fingers on the handle. If he lost consciousness now it would blow him to pieces within seconds.

Bill knew he had to act quickly before he passed out. Bleeding to death was one thing, but he had no intention of being blown to smithereens. He fumbled frantically in his pocket for the field dressing that every soldier was equipped with before going into battle, but rather than attempt to use it on his stomach wounds, he took the bandage and wrapped it around the grenade, tying the spring down so that the bomb couldn't go off. Once it was secured, he finally passed out.

As he relinquished his grip on consciousness, Bill was surprised to find himself feeling utterly at peace. He was sure that he was dying, but it didn't seem so bad after all. His eyes had been spattered with blood and everything around him seemed to be bathed in a soft orange glow. Serenely, Bill closed his eyes and prepared to meet his maker.

When he woke up several hours later to find that he wasn't dead after all, Bill was astonished. It was getting dark, and he could see a German patrol approaching in the distance. Bill had no desire to be taken as a prisoner, knowing that as a sniper he might be singled out for especially cruel treatment, and since his stomach wound seemed to have stopped bleeding he was able to crawl back towards the British lines.

Along the way, Bill came across a South African patrol that helped get him to an ambulance. When it was clear that he was no longer in mortal danger, he was taken on board a paddle steamer, the *Queen of the Belgians*, which was heading across the Channel back to England. But as if Bill hadn't suffered enough already, halfway through the voyage the crew began attaching lifebelts to his stretcher – a German submarine had been spotted not far away, and if it engaged the boat, the plan was to throw the patients overboard.

Fortunately, the *Queen of the Belgians* made it back to England in one piece, and Bill soon recovered from his injuries. He learned, too, the incredible stroke of good luck that had saved him from dying on the battlefield: while the first German bullet had indeed entered his abdomen, causing him to begin bleeding heavily, the second had impacted his ammunition pouch instead, setting fire to a section of his tunic and cauterising the wound. Bill's survival was nothing short of a miracle.

The attack on the Butte de Warlencourt was the Post Office Rifles' final contribution to the Battle of the Somme. It had been a dismal failure, and over the following weeks no other battalion fared any better. Every attempt the British Army made to take the mound came to the same unsatisfactory conclusion, and the Butte continued to mark the limit of the Allied advance.

Once the Post Office Rifles had been relieved, they returned to Albert, where their dead comrades' belongings were spread out on the lawn of the basilica. Certain items had already been reserved for the next of kin, but everything else was up for grabs, and the survivors began helping themselves to socks, underwear, jumpers and more – all under the watchful gaze of the Golden Virgin, still hanging precariously from the side of the cathedral. Each soldier was given a mug of tea and a large chunk of bread for sustenance, and many were so exhausted from the battle that they lay down and slept on the town's cobbled streets.

After a few days' rest, the men were put on trains heading north to Belgium, en route to the Ypres Salient. Since they had arrived on the Continent over a year and a half earlier, all their battles on the Western Front had been fought in France, but now they were going to see Flanders. There were changes in the chain of command as well. Colonel Whitehead was sent home sick to England, leaving Captain Peel temporarily in charge.

I heartily congratulate you upon the great success achieved by my gallant troops during the past three days in the advance on both sides of the Ancre.

This further capture of the enemy's first-line trenches, under special difficulties, owing to the recent hot weather, redounds to the credit of all ranks.

Telegram from King George V
to Sir Douglas Haig, 15 November 1916

The Post Office Rifles were settling in to their new routine in Belgium – a week in the trenches followed by a week in support – when the Battle of the Somme finally came to an end in November 1916, following British success at the Ancre. Overall, the battle was declared an Allied victory, but it had been a terribly costly one. In four and a half months the Army had advanced just six miles, with a total territorial gain less than two-thirds the size of the Isle of Wight. But the casualties were on a scale never seen before in war – Allied and enemy losses combined were over a million men killed, wounded or missing.

Strategically, the Somme had been a success, in so far as the gradual advance had worn down the German Army, whose leaders were now contemplating plans for a measured retreat on the Western Front. As early as September, the Germans had started work on a fortified trench system known as the Hindenburg Line, or *Siegfriedstellung*, which they could fall back to in the event of another Allied push. But in Britain, the battle had become a byword for the senseless waste of human lives, and the military policy of attrition was becoming increasingly unpopular. Over a hundred thousand British men had lost their lives on the Somme. How many more would have to be sacrificed before the war could come to an end?

It was in part due to the controversy over the battle that the Prime Minister, Herbert Asquith, was forced to resign on 5 December, thanks to some clever manoeuvring by his long-time rival, David Lloyd George. Since taking over as War Minister six months earlier, when Lord Kitchener's warship was sunk by a German mine, Lloyd George had begun to despair at Asquith's weak leadership – he felt that for Britain to stand a chance of victory, the country needed a Prime Minister with more vision and drive. Two days after Asquith's resignation, Lloyd George himself was settling in to Number 10 Downing Street.

The winter of 1916 was unusually bitter – one of the coldest on record. For the Post Office Rifles, who were now based near Hill 60 in the Ypres Salient, the harsh weather was just one more trial to endure. While some men struggled with the extreme conditions, others embraced them. Lieutenant Berry had developed an impressive morning ritual, in which he was able to wash, shave, get dressed and eat breakfast all without emerging from the mountain of blankets he slept under every night. Captain Fenwick, on the other hand, would get up bright and breezy every morning and break the ice in a bucket of water he had left outside his dug-out, before enjoying a bracing wash in the open air.

Not everyone appreciated the invigorating effects of cold water. One bathing day, the men of the battalion stripped down in a little changing hut and dashed – stark naked – 40 yards along a duckboard trail to the nearby shower building. They lined up hurriedly under the rows of hoses that ran along the ceiling, shivering with cold and hopping up and down on the spot impatiently. But when the shower operator sitting in a little box up above pulled the lever to release the water, he forgot to turn the hot tap on first. The men howled as they were drenched in an icy deluge, until the operator realised his mistake and adjusted the temperature.

After the heavy losses at the Butte de Warlencourt, the Post Office men were once again welcoming new recruits. Among them was a postman from Wootton Basset who had left a wife and six children back home to come out to the front. 'Old Fred Hunt', as he was known in the battalion, was actually only in his forties, but to men still in their teens that seemed positively ancient. In any case, he was too old to be conscripted – when one of his new comrades asked him what had inspired him to volunteer, he replied, 'I could not leave the youngsters to come and fight for me and my family, while I just walked around delivering letters.'

Sadly, Fred's belief that he was right to join the fight was not shared by those in authority. When the battalion was inspected by Lord Plumer, the general declared that an 'old' fellow like Fred had no place in the front lines – and, much to the former postie's disappointment, had him transferred to the Salvage Corps instead.

Meanwhile, another new arrival was struggling to make a good impression on the battalion's temporary commanding officer, Acting Lieutenant Colonel Peel. Captain Boss was one of a handful of officers recently transferred from the Northern Cyclist Battalion, and had never seen service overseas. His knowledge of trench warfare was based entirely on what he had learned at the training camps in England, and he had come over to the Western Front, as he later described it, with a belief 'that front-line troops almost daily went "over the top" with bayonets fixed and giving voice to blood-curdling yells'.

Despite Boss's lack of experience at the front, his promotion to captain had gone through earlier than that of any of the Post Office Rifles' officers, so he was automatically put in command of No. 1 Company. He applied himself with energy and enthusiasm, but was unable to disguise his naivety. When Peel sent him up to reconnoitre and provide a report on a set of front-line trenches, Boss failed to note down any information about the cooking arrangements, forgetting the crucial maxim that any army marches on its stomach.

Peel was not impressed with Boss's report, and summoned the young man to his office. 'I think it would be better if Captain Davies were to have No. 1 Company,' he told him. 'You can take No. 3 Platoon instead.' Boss was disappointed, but he didn't feel able to argue, since he knew he would only make more mistakes. 'Yes, sir,' he replied, swallowing his pride, and was duly demoted to platoon commander.

As December wore on, the Post Office men began to reconcile themselves to the fact that they would be spending Christmas in the trenches once again. As had happened a year earlier, word was sent down from on high that any fraternising with the Germans was expressly forbidden – in fact, the men were advised to refrain from any audible celebration at all, in case it put the enemy in a festive mood.

There was no grand feast to be had at the front line either – only a dinner of boiled rice and jam – but at least the sector was relatively quiet. The bitter cold that the men had to put up with now was nothing compared with the horrors of their last Christmas spent in the Hairpin, when they had been under constant threat from a German sniper and worried about being blown sky-high at any moment.

As had happened the previous year, REPS had organised extra Channel crossings to cope with the seasonal increase in mail, and the men were soon unwrapping packages from home. Bill Harfleet was delighted to receive a letter from his grandmother containing a shilling, which he converted into the local currency and used to buy 50 full-size Woodbines. Bertie Whitehurst, meanwhile, received a large parcel from his mother. Inside were a couple of oranges, four Pearmain apples and a fruitcake that she had baked herself. The gift was particularly generous given the food shortages on the home front, where butter, sugar and fruit were all increasingly hard to get hold of.

In the trenches, the men sometimes slept in 'funk holes', small shelters scraped out of the wall that could accommodate a couple of soldiers at a time. Bertie shared his with a Welshman by the name of Billy Williams, and the two men tended to share anything they received from home as well. Naturally, Bertie's cake fell under this arrangement, and before long he and Billy were tucking into it together.

When the time came for them to do their sentry duty on the fire step, Bertie wrapped the remainder of the cake back up again and tied the parcel closed with some string. Then he tucked it carefully into a corner of the funk hole.

There wasn't much to see over no man's land that evening. It was a clear, frosty night, but other than the occasional British Verey light going up, little caught the men's attention. After two hours they returned to their funk hole and Bertie reached inside for the rest of the cake. But all he found were a few scraps of brown paper, along with the distinctly nibbled remains of the apples. While he and Billy had been on duty, the local rats had enjoyed a Christmas feast of their own.

For the British soldier in the trenches of the Western Front, rats were a perennial problem, rivalled only by lice for their ability to infuriate and appal. Not only would they snatch any food left unattended, they would bite the flesh right off dead soldiers, and sometimes try their luck with the living as well.

Men frequently awoke in the night to find a rat gnawing on their hair – one Post Office man suffered such severe wounds to his forehead that he had to be sent off to hospital.

Across all ranks, the rats were equally despised. Peel expressed his hatred of them in a letter to his wife Gwendolen:

> *I am being plagued by rats. All these places are infested by them, including my present-humble sleeping apartment – & as the sight of a rat gives me the shivers & the thought of touching one makes me physically sick I don't appreciate the idea of their running over my bed.*

Some men attempted to take matters into their own hands. Rifleman Robinson's diary includes the following entry from April 1915:

> *Easter Monday. Pass time by trying to bayonet rats. Relieved by A Company at 4.30pm.*

While the Germans might be the enemies the men had come to the Continent to fight, the rats offered a popular second front.

There was no white Christmas in the trenches, but as the New Year arrived it brought with it a flurry of snow. Soon everything around was thickly coated in it, and the men were kitted out with white camouflage outfits. General Gorringe, who had commanded the 47th Division ever since Barter's departure after High Wood, took the cold weather very seriously, and ordered that each man in the trenches should be given a hot meal or drink at least every four hours.

It was a popular move, but not enough to keep the men from growing miserable in the horribly cold conditions. During the daylight hours they would long for night to fall, when at least there was the prospect of work out in no man's land to keep their bodies moving. In the day, there was no physical labour, only shivering wretchedly in the snow.

The men had not been forgotten about, however, and one evening they received a visit from an old friend. When Fred Hunt had gone off duty at the Salvage Corps that night, instead of heading back to his billet to rest, he had begun the long trudge up to the front line, where he knew the Post Office Rifles were stationed. The former postman had an important delivery to make – a large jar of rum that he had salvaged that day. 'As soon as I saw it, I just thought of the boys,' he explained. 'And I decided that by God's help they should have it.'

With his present delivered, Fred went on his way again, warmed by the gratitude of his former comrades. The men were delighted with the rum, but even more so with the kindness of Old Fred's gesture. As one of them later recalled, he was 'a hero with no medals' – and one of the best men that they had ever served with.

CHAPTER 13

'ACTION!'

—

No. 14 Stationary Hospital
BEF, France

My dear Lord Emmott,

Very many thanks for your letter of the 23rd. I don't know myself what my present rank is, & have written to ask! I am perfectly well, & it is absurd for me to be here. I show no sign of feeling, & myself think I have never had, the suspected disease. ... I only hope all that we hear about Germany's internal condition is true. We of course see no signs of that, and that of course is what people naturally go by. It's the most important side of it. The German Peace Move is as clever as the Yankee one is contemptible. I don't think the Hun move will have much effect on any one but it was well worth making. The Yankee showed his true colours – he only cared for how he stood, & what he was likely to make or lose in another man's war. Loathsome people.

Best love to you all,

Home

Letter from Captain Home Peel to his father-in-law Lord Emmott, 30 December 1916

IN DECEMBER 1916, Peel had been invalided out of the trenches, suffering from a suspected case of scarlet fever. But, laid up in a hospital bed, he hadn't exactly embraced the idea of rest and recuperation. Instead, he had kept himself busy firing off letters to his family in England. He had always enjoyed a bit of political gossip and was fascinated by the recent change in government, not to mention the impact it might have on the Army – and he was also typically cynical about two recent attempts to persuade the new Prime Minister to make peace. The American proposal was, as far as Peel was concerned, transparently self-interested: President Wilson feared that if the war went on much longer, the United States would be drawn into it – his hope was that an armistice could be reached before any of his own country's blood was spilled. The German offer, meanwhile, seemed pretty disingenuous, since it hinged on them keeping territorial gains they had made during the war. Unsurprisingly, Lloyd George had rejected both proposals.

By the time Peel returned to Belgium after his spell in hospital, Major Vince was commanding the Post Office Rifles. Peel went back to his former role of adjutant, which in many ways suited him better than command – thanks to his pre-war career as a civil servant, he felt content surrounded by mountains of paperwork. Vince, meanwhile, was more of a natural leader, and the Post Office Rifles meant the world to him. The battalion couldn't have hoped for a pair of officers better suited to their positions.

On 18 March 1917, the men from the Post Office celebrated two years since they had first arrived in France. There was a lavish dinner laid on at Devonshire Camp, open to the 90-odd original 'survivors'. The guest list restriction was not taken too seriously, however, and in the event more than 180 men turned up. No one seemed to mind about the gatecrashers – after a year in which over 500 of the battalion's men had been killed, it was good to see so many of them together and enjoying themselves.

While the First Battalion were celebrating the completion of two years' service on the Western Front, the Second was just beginning to settle in. After six months of waiting around in Wiltshire for their ticket to come up, they had finally set forth across the Channel on 27 January, a full two years after the Third Battalion had been formed in order to free them up for active service.

Now, though, there was no messing about. After a brief introduction to life in the trenches, courtesy of the Sherwood Foresters, they found themselves involved in a great advance. In March, German forces had begun a careful retreat to their new stronghold, the heavily fortified Hindenburg Line. As British troops moved forward to take up the old German positions, the Second Battalion got its first look at the enemy trenches. Many had been booby-trapped, with supplies of water laced with poison and duckboards primed to explode when trodden on. German helmets – one of the more popular souvenirs among the British forces – had been left hanging temptingly on hooks along the wall, but one touch would trigger an explosion and put an end to any hapless trophy-hunters.

The new battalion of Post Office men soon grew wise to the German tricks. When they came across a brazier standing outside a dug-out, fully primed and ready to cook their dinner on, they had a feeling that it was too good to be true. Carefully dismantling the stove, they made a discovery that confirmed their misgivings: hidden among the coke and wood shavings was a wad of high explosive. It was just as well the Post Office men hadn't lit that particular barbecue – if they had, the only meat on the menu would have been them.

With both the First and Second Battalions now serving in the field, the Third Battalion was solely responsible for training up new Post Office recruits – over the course of the war, it sent out over 5,000 men to the other two battalions. But the traffic was not always one way, since many soldiers injured in France and Flanders were transferred back to England as instructors.

Among them was Lance Corporal John McIntyre, the Newcastle lad who had suffered a bayonet wound through the leg at High Wood and had spent two nights in an abandoned trench before being rescued. McIntyre had just completed a three-month convalescence when he was sent to join the Third Battalion in January 1917.

Having been lucky enough to escape the horrors of the front lines, he would have been forgiven for expecting a spell with the training battalion to be relatively free of danger. But as it turned out, even in Blighty, the Post Office men were never entirely out of harm's way. During their initial training period at Blackheath in London, a group of riflemen had been hit by a bus as they returned from a march late at night. The accident had resulted in 30 casualties, some of them fatal, and as a result the Army had introduced a new regulation that all troops were to carry red lanterns while marching in built-up areas after dark.

By the time Lance Corporal McIntyre joined the Third Battalion it was based at Blackdown Camp, just north of Aldershot, where the men were training on a set of extremely realistic German trenches, built by the inmates of the local prisoner-of-war camp at Frith Hill. McIntyre's job was to train his fresh recruits – many of them volunteer 'A4 boys', too young to be sent out to the front yet – in the technique of lobbing bombs into the trenches to clear them of enemy soldiers.

Since the original contingent of Post Office men had completed their training at Abbots Langley, the Army had given much thought to best practice where the throwing of grenades was concerned. In the heat of battle, grenadiers could easily become overexcited, using up all their precious bombs in a wild spree, rather than carefully considering how to make the most of every explosion. The new watchwords were moderation and restraint – as one Army memo put it, 'Haphazard and promiscuous grenade throwing does not produce satisfactory results, and should not be permitted.'

The training facilities around Aldershot were a popular destination for VIPs – not least King George V, who visited regularly to inspect the troops – and when guests arrived at Blackdown, they were often shown the Post Office Rifles at work in the impressive German trench system. When the celebrated American film director D.W. Griffith came to the area looking for some soldiers to perform in his latest movie, the Third Battalion was the obvious choice to assist him.

At 42, Griffith was already a Hollywood sensation. Only two years before, his three-hour epic *Birth of a Nation* had become the first commercial blockbuster of the silent-movie era, breaking all box-office records. After a screening at the White House, President Wilson had described it as 'like writing history with lightning'. The director had been fascinated by the Great War ever since the first shots had been fired, but had yet to commit his own vision of it to celluloid.

In late 1916, around the time when Wilson was campaigning for re-election on an anti-war ticket, the British War Office made Griffith an offer he couldn't refuse. If he would make a film that might encourage America to join the war, they would support him with both men and equipment. As it turned out, by the time Griffith and his 17-strong crew rolled up at Blackdown, on a warm summer's day in 1917, America had already declared war on Germany and was beginning to send soldiers to Europe, but the War Office still honoured the agreement.

To the Post Office men, Griffith brought with him an air of Hollywood glamour and excitement. The premiere of his latest film, *Intolerance*, had been met with a seven-minute ovation at Drury Lane, and had seen the highest-ever UK gross for an opening night. Rumours abounded about the new project the great director was working on, a sweeping drama called *Hearts of the World*. Some claimed that he had already tried and failed to film his battle scenes elsewhere: a reconstruction using actors in America had been deemed inauthentic, while his attempt to shoot footage at the front lines in France had been hindered by genuine German shelling – hence the decision to make the film with real-life soldiers but in the relative safety of a training camp.

The British Army had been involved in performing for the camera before. The phenomenally successful documentary *The Battle of the Somme*, which was seen by over 20 million people in its first six weeks and played in over 2,000 cinemas, had included a number of shots 'faked' behind the lines with the assistance of the Third Army Mortar School. This time, however, the troops would be participating in a drama. Griffith's story concerned an American soldier in the French Army, and the Post Office Rifles were playing average '*Poilus*'. (In France, the '*Poilu*' was the equivalent of the British 'Tommy' –

the word literally meant 'hairy one', referring to the fabulous beards and moustaches the French soldiers traditionally sported.)

In place of their regular khaki battledress, the Post Office men were kitted out in the light blue of the French infantry. Once the men were all dressed and in position, they awaited orders from the director's megaphone. With his bow tie and smart tweed suit – a recent acquisition from London that he had rather fallen in love with – Mr Griffith was a very different sight to their usual brass-hatted authority figures.

Like many engagements on the Western Front, the mock battle Griffith was orchestrating required a preparatory artillery bombardment, and for this Lance Corporal McIntyre and the other bombing instructors were asked to bring their expertise to bear. The plan, devised by an American bombing officer, was to lay a series of underground charges, made of gunpowder packed into light containers, which would simulate the effect of a barrage when they exploded at the appropriate moment. Meanwhile, fake shrapnel blasts would be generated by hurling ammonal balls from a row of trench catapults, with fuses primed to detonate in mid-air.

In charge of assembling the specialist bombs was a team of 11 men led by Sergeant George Kennedy, a 35-year-old former postman from St Helier in Jersey. Several lorry loads of explosives had arrived from the batteries depot and were being stored in the magazine or 'bomb hut', while five barrels of gunpowder had been placed in an adjacent compound.

While the Post Office men dressed as *Poilus* prepared for the performance of their lives, Sergeant Kennedy and his team were in the bomb hut preparing the explosives. But before Mr Griffith had even called 'Action!', tragedy struck. Something caused the gunpowder in the store to ignite – a court of inquiry later ruled that it could have been a spark from someone's boot tip – and when it went up, the fire soon spread to the hut next door, with the 11 men still working inside.

The bomb hut exploded, sending shovels, picks and bomb casings flying in all directions, and causing the ground to shudder 500 yards away. There were terrified shouts from the German prisoners who were being held nearby. Some of the Post Office men rushed forward to assess the damage, stepping over the scattered debris until they got to what was left of the hut. What they found inside was a grisly sight: Sergeant Kennedy and two of his NCOs had been killed, and four more men were badly burned from the chest upwards.

But, remarkably, the horrific incident didn't cause the film shoot to be cancelled – in fact, it barely made an impact on Mr Griffith's shooting schedule. As the injured men were carted off to hospital, and the dead bodies were removed to the morgue, replacement explosives were sent for from the batteries depot, along with a replacement team to assemble them.

With the cameras rolling, the timed explosions went off as planned, creating a pretty convincing artillery barrage. The fake shrapnel detonated satisfyingly in mid-air, and Lance Corporal McIntyre and some fellow bombers in the German trench hurled grenades over for good measure. Although some of them rolled dangerously close to the young riflemen who were acting the part of the French soldiers, there were no further serious injuries – just a few cuts and bruises caused by flying stones, which if anything lent an air of authenticity to the whole performance.

Mr Griffith was delighted with the footage he had captured, and was so impressed with the work of the bombers that he decided to set them a further challenge. His attention had been caught by a magnificent old oak tree that stood nearby, and with his natural instinct for Hollywood spectacle, he knew just what to do with it. 'I want you to blow that thing sky-high,' he told the bombing team.

The bombers primed the ancient oak with slabs of guncotton and retreated to a safe distance. But when they lit the fuse and Mr Griffith called 'Action!', for some reason the explosives didn't go off.

'Cut!' the director yelled through his megaphone, and the bombers cautiously returned to the tree to investigate. They went for a second take, and then a third, but the tree resolutely failed to explode. By this point everyone was getting impatient and the bombers' fellow soldiers were starting to tease them.

Finally, on the fourth take, the guncotton did its job correctly. As the explosive detonated, the vast oak tree was heaved up into the air, before coming back down to earth with a heavy thump. Rather incongruously, it landed, perfectly upright, only feet away from its own blasted stump.

For a moment everyone held their breath, wondering if the shot would be ruined as the tree refused to fall on its side. Then, after a few moments, the giant oak began to totter, and with a great crash it came down to the ground.

'Gee boys, that was great!' Mr Griffith shouted excitedly, and the bombers breathed a sigh of relief.

The director left the camp with a spring in his step, confident that he had secured the footage he needed for his movie. The riflemen who had performed the role of the French infantry were not exactly treated like movie stars – their pay came in the shape of 10 Woodbines each plus enough cash to buy a couple of pints in the pub. But there were no complaints. The men were satisfied knowing that they had done a good job for their temporary American commanding officer, and thrilled to think that they had played a small part in Hollywood history. On the wave of exhilaration they were riding, it was almost possible to forget that three men had died for the sake of a movie.

Chapter 14

An unpopular hero

—

My darling,

Very many thanks for the parcel which has arrived and the contents of which are most satisfactory & excellent. We've just had a battle of which you will have heard by now – the whole thing was a great success & so far as this Brigade was concerned everything went to perfection. The C-in-C told us the Brigade had the most difficult job of any in the show, & as we carried it out completely, taking all objectives, nothing could have been better. We got a lot of prisoners, & had only very moderate casualties. The 8th did splendidly. We are still in the line. I'm very fit but pretty busy. Best love to you all.

Your loving Home

Letter from Captain Home Peel
to his wife Gwendolen, 9 July 1917

AFTER A BITTERLY COLD WINTER spent in the trenches around Ypres, the First Battalion of the Post Office Rifles greeted the arrival of spring with relief. But before long the men began to notice that visits to the front lines from red-hatted staff officers were growing increasingly frequent – a sure sign that something was brewing. They waited anxiously for orders to come through for the next big attack.

While the British Army was ready for action, the French was in a state of utter chaos. Following a disastrous attack in April at the Chemin des Dames, a ridge just north of the Aisne River, the French soldiers had begun to mutiny, disobeying orders and abandoning the front lines. At the same time, although American troops were now on their way to Europe, it would be another year before they were ready to participate in a major advance. In the meantime, it was up to the British and colonial troops to hold the Western Front.

Unfortunately, just sitting still and waiting things out was not a viable option. The fear was that, if the British didn't attack soon, the enemy would. Aeroplane reconnaissance indicated that the Germans might be planning an operation, and Sir Douglas Haig – recently promoted to field marshal as a 'New Year's gift' from the King – believed that it was important to act fast. His plan was for a two-stage attack around Ypres. The main event would be an advance onto the Passchendaele Ridge to the northeast, but first he intended a limited push south of Ypres to straighten out the bulge around the town – a shorter trench line there would mean fewer men needed to hold it, and hence more manpower available for the second attack.

For the initial battle, Haig had his sights set on the Messines Ridge, a natural vantage point from which the enemy currently had a good view of the British rear lines, something that had long caused unease in the Army. For almost two years, troops in the area had been preparing for an attack, digging a series of underground mines well below the enemy lines, packed with over a million pounds of explosives. Combined with the usual artillery barrage, the mines were intended to deal the Germans a knockout blow before the infantry began to advance.

The Post Office Rifles would be moving forward as the right flank of the 47th London Division, taking a series of German trenches near the canal that ran between Ypres and the town of Comines to the southeast. The Shiny Seventh would be on their immediate left, and, assuming all went well with the first part of the operation, the Cast Iron Sixth and Civil Service Rifles would be waiting to come forward three hours later and attempt to make further gains.

There were four enemy trenches within the Post Office men's section – known as Oak Trench, Oak Support, Oak Reserve and Oak Switch – as well as a heavily fortified road called the Dammstrasse. The road led up to a building known as the White Chateau, which was one of the Shiny Seventh's objectives. As with many wartime landmarks, the name was woefully out of date. In reality, the 'chateau' was little more than a giant mound of smashed bricks and iron girders, in the midst of which the Germans had built a number of concrete pillboxes.

The rehearsal for the Battle of Messines was exhaustive. Lieutenant Colonel Maxwell, back in command of the battalion again, led the Post Office men through a series of practice runs on taped-out courses at Steenvoorde, a small town just across the border in France. The attention to detail was meticulous – thanks to detailed photography from the Air Force, the locations of machine guns and hidden barbed wire had been accurately marked on the course, so when the men went over the top they would know exactly what to expect.

Meanwhile, to simulate the creeping barrage behind which the Post Office Rifles would advance, men from the transport section rushed forward in bursts, waving white flags to indicate shells falling. The Army had learned from previous battles in which the infantry held back too far behind the barrage, allowing the enemy time to recover and emerge from their dug-outs before they reached them. The new system was designed to ensure that their timing was perfect.

There were other innovations, too, in the preparations for the battle. For the first time, officers were ordered to wear the tunics of regular soldiers, in an attempt to prevent them being singled out by enemy fire, while an elaborate system of code words was circulated to be used in communications. Innocent-sounding surnames were substituted for key information: 'Hayward' was code for 'Troops on right held up', while 'Hayes' indicated the same problem on the left. 'Am held up by enemy fire' was signalled by 'Strudwick', while 'Bombs wanted' was 'Briggs'. Some of the code words seemed more obviously appropriate than others – the code used to request further artillery support was 'Gunn' – although if you needed a tank you asked not for 'Carr' (which indicated 'Casualties heavy') but 'Tarrant'.

Secrecy was crucial to the success of the operation. Although it must have been obvious to the Germans that some kind of attack was imminent, every effort was made to keep the date and time from falling into their hands – something which, judging from the German prisoners who were captured and interrogated, was achieved with remarkable success.

Once again, the Post Office Rifles would be going into battle with a number of new arrivals in the ranks, and not all of them were strictly speaking Post Office men. One less than popular addition to the battalion was Corporal Thomas Bottomley, a short, pugnacious man from Staffordshire who had been transferred from the Royal Berkshire Regiment. Perhaps Bottomley felt that as an outsider he had to prove himself, or perhaps he was just naturally belligerent. Either way, he always volunteered for the most dangerous patrols and seemed ill at ease during quieter moments in the trenches, when most men were thankful for a respite from mortal danger.

The men of the battalion soon grew to dislike Bottomley intensely. They found him aggressive and rude, a loose cannon whose unpredictable behaviour was a danger to everyone around him. The live-and-let-live philosophy was utterly alien to him, and he often took it upon himself to fire rifle grenades at the Germans, without provocation or warning – something that inevitably brought about reprisals. The result was that most men tried to stay as far away from him as possible. He was just too much of a liability.

Unsurprisingly, when volunteers were requested for a regular fighting patrol, Bottomley was the first to step forward. The group of 14 men operated independently of the platoon system and were sent out into no man's land at night to attempt various dangerous objectives, such as raiding an enemy trench for prisoners to interrogate, or engaging German night patrols. But not all their missions were combative ones, much to Bottomley's disappointment.

Late one still and quiet night, the fighting patrol was out in no man's land reconnoitring the German trenches opposite, the men doing their best to avoid being noticed – when Bottomley decided to spice things up a bit. He pulled the pin out of one of his grenades and lobbed it at the enemy lines. Almost immediately, the Germans sent up an SOS flare, calling on their artillery to fire. Soon shells were raining down on a section of the British line held by the Cast Iron Sixth, who fired their own flare, calling on the British artillery to retaliate. Before long, all hell was let loose, with dozens of shells falling on both sides.

The men of the patrol hurried back to the British trench, but Bottomley remained out in no man's land on his own. He finally emerged an hour later, uninjured and unapologetic, just as the bombardment was dying down. In the meantime, the Cast Iron Sixth had suffered severe casualties in the shelling, so no one was particularly pleased to see him.

By the time the Post Office Rifles moved up into position for the Battle of Messines, Bottomley was itching to go over the top. 'I'm out for a VC or a wooden one this time!' he told Bill Harfleet excitedly. The Victoria Cross was the Army's highest award for bravery, and no Post Office Rifle had yet won it. The wooden cross, on the other hand, signified membership of a less exclusive club: the 700-odd men of the regiment who had already been buried in the field.

At 3.10am on Thursday 7 June, the mines under the German front line were detonated. The ground of the British trenches shuddered as streaks of fire burst into the sky, casting a red glow over no man's land. In a matter of moments, 10,000 German soldiers were either dead or dying, some vaporised by the force of the blast itself, others buried alive under the tonnes of earth and clay. Many of those who survived were reduced to gibbering wrecks and emerged from their lines begging for surrender.

It was the largest manmade explosion in history. The sound was clearly audible as far away as London, and for the men waiting to go over the top only a mile away it was literally deafening. There was no point blowing a whistle to signal the advance – instead, platoon sergeants tapped the men on their shoulders and waved them over into no man's land.

The combined effect of the 19 mines, along with the creeping barrage that followed, provided the best possible conditions for the infantry. The Germans were so stunned and demoralised that many put up little fight at all. Some were still cowering in their dug-outs when the British bombers arrived and began hurling grenades through the doorways.

The Post Office Rifles made good progress. Within an hour they had secured all four lines of the German trench system, and were beginning to consolidate their gains. But on their left, the Shiny Seventh had not been as lucky. A sniper holed up in what was left of the White Chateau had already taken out a number of their soldiers. Now a machine gun nestled somewhere in the ruins of the building began firing on the Post Office men as well, enfilading them as they took up their new positions.

A handful of Post Office men rushed to help the Seventh Londons take the chateau, but attempt after attempt ended in failure. The advance, which until now had seemed to be going so well, was suddenly in jeopardy. Unless someone could silence the machine gun, there was no telling what damage it could do.

The men of both battalions looked on in dismay as the gun continued firing wildly, spraying bullets all over the battlefield. Then suddenly, and unexpectedly, it fell silent.

The men cautiously approached the White Chateau, and made their way to where the firing had come from. Draped over the machine gun they found the body of Corporal Bottomley. He had evidently seized control of the gun and had managed to turn it on the Germans, for their dead littered the ground all around him. But before long he too had succumbed to the wounds he had sustained, and he had died there, alongside his enemies.

It was the kind of heroic end that Bottomley had dreamed of, although with no survivors present to offer a first-hand account of his actions, he received no medals for his bravery, even posthumously. The comrades who had formerly despised him, however, were left with a new-found sense of respect. Bottomley may never have been a Post Office man himself, but he had saved the lives of plenty of them, and had helped them to secure a triumphant victory.

Overall, the Battle of Messines was a phenomenal success, perhaps the single most effective British engagement of the war. It was a textbook example of good planning and careful rehearsal, and both the artillery and the mines had performed their roles perfectly. By nightfall, three lines of enemy trenches had been taken across a nine-mile front, and over 7,000 German soldiers had been taken prisoner. The number could have been higher were it not for the cruelty of one British soldier, who was seen by the Post Office men turning his machine gun on a group of Germans who had already been disarmed, and mowing them down in cold blood.

For the Post Office Rifles, success had come at a fairly modest cost, certainly compared with the horrors of High Wood and the Butte de Warlencourt the previous year. The battalion had lost only 42 men killed, among them the controversial Corporal Bottomley. When the men were relieved a couple of days later, they celebrated their victory with a swim in the nearby canal, doing their best not to think about how many bodies might be lurking under the water.

While the men rejoiced at their success in the recent battle, among the officer class there was the usual jostling for position. Captain Peel was temporarily promoted to brigade major, meaning that he was in charge of operations and intelligence for not only the Post Office Rifles but the Civil Service Rifles and the Sixth and Seventh Londons too. He soon fell in love with the new role, which carried more responsibility than his previous job as adjutant. But as time went on he began to realise that the Army saw him as only a fill-in, keeping the seat warm until they sent a new man from England to take over.

Anxiously, Peel wrote to his most well-connected friends back in Blighty, including Gwendolen's father, Lord Emmott. His hope was that one of them could persuade Lord Derby – the Secretary of State for War, and as it happened a former Postmaster General – to personally recommend him for the position. 'It's the one job in the British Army I want,' he explained to his father-in-law:

> *I know well, even intimately, all the commanding officers and (I write frankly) am liked by & get on well with them. I've served in every officer rank from platoon commander to CO inclusive with them, have acted as Staff Captain & Brigade Major & have been through*

Festubert, Loos, Vimy, the Somme, & this last big show with them. I am recommended for the job to the extent that all from the Brigadier to the Army are trying to get it for me. So it's not a sham or a put-up job. But you've no idea of the difficulties – e.g. the way people from home are shoved in over the heads of us who've been at it all the time out here.

Lord Emmott did his best for his son-in-law, but his efforts were not crowned with success. It turned out that neither his contacts nor Peel's had the power to halt the wheels of the Army bureaucracy. Just as Peel had predicted, the job went to a man sent out from England.

'I'm very sick about it, but it can't be helped,' Peel told Gwendolen sadly. But to her father he expressed more of his anger, in particular concerning Lord Derby's Private Secretary Herbert Creedy, who had written to explain why the War Minister had refused to get involved in the decision:

Creedy's answer is of course all rubbish and merely the parrot cry of the typical official. To begin with, it is not the case that the War Office do not interfere. If you ask GHQ [General Headquarters] for anything, they refer you to the WO; & if you ask the WO they refer you to GHQ – and so the see-saw goes on, and the sufferers from it are legion. Secondly, official interference from the WO was not asked for nor expected, but merely a personal word from one head to another which is done, always has been done & always will be done so long as humanity exists, & the method of doing it is known to every Private Secretary who is worth a damn, which Creedy never was in spite of his CBs and CVOs & Legions of Humour.

After which explosion of temper you will not be surprised to hear that the appt. has gone to the other man, on a direct order that the next vacancy was to go to the top on the list from the Cambridge staff school at home. If you ask GHQ where the order emanated from they will tell you WO, & the estimable Creedy if asked will tell you it came from GHQ.

Peel felt understandably bitter about the whole affair, but there was one consolation to the outcome. With the new officer on his way from England to take over Peel's job, he found himself eligible for some home leave. 'I'm very tired, and want a rest badly,' he wrote to Gwendolen on 21 July. Less than a fortnight later, he was back in London and boarding a train to St Ives, where his wife and two children – not to mention their beloved 'Mr Dog' – were staying. For a short while, at least, the whole family was to be reunited.

Chapter 15

Passchendaele

—

His Majesty The KING has been graciously pleased to approve the award of the Victoria Cross to the undermentioned Officers, Non-commissioned Officers and Men: —

No. 370995 Sgt. Alfred Joseph Knight, Lond. R. (Nottingham). For most conspicuous bravery and devotion to duty during the operations against the enemy positions. Sgt Knight did extraordinary good work, and showed exceptional bravery and initiative when his platoon was attacking an enemy strong point, and came under fire from an enemy machine gun. He rushed through our own barrage, bayoneted the enemy gunner, and captured the position single-handed. Later, twelve of the enemy with a machine gun were encountered in a shell hole. He again rushed forward by himself, bayoneted two and shot a third, causing the remainder to scatter ... His several single-handed actions showed exceptional bravery, and saved a great number of casualties in the company. They were performed under heavy machine gun and rifle fire, and without regard to personal risk, and were the direct cause of the objectives being captured.

Supplement to *The London Gazette*,
8 November 1917

THE FIRST BATTALION of the Post Office Rifles had triumphed in the Battle of Messines, but for the next stage of Field Marshal Haig's grand plan it was the Second Battalion that was called on to play a part. By the time the battalion arrived in Belgium, the Third Battle of Ypres – known today as 'Passchendaele', after the village that was its ultimate objective – had been under way for a month, and had already descended into a disaster to rival the Somme.

This time it was the weather that was largely to blame. The timing of the attack could not have been less fortuitous – the rainfall in the area during summer and autumn of 1917 was five times worse than it had been for either of the previous two years. Men in the trenches were often up to their waists in water, and in no man's land the situation was even more grim. Injured men could be caught out by a new burst of torrential rainfall, drowning in shell holes that they were too weak to struggle out of.

To make matters worse, the drainage system in the area was extremely delicate, with an unusually high water table, and the fortnight-long artillery bombardment that preceded the battle had turned the ground into a kind of murky porridge. Men who had already seen action at the Somme had a rough idea of the quagmire that awaited them, but Passchendaele was far, far worse than anything they had seen in France. Tanks found the ground completely impassable, and it wasn't much better for the infantry. One soldier who fought in the battle wrote at the time, 'Fancy fighting Germans for a land like this. If it were mine I'd give them the whole damn rotten country.'

The Second Battalion had experienced pretty bad mud already. Going up the line in March 1917, a signalman by the name of Rogers had accidentally stepped off a duckboard trail and had begun to sink into the black slime. Rifleman Kingston had knelt down and tried to help him, removing the kit Rogers was carrying a piece at a time. But his kind gesture drew the irritation of one of the battalion officers. 'You're exposing yourself and the rest of us to danger,' Kingston was told. 'If you want to help him, you're going to have to wait until nightfall.'

The rest of the men moved on, but Kingston stayed behind with Rogers, who was gradually sinking deeper into the sludge. When darkness fell, he began working to get his comrade free.

Rogers was buried in mud up to the waist, and the only way Kingston was able to get him out was by cutting off his waders and trousers. Eventually, he was able to slither out of them and clamber up from the slime onto the duckboard trail. He looked quite a sight – covered in the filthy muck from head to foot, with full military uniform on his top half and nothing but his underwear down below.

But Kingston already had a solution. 'Take your jersey off,' he told him. Rogers removed his tunic, and then the jumper he was wearing underneath it. Then, under Kingston's instruction, he held the garment upside down and stepped into the arm holes. It was an unorthodox pair of leggings, but it was better than nothing.

Not all mud-related crises ended so happily, however. Rifleman Harvey of the First Battalion witnessed another man slide off a duckboard into the mire. When two of his comrades were unable to pull him out between them, they attached a chain to a pair of mules and tried to get him out that way. Through the layers of mud, Harvey heard a crack as the man's spine was broken in the attempt. The mules got him out, but he died not long after.

In the ground around Ypres, the Second Battalion started to witness such horrors on a regular basis. One day, when they were on the move, a man slipped and fell into the quagmire. His friends begged their sergeant to stop and try to rescue him, but as their comrade began to slide out of sight there was nothing they could do. Several men wept as the man was shot by a former colleague from the Post Office: a bullet in the head was considered preferable to suffocation by the mud.

In August, the appalling weather led to a temporary halt to the battle, but by the end of the month the sun had begun to shine once more, and Field Marshal Haig was determined to try again. He ordered another massive artillery bombardment, this time lasting a full three weeks, and on 20 September, at 5.40am, the next big push began. This time the Second Battalion was one of the units going over the top.

Their objective was to capture a section of the German line leading up to Wurst Farm, as part of the Battle of the Menin Road Ridge. The section the Post Office Rifles were charged with taking contained three enemy strongholds, known as Hubner Farm, Genoa Farm and Marine View. The plan was to seize these key points first, and then to force the rest of the Germans in the line to surrender.

As was now becoming increasingly common practice, the objectives had been marked out on a training ground, and a scale model of the battlefield had been prepared, complete with viewing galleries 20 feet above the ground from which the men could study it. By the time the Post Office Rifles assembled for battle on the night of 19 September, they knew exactly what they were supposed to be doing.

By 3am, the men were in position and ready to go over the top. In the lull before the whistle was blown, their minds began to wander. One of the Post Office sergeants, Alfred Knight, was imagining what it must feel like to be a man condemned to execution, trying to get a final night's sleep before taking the walk up to the hangman's noose. It didn't seem a million miles away from the situation he and his men were in now.

Knight was a 29-year-old man from Birmingham who had worked for the Post Office as a clerical assistant in the North Midland Engineering District. He had already been highly praised for his bravery during an attack in France four months earlier – his promotion to sergeant had come about thanks to 'gallant conduct' in helping wounded comrades to safety under heavy fire. But no one could possibly have predicted the extraordinary acts of heroism he was about to commit at Wurst Farm Ridge.

The moment the creeping barrage opened up, the men of the Second Battalion hurled themselves out of their trenches and began the dash across the slippery ground of no man's land. Keeping good note of their training, they hugged the barrage close, and at times the shells were falling less than a dozen yards in front of them. They made fast progress across the terrain, but the casualties were heavy. Soon both No. 1 and No. 3 Companies were without any officers at all – every one of them had been either killed or badly wounded.

Sergeant Knight, though, seemed to be protected by some kind of magic charm. He was carrying on his person every one of the various objects that were popularly supposed to stop a bullet – and, as the morning wore on, every one of them did: a cigarette case, a miniature picture frame, and even a book were all torn or smashed to pieces, but the sergeant remained free from injury.

It was certainly not for lack of bravery. When Sergeant Knight saw a group of men from No. 2 Company under fire from a German machine gun, he stormed up to the gun emplacement and captured the position single-handedly. Then with a cry of 'I'm after this, boys!' he charged on to a second machine-gun post, shooting and bayonetting several enemy troops there and causing the rest of them to scatter.

But all the heroism in the world was no use against the force of the mud. Soon the sergeant lost his footing and found himself buried up to the waist, his face and tunic spattered all over. There was another stronghold up ahead and a group of Germans there were shooting at some of Alfred's comrades. Without stopping to consider his own safety, he opened fire on them, and soon half a dozen lay dead.

The remaining Germans returned fire immediately and Alfred felt the bullets ping off his helmet. He watched, transfixed, as the spray from a machine gun drew patterns in the mud all around him. But somehow he was able to extricate himself and clamber up to relative safety.

With hardly any officers left on the battlefield, Alfred rounded up a group of survivors and issued his own orders. He could see a platoon struggling to take one of the farmhouses, so he brought his band of men up to offer assistance, firing on the enemy's flank and giving his comrades the chance they needed to claim victory. As one eyewitness later commented, 'It is not exaggerating to say that the entire command of the troops in these operations fell on Knight, and had he failed, the chances are that the whole of the work put into that particular push would have been in vain.'

Alfred Knight's heroism and quick-thinking paid off handsomely. Before long the battalion had secured all three strongholds, and the Germans were beginning to surrender. It was a costly battle for the Post Office Rifles, with 90 men killed and many more seriously injured, but, thanks in large part to Sergeant Knight, the operation had been a success. More generally, across the eight-mile front of the advance, things had gone well too, and by noon most of the Army's objectives had been taken.

For his part in the Battle of Wurst Farm Ridge, Alfred was awarded the Victoria Cross, the highest honour for gallantry in the British Army. When he returned home on leave to receive the medal from King George V, he found himself treated as a celebrity. In his home town of Birmingham he was feted with a ceremonial presentation, and invited to address the assembled masses.

When members of the public asked him what they could do to help the men at the front, Alfred had a simple answer for them. What the men valued more than anything else, he told them, were letters. If the people in the crowd wanted to help boost morale in the trenches, the most important thing that they could do was to pick up a pen and write. It was hard to imagine that the celebrated war hero had once been a mere clerical worker, but in his heart Alfred was still one of the men from the Post Office.

While Alfred was back in Blighty giving speeches, for his comrades in the Second Battalion, the horrors of the Western Front continued. A month after the attack at Wurst Farm Ridge, they were ordered back into the front line to participate in the battle for Passchendaele itself. It was to be a night operation, with the Post Office Rifles going over just before dawn. Once again they had been given a series of enemy strongholds to conquer, all of them former farms or houses.

There was no trench from which to launch the attack – instead, the men followed a fragile duckboard trail through fields of sinister black slime until they reached a white line taped out on the ground. Here, they silently prostrated themselves, clinging to the muddy earth beneath them or hiding behind the lip of a shell hole as they waited for the signal to advance.

For the men from the Post Office, the attack was an unmitigated disaster. Even before they began to move forward, many of them were caught by the shells of the creeping barrage, which were falling dangerously close to their positions. As soon as they did start to advance, they found themselves stuck in impassable mud, and while they struggled to heave their legs out of the morass they were sitting ducks for enemy snipers.

The lucky ones made it to the relative safety of a shell hole, but once the sun came up and the Germans could see clearly across the battlefield, there was little chance of advancing any further. At the slightest hint of movement, they would be hit by a torrent of gunfire.

Rifleman Fred Shewry was one of the men left cowering in a shell hole for the rest of that long

October day. Every so often a shell would fall nearby, almost deafening Fred and the men who were with him, and showering them with a fresh layer of mud and slime. All around, they could see the remains of what had once been their comrades.

For some, the endless waiting, soaked through and exposed to the bitterly cold air, became too much. 'I can't stand this any longer,' one man told Fred, before standing up and making for a nearby British pillbox. He got only a few steps away from the shell hole before he went down, shot through the head by a sniper.

As darkness fell, Fred and the other survivors made their way carefully back to their starting positions. They crawled on their hands and knees, often sinking up to their armpits in the mire. At one point, Fred's rifle was swallowed by the mud, and try as he might he was unable to get it back. He felt desperate, like a fly trapped on flypaper. Eventually, however, Fred and his comrades reached the safety of the British positions.

The surviving Post Office Rifles had little hope of taking any of their objectives now, with so many men out of action. In the day's failed attack, over 120 of them had been killed – and the battalion had not gained a thing. Among the dead was the thousandth Post Office Rifleman to perish since the start of the war: Lance Corporal Bailey, a 24-year-old former postman from Walworth in south London.

The men felt deeply dispirited, both at the terrible losses they had sustained and at their failure to make any headway in the battle. But when they were visited by their divisional commander a few days later, he seemed to be in a surprisingly upbeat mood. 'I always thought you were a lot of stamp-lickers,' the general told them frankly, 'but the way you fought – you went over like bloody savages!'

The men soon learned the reason for the general's good spirits. As it turned out, the Army had never intended the Post Office Rifles to capture any of their objectives. Their attack had been nothing more than a diversion, designed to draw the Germans' attention away from the real advance being made by some Canadian units.

Since the Canadians had ultimately proved successful in taking the village of Passchendaele, the general was delighted, but the Post Office men were left with a bitter taste in their mouths. As they saw it, over a hundred of their lads had been killed in an attack that had been designed to fail. Some blamed the battalion's own commander, Lieutenant Colonel Derviche-Jones (known unofficially as 'Kill-Boche Jones' for the bloodthirsty speeches he made before every battle). They felt that he had been too quick to offer his men up as a sacrifice, just to please those above him in the chain of command.

The Second Battalion had been on the Western Front for less than a year, but disillusionment had already begun to set in.

Chapter 16

Farewell to the First Battalion

—

L'Affaire Cambrai

'Whose fault is it? Can it be you?'
Says WO to GHQ.
  'Of course not me, I'll ask the Army,'
  Says Haig, 'poor Bungo must be barmy.'
'Not me,' says Byng, 'I'll ask the Corps,
And, if it's them, give them what for.'
  Corps treats the matter with derision
  And sends a strafe to each Division.
Umpteen Divisions make parade
Of innocence & strafe Brigade.
  Brigades, thrice umpteen, squeaking 'Rats!'
  Strafe twelve times umpteen broken Batts,
Who curse, with much unseemly noise,
Forty-eight times umpteen Coys.
  Indignant Coy Commanders soon
  Pass on the curse to each platoon,
Who show immediate predilection
To pass it on, one curse per section.
  Sections, 'yond which it cannot pass,

Each choose a man & kick his ----.
And that's the proper Army way
Of dealing with l'Affaire Cambrai.

Poem written by Major Home Peel in a letter to his
father-in-law, Lord Emmott, 21 February 1918

WITH THE BATTLE of Passchendaele still rumbling
on in Belgium, and swallowing men at a horrifying
rate, General Julian ('Bungo') Bing was looking for a
knockout blow that would create problems for the
enemy in France. The result was the Battle of Cambrai,
an attempt to break through a section of the heavily
fortified Hindenburg Line. Initially it was a stunning
success. Instead of an artillery bombardment, it
opened with a tank attack, and for the first time the
new vehicles proved what they were capable of. More
than 450 tanks were involved in the operation, and
when they began to storm the German lines in the
early morning of 20 November, the enemy was so
horrified that many gave up without a fight. By the
end of the first day of the battle, the British had
pushed forward four miles and had taken 7,500
prisoners. Back home in England, church bells rang
out for the first time since the beginning of the war.

But the sense of triumph was short-lived. On
subsequent days, the British failed to match the
momentum of the initial push, and they never made it
to their ultimate objective, the town of Cambrai itself.
When the Germans counterattacked on 30 November,
they caught the British forces off guard, and by the

time the battle ended a week later, almost all the new gains had been lost again. While the British clung on to a small captured section of the Hindenburg Line, elsewhere the Germans had pushed forward into Allied territory, and a front line that had once been relatively straight now resembled an awkward zigzag. In a matter of weeks, the battle went from a source of national pride to a fiasco, and – as Peel described in his typically sardonic poem – the Army began playing the blame game.

The Post Office Rifles were not involved in the initial stage of the battle, but a week later the First Battalion was called on to help defend an area known as Bourlon Wood. At the time, the men from the Post Office had been looking forward to an exotic new posting in Italy, and when the plans were changed at the last minute they were understandably disappointed. 'You thought you were going to spend the winter with the ice-cream merchants, eh?' was a popular joke in the battalion, as they tramped through heavy rain and icy winds towards the front line.

Thanks to some requisitioned double-decker buses, the battalion reached the Hindenburg Line by 28 November, and when the German counterattack began two days later they were ordered forward to positions in the wood. Following the road towards Cambrai, they came across an abandoned sugar factory that had recently been held by the enemy, and here they were greeted by an eerie sight. Inside were two German corpses that seemed to have been frozen on the spot: they were both sitting bolt upright and one of them was holding a slice of bread and jam up to his mouth.

There was no time to dwell on the uncanny tableau, though. Before long, the men from the Post Office had taken up their positions within the wood and were making good progress against the enemy. On the night of 2 December, they advanced on a German trench, catching the men there unawares. Many of the Germans surrendered, assuming that the Post Office Rifles were part of a much larger attack. Others rushed off along a duckboard track that led further into the wood, trying to reach their positions in the rear.

Tommy Thompson, the former Debenhams clerk who had managed to talk his way into the Post Office Rifles, was ordered to fire on the track with his Lewis gun, covering the area with a continuous spray of bullets. In the dim moonlight, he could hardly see what he was doing, but it was clear from the occasional screams that he was on target.

It was only when dawn broke the following morning that Tommy saw the carnage he had caused. The track was littered with scores of German bodies, all of them lying face down with bullet holes in their backs. When a German Red Cross officer came and begged permission to bury his comrades, Tommy felt a deep sense of shame.

For the Post Office Rifles, the Battle of Bourlon Wood was a great success. But – as had happened so many times before in the course of the war –

their own victories were not matched by units elsewhere. A day later they were relieved, and the British forces began to withdraw as part of the embarrassing climbdown that Peel had christened 'L'Affaire Cambrai'.

For the men of the First Battalion, the disappointment would prove to be final. They didn't know it at the time, but they had fought their last battle together.

There is no objection to the following being written on Field Service Post Cards: –

'A Merry Christmas and a Happy New Year'

Attention is called to the fact that the sending of Christmas and New Year Cards, books, photographs, etc., to enemy or neutral countries is forbidden.

General Routine Order 2766, 4 November 1917

After two miserable Christmases in the trenches, the Post Office Rifles were delighted to be spending the holiday season away from the front lines. Late in the evening of 22 December, they arrived at a village that rejoiced in the distinctly festive name of Méricourt-l'Abbé. The quiet little community couldn't have been a more perfect antidote to the horrors of the battlefield, and when the men from the Post Office arrived well after midnight, the streets were already coated in a blanket of snow, like a scene from a picture postcard.

The Post Office men were jubilant. For once they enjoyed a slap-up feast on Christmas Day itself, accompanied by plenty of traditional carols, and even more plentiful supplies of rum. They also shared in the festivities of the village, watching with delight as the French children played in the snow.

Not everyone was in such good spirits, however. Although Home Peel had finally been promoted to brigade major, the position he had been so bitter at missing out on before, he had recently received some distressing news from England. His sister Helen had contracted meningitis while she was working as an ambulance driver for the Voluntary Aid Detachment, and had died only a fortnight before Christmas, with their father at her bedside. Peel had grown used to his men in the trenches being plucked by death without warning, but it did nothing to prepare him for the shock of a sudden loss in his own family.

The war that was supposed to be over by Christmas 1914 had now rumbled through its fourth Yuletide without coming to the promised conclusion. But for the men of the Post Office Rifles, it certainly felt like a time of endings. In January they received the shocking news that the First Battalion was being disbanded, as part of a general reorganisation of the Army hierarchy. While the headquarters section and one of the four companies would be absorbed into the

Second Battalion, the majority of the men were to be dispersed among other fighting units.

On 29 January, the battalion held another special meal, although this time the mood was more sombre. Lieutenant Colonel Vince gave a speech thanking the men for all their efforts over almost three years, and reminding them of their numerous successes.

Four days later, on a cold and frosty morning, the First Battalion gathered for their last ever inspection. Vince was seated on his charger, with tears in his eyes, but this time he couldn't bring himself to speak. Instead, he personally inscribed the final entry in the official War Diary:

> *The Battalion is gone, and its officers and men scattered abroad. But the spirit of the Battalion – that same spirit which carried it through over two and a half years of hard fighting – will always remain in the hearts of all those who have served in and for it. 'Olim meminisse iuvabit.' [One day, this will be pleasing to remember.]*

One day, perhaps, but in the meantime all the Post Office men were left with was a profound sense of loss. Those former messenger boys and postmen who had been so proud to serve with their colleagues would now be fighting alongside men who knew nothing of their pre-war lives. As one of them put it, 'many a Post Office worker was marching to his new Regiment, to give his loyal support, and in many cases his life, for a battalion that was not his own.'

One of the chaplains of 140th Brigade was so moved by the end of the First Battalion that he wrote a poem about it, 'In Memory of the Post Office Rifles':

> *The silver bugles, where sound they? Where march*
> *the PORs?*
> *Does Fortune favour still the lads whose badges shone*
> *like stars?*
> *The silver bugles sound no more. The Battalion alas*
> *is dead.*
> *Gone are the men whose faithful hearts their willing*
> *blood would shed,*
> *Blood for the Allies' sacred cause, no road echoes*
> *their tread.*

The chaplain wasn't the first man at the front to put his affection for the Post Office Rifles down in verse. The men of the battalion had long since composed their own song, written to be sung when they triumphantly returned to London at the end of the war. Its tone was rather less grandiose than that of the chaplain's offering, but their pride shone through nonetheless:

> *Can't you hear them coming,*
> *Coming back to London Town?*
> *Boys of the Post Office Rifles,*
> *The boys who won renown.*
> *They have faced the bullets,*
> *The shells and whizz bangs too,*
> *And all they had for dinner*
> *Was bully beef stew.*

In dark days, the song had become a source of hope to men who longed for the time when they would finally return home for good, with the war over at last and the enemy vanquished. Now, though, there was to be no such celebration – whatever the outcome of the war, the men from the Post Office would not be returning together.

As winter turned to spring in the early months of 1918, it began to look like the war might be coming to an end rather swiftly after all. But what was more doubtful at the time was whether the Allies were still capable of winning it. Following the Russian Revolution the previous year, Lenin had pledged to pull out of the war as soon as possible, and on 3 March a peace treaty was finally signed at Brest-Litovsk. With the war in the East concluded, the Germans were able to focus their attention – and, more to the point, their troops – on the Western Front. For the first time since the start of the war, they found themselves outnumbering the French and British forces, to the tune of about 200,000 men. So far, only one American division had landed in France but more would be arriving soon, so the Germans had only a limited window in which to make the most of their numerical advantage and strike a decisive blow. They decided to gamble everything on one final throw of the dice.

The German Spring Offensive, or *Kaiserschlacht*, was targeted at British positions in the Somme region, with the goal of splitting them from their French allies.

Although the details of the attack remained secret, there was no doubt that it was coming, and given the overwhelming strength of the German Army, it was going to prove the toughest fight of the war. As Field Marshal Haig later wrote in a communiqué sent to all British forces:

> *There is no other course open to us but to fight it out. Every position must be held to the last man: there must be no retirement. With our backs to the wall and believing in the justice of our cause each one of us must fight on to the end. The safety of our homes and the Freedom of mankind alike depend upon the conduct of each one of us at this critical moment.*

As the Germans geared up for the attack, the Allies hurriedly readied their defences, and all over the Western Front trench systems were fortified and deepened. For the French and British soldiers who stood in the face of the coming onslaught, there was only one small consolation: with the enemy putting so much into one offensive, if it did somehow fail it might prove to be the last gasp of the German Army.

At 4.40am on 21 March 1918, a devastating German barrage began: over the next five hours, more than a million shells landed on Allied positions. It was the heaviest bombardment in the entire course of the war. The men holding the front lines knew that the moment of truth had arrived – all that remained was to wait for the German forces to come over the top.

In some respects, the recently expanded Second Battalion – now known simply as the Post Office Rifles – was lucky. On the morning of 21 March, they were the only unit in their division that was in reserve, so they missed out on the initial German assault. That evening, however, they were ordered forward to defend a section of the St Quentin Canal, which the Germans would have to cross if they were going to advance any further.

It was a foggy night, but by the faint light of the moon the men made their way forward, arriving at the canal around midnight. The Germans were firing shells across the water, but hadn't yet attempted to cross it. The Post Office men waited patiently in a series of shallow trenches on the western side of the waterway, while some of their colleagues began blowing up the bridges that linked the two sides.

As dawn broke, the fog showed no sign of lifting, and in the poor visibility the men couldn't make out any enemy positions. They passed an anxious few hours, waiting for the inevitable attack. But gradually the morning wore on, and it still hadn't come.

What the men from the Post Office didn't know was that the Germans were trying a new strategy. A hundred of their soldiers had clothed themselves in the uniforms of captured British men, and thanks to the fog they were able to slip across the canal unnoticed and take up a position on the left flank of the Post Office Rifles. At 1.15pm, when the main enemy attack began across the canal, these wolves in sheep's clothing were well placed to deal a devastating blow. The Post Office Rifles found themselves under fire from two directions at once – before long, two company commanders were dead and a large number of men had been taken prisoner.

Rifleman Walter Young, one of the battalion's stretcher-bearers and a former assistant postman, set off with his colleague to search for casualties on the battlefield. Before long they found themselves under fire. The two men dropped to the ground as the bullets whizzed by their heads, crawling to a nearby clump of tall grass in the hope that it would provide a little camouflage, and dragging their stretcher behind them.

Up ahead they could see the road that led back to the British first-aid post. Walter decided to chance it – he raised himself up to a stooping position and began to run. Within seconds a bullet smashed through the rim of his helmet. Walter was sure he had been hit in the head, and raised his hand up to feel for blood, but he couldn't find any. His ears were still ringing from the impact when a second bullet ripped through his left hand. 'I'm hit,' he shouted, as he fell down to the ground.

Walter began crawling as fast as he could back towards the British lines. He couldn't believe his luck: the hole in his hand was a perfect Blighty wound – his very own ticket back to Britain. But it wouldn't be any use to him unless he made it out of the battle alive.

Up ahead, he could see a group of figures with rifles heading in his direction. He was sure they must be friendly troops, since the Germans had been nowhere near his position. 'I say!' he shouted, hoping to attract the men's attention. But as they came closer, emerging from the fog, Walter could scarcely believe his eyes. The long grey coats and tortoiseshell-shaped helmets were unmistakable. 'Germans!' he gasped under his breath.

It was too late. The men were already on top of him, with their bayonets at the ready.

Very calmly and slowly, Walter rose to his feet. The lead German lowered his rifle and beckoned for the Englishman to follow him.

Over the next few days, the men from the Post Office began to retreat. By late afternoon on 22 March, the Germans were pouring over the Crozat Canal, and the British forces retired to a position just west of the town of Tergnier. The following day they fell back to Noreuil, and then again that night to Chauny. At each stage they put up the best fight they could before retiring – on 23 March alone, 43 men were killed on the battlefield.

When the First Battalion of the Post Office Rifles was disbanded, Major Peel had stayed behind with their old brigade, and it too was making a series of staggered retreats. For men used to the mechanics of trench warfare, the sudden shift to a war of movement – in which the battle lines, and even the direction of attack, were often unclear – had come as a shock. The British Army's retreat was chaotic, with men scrambling across the French countryside and heavy vehicles barrelling along the roads as fast as they could.

On the afternoon of 24 March, Peel was with the brigadier general and a handful of scouts and signallers en route to Martinpuich, a town just the far side of High Wood. They hadn't eaten for several hours, so when the general announced that he was peckish the small group stopped by the side of the road for some refreshment from their mess cart. When a party of around 60 men was spotted approaching from the southeast, Peel gave them a cursory glance through his binoculars and decided that they must be some of the division's own troops who had been separated from their comrades.

After everyone had eaten, the group set off again, with the mess cart trundling along behind them. It was only as they began to approach a nearby village and got a closer look at the men they had seen before that Peel realised he had made a terrible mistake. They were no British stragglers, but an enemy patrol.

Aside from a couple of men with revolvers, the British party was unarmed, and the officers were wearing cloth caps instead of tin helmets. As soon as the Germans saw them they began to open fire. Peel and his colleagues knew it would be suicide to try to make a stand, outnumbered five to one and with barely any weapons to speak of. Their only hope was to get away as quickly as possible – if they could hide out long enough for the enemy patrol to lose interest, they might be able to meet up with some friendly units later on.

The men of the party scattered as fast as they could. Peel turned and began running back the way they had come along the road, with the brigadier general right behind him. They caught up with the mess cart, which had itself performed a turning manoeuvre and was beginning to pick up speed as the driver whipped the horses frantically.

Peel ran alongside the cart, his chest heaving as his feet pounded the rough dirt track. He was about to leap on board the vehicle when the cart started to crack up. It had not been designed for racing, and the poor condition of the road was proving too much for it. The wooden shafts snapped under the strain, and the cart came to a shuddering halt.

Before long, half the British party had been taken prisoner and the captives were being led away by the Germans. But at least they were safe for the time being. They only hoped the same could be said for Major Peel. The last anyone had seen of him, he was still running – badly out of breath – away into the distance.

CHAPTER 17

THE END GAME

—

Dear Madam,

On my way to the fighting lines I found the body of Capt. H. Peel, who I gather, from the letters which were lying on his side, was your husband.

Although enemy & sometimes deeply hurt by the ridiculous tone of your home press, I feel it is a human duty to communicate to you these sad news.

Capt. Peel was killed in action near Longueval & died, as it seems by the wounds received, without suffering.

I have the honour to remain, dear Madam,

Faithfully yours,

E.F. Gayler

> Letter from a German soldier
> to Gwendolen Peel, 29 March 1918

WHEN A SOLDIER DIED on the battlefield, his family could expect to receive certain items of correspondence: a telegram from the War Office, the Army's official B 104-82 form with the relevant details filled in by hand, and a condolence letter from an officer who served in his unit. But a note from an enemy combatant was another matter entirely. E.F. Gayler's letter had been sent five days before Gwendolen's official War Office telegram, and that told her only that her husband was missing, since no British soldier had yet seen his body. But the German man had been able to identify him thanks to the letters he carried on his person – letters, presumably, that had been written by Gwendolen herself.

To begin with, the War Office was not totally convinced that Gayler's letter was genuine. After all, if the Germans weren't above dressing in British uniforms to fool their enemies on the battlefield, who was to say they might not send misinformation about casualties as well? But any lingering hopes that Peel might be secretly holed up in a German prisoner-of-war camp were soon put to rest. Lieutenant R.L.G. Goldsmith, who had been with him at the end, wrote from Block VII Hut 68 at Rastatt prisoner-of-war camp in Baden:

> *If you can find out from the War Office the address of the widow of Capt. Home Peel ... and let her know he died quite peacefully it would be doing her a great kindness. He was killed at my side about 7.30pm on the 24th.*

The message from the English lieutenant was a thoughtful one, but it was within the realm of an officer's normal behaviour. The German note, on the other hand, was very unusual. Keen to find out as much as Gayler could tell her, Gwendolen wrote back to him, thanking him for his letter and asking if he had any more information about how her husband had died. The German could offer no insights into Peel's last moments, but he did tell her the precise spot where he was buried, and offered to speak to the local authorities the next time he was in the area to ensure that the grave was clearly marked.

Judging by the letters that he wrote to Gwendolen, E.F. Gayler could hardly have been more different from the image of the German soldier put forward by the British propaganda machine: the murderous, ape-like 'Hun' that left a trail of rape and pillage in its wake. He was, in fact, something of an anglophile – he had spent almost two years working for a company in Sheffield before the war, and had celebrated his 21st birthday in the city. 'I shall be much obliged if you will kindly remember me to my Sheffield friends & let them know that I am still in good health,' he begged Gwendolen in his second letter.

Any suspicions that Gayler's letter had been written for propaganda purposes were dispelled when those who had known him in England were interviewed. His old landlady, Mrs Tear, an elderly Scottish woman, could not speak too highly of the young man, while his former colleagues pronounced him 'the nearest approach to a gentleman that a German could be'. Clearly, he was a man of great compassion and decency. He signed off his second letter to Gwendolen, 'with all my sympathy at your sad loss'. Almost four years into a war that had claimed the lives of 10 million soldiers, the currency of grief was universal.

On 15 May, Home Peel's obituary was published in *The Times*. Gwendolen found herself deluged with condolence letters, including one from someone who had not always seen eye to eye with her husband but who had eventually come to respect and even care for him – Eric Gore Browne:

My Dear Mrs Peel,

This is a very difficult letter to write because I cannot tell you just what I am feeling for you. A letter is such a poor thing but I want you to know how I am feeling for you from the bottom of my heart. I knew Home so well and we have had such splendid times together. He did not really like soldiering but he never let anybody know, and he was so gloriously brave and devoted to the Battalion, and he gave himself wholeheartedly to it. I cannot realise that I shall never see him again. I never saw him downhearted and he used to help us all every moment we were together. I want you to know that nobody feels more deeply for you than your always,

E.G.B.

Major Peel had been killed on Day Four of the German Spring Offensive, but it was almost a fortnight before the first stage of the mighty assault came to a halt. In that time, the Germans had advanced up to 40 miles in places, recapturing all the land they had lost in the four and a half months of fighting on the Somme, as well as the town of Albert with its famous golden statue. Days later, they began a second campaign, this time in Belgium, and within another fortnight they had taken back both Messines and Passchendaele. In the space of a month, the outcome of every successful battle the Post Office Rifles had fought during the last two years had been reversed, and the Germans had finally achieved something that had eluded the Allies in almost four years of war: a major shift in the geography of the Western Front.

In the first two weeks of the German advance, they had taken over 90,000 Allied prisoners. Among them was Rifleman Walter Young, the Post Office Rifles stretcher-bearer who was captured near the St Quentin Canal. After being made a prisoner, Walter was moved, along with a number of British and French soldiers, to a town behind the front lines. They were searched for offensive objects such as scissors and knives that might be used to effect an escape, and were given a series of inoculations. A couple of French medics who had also been captured took a look at the bullet wound in Walter's hand.

The prisoners were put on a train to a German rest camp, where Walter shared a hut with another British soldier. Like him, the man had what would normally be considered a perfect Blighty wound, having been shot through his arm near the shoulder. But the injury had not been treated properly – it smelled awful and the soldier was in a wretched state. After a couple of days he collapsed unexpectedly and died. Walter was one of a small group that attended his funeral – it was held by a German chaplain, with another British prisoner saying a few prayers.

After a while, Walter and the other prisoners were put on a train again, this time to a camp in Germany itself. They were reasonably well treated, but the conditions were far from comfortable and they were fed only just enough to keep them alive. Before long, the Germans put them to work – first Walter joined a party that had taken on a job previously performed by horses, dragging a cart of empty tin cans to a factory in Darmstadt, five miles along an old cobbled road. Next, he was sent to help strengthen the sleepers on a nearby railway line.

But the Germans had saved the worst job for last. Walter's boots were confiscated and he was given a pair of wooden clogs to wear instead, before being put on yet another train. It passed through a grim industrial district where tall chimneys pumped the air full of smoke, before suddenly coming to a stop between stations in the middle of the countryside. Walter and his fellow prisoners were marched along old winding roads, their feet aching more and more with every step as they wondered where on earth they were being taken. Then finally, exhausted and miserable, they arrived at their destination: a German coal mine.

Walter's job here was to assist one of the burly miners, who would indicate with gestures what he wanted his new English skivvy to do – loading lumps of coal he had mined into containers or pushing heavy cartloads to the lift that would take them up to the surface. They worked eight-hour shifts, alternating between 6am to 2pm one week and 2pm to 10pm the next.

Every worker in the mine was given his own numbered lamp, which he had to collect from a foreman at the start of each shift. Walter's was No. 488, and he soon learned how to say it in German: '*Vierhundertachtundachtzig*'. In fact, he found that with only a few words of the language, he was able to communicate with the German miners quite well. One morning a group of them turned up with a newspaper, waving it around and shouting 'England kaputt!' in an attempt to wind up the British prisoners. 'Nein, England nicht kaputt,' Walter protested boldly. There was a little more chat back and forth about which of their two sides was done for, before the group settled on 'Alles kaputt!' – a statement that both Englishmen and Germans were happy to agree on.

The German miners were very much a mixed bunch – while some were quite friendly, others were downright hostile. At one point, Walter was working with a particularly grumpy old man who suddenly started shouting at him in German. Walter had no idea what he had done to annoy him, but eventually the German grew so angry that he hurled a piece of wood at his head – fortunately, Walter ducked just in time to avoid a knockout blow.

Not that the English prisoners were much better than the Germans. The grim conditions at the mine – where the prisoners were herded like cattle and barely ever saw the outside world – seemed to bring out the worst in them. There were frequent fights, and very little of the usual camaraderie of the Tommies abroad. Walter had always found making friends relatively easy, but here he felt utterly alone.

It was the most wretched time of his life, worse even than the darkest days in the trenches. For months on end, he received no letters or parcels from home, no indication that anyone even knew that he was still alive. He had seen from watching the other prisoners that parcels were something of a mixed blessing – when one of the men did receive food or clothing, it was often stolen, and disagreements would quickly turn to violence. But at least men whose families sent them soap were able to get the coal dust off their skin at the end of a shift. Walter was living in a permanent state of filth.

Despite the depressing situation, however, he refused to let himself be ground down, and after a while he came up with an idea that he hoped would spread some goodwill among the prisoners. The only reading material Walter had with him was a New Testament he had brought with him to France and a copy of the Book of Common Prayer that a German Red Cross officer had given him, having found it in the pocket of a dead British soldier. They weren't much to keep him entertained during months of unremitting boredom, but for what he had in mind now they were all that he needed.

Walter persuaded the German guards to let him organise an impromptu Sunday evening service in the men's shower room, which was the best the mine could offer for a chapel. He put up a notice inviting all English-speaking prisoners to attend, expecting that half a dozen might come if he was lucky. In the event, more than 40 people turned up, including several French and Russian prisoners, and a man with a violin who offered to play the hymns. It was hard to hear the music over the loud hissing noise of the boiler, and with no hymn book the men struggled with the words, but they belted them out as best they could. Walter had never enjoyed public speaking, and in his ragged and dirty clothes he didn't exactly look the part of a priest, but somehow he found the confidence to address the congregation.

Walter was touched by how many people had turned up for his improvised devotional, and the other prisoners clearly appreciated how much effort he had gone to. As he had hoped, the service helped to bring everyone a little closer together, and it soon became a regular weekly fixture.

In the coal mine, news of the outside world arrived slowly, but gradually Walter and the other prisoners began to realise that the situation on the Western Front was changing. By summer it had become clear that, although the Germans had achieved a devastating advance – they were now so close to the French capital that a million Parisians had packed their bags and left – they hadn't quite managed to deal the knockout blow that was needed to win the war once and for all. Their forces were overstretched, with supply lines struggling to cope with the demand for food and ammunition, and the casualties they had sustained were horrific, running to almost half a million men.

On 15 July, when the Germans attacked across the River Marne, the Allies were ready for them. The German artillery bombardment fell on trenches that had already been evacuated, and the French counter-bombardment hit back hard. Within a few days, British, French and American divisions were attacking together, and driving the Germans back across the river – on the first day alone the Allies advanced four miles. They pushed the Germans back to their starting positions and then carried on pushing. The Spring Offensive was finally over.

For the German Army it was the beginning of the end. On 8 August, at Amiens, the Allied forces launched their final campaign, the 100-day-long offensive that would finish the war. The Post Office Rifles were involved right from the start. On Day One of the operation – 'the black day of the German Army' as General Ludendorff described it – they fought at Mallard Wood. Things got off to a bad start when the petrol can containing one company's rum ration was hit by a stray German bullet, but the men quickly emptied their water flasks onto the ground and poured into them as much of the precious liquid as they could salvage. The battle itself was a tremendous success – advancing through heavy mist, the Post Office men captured several machine guns and trench mortars and took over 500 prisoners, in an action that cost them only 11 lives.

Later that month the battalion was in Billon Wood, where the men fought through an intense thunderstorm and once again secured all their objectives. Two days later it was Marrières Wood, in which they captured not only 150 prisoners but 40 'enemy pigeons'. (Birds taken captive during the war were a popular attraction on the home front, where they were paraded in the streets like humiliated prisoners.) Next came Hem Wood, and the third attack in only five days. Once again, it was a success and over 200 enemy soldiers were taken alive.

Although German prisoners were captured in record numbers during the 100-day Allied advance, not all British soldiers were prepared to show mercy to men who had been doing their best to kill them for the past four years. Rifleman Vincent Richardson saw a man from another regiment raise his rifle to a group of surrendering troops who had their backs to him. 'If you kill one of those men I'll put a bullet right between your eyes,' Vincent hissed at the other man, who swore at him before angrily sloping off.

As the days and weeks wore on, the Allied advance continued relentlessly. Meanwhile, far behind the lines in Belgium, the Germans were beginning to talk about a peace plan, doubtful that victory was even possible any more. General Ludendorff, the second in command of the German Army, advised the Kaiser to beg for an armistice. By 5 October, when the Allies finally broke through the Hindenburg Line, the writing was on the wall. The Germans formally approached President Wilson and begged to negotiate terms.

As the cogs of diplomacy turned, the Allied forces continued to advance. By 14 October, the Post Office Rifles were stationed in Courrières, seven miles east of

Lens. The next day they crossed the Canal de la Deûle into Oignies. Then it was Bersée, Wattines, Nomain and Maulde – almost 30 miles in less than a fortnight. The days of static trench warfare were behind them.

On 8 November – the same day that British, French and German representatives converged on a railway carriage in the Compiègne Forest to begin formal negotiations for peace – the men from the Post Office arrived at Flines-lès-Mortagne. The next day they were at Callenelle, just over the border in Belgium, and the following night at Beloeil. The men had grown used to the inexorable march eastwards, and on the morning of 11 November they were on their feet again, setting off on the four-and-a-half-mile trek to the small Belgian town of Waudignies. But before they arrived at their destination, they were met on the road by an old friend. Their former commander Maxwell, now a brigadier general, had galloped up personally to tell them the news: the armistice papers had been signed early that morning, and in an hour's time the war would come to an end.

As soon as they heard the momentous news, the men began whooping and cheering. At long last, the moment they had dreamed of had arrived – almost three and a half years since the first of them had crossed the Channel and set foot in France. After all the ordeals they had endured in the intervening years – the mud, blood and tears, the exhaustion and the horror – they could scarcely believe that it was true. Only a few months before there had been talk of the war spilling over into 1919, as the weather turned cold and the two sides burrowed into their trenches for yet another bitter winter. Now a very different future faced the men of the Post Office Rifles – a future of peace, of a return to loved ones back home, of lives broken off that could at last be resumed.

By the time the Post Office men arrived at Waudignies, the news of the armistice had become public knowledge. Men and women were thronging the streets, their faces streaked with tears. Children threw garlands of flowers at the soldiers' feet, as their parents pressed cups of wine into their hands. There was singing and dancing, and many heartfelt speeches from the locals. Some of them rushed up to the English visitors and threw their arms around them.

But while 11 November 1918 was a day of joy and celebration, there was room for sadness too in the minds of the Post Office men. They thought of the comrades who had been less fortunate than themselves, those who hadn't made it all the way. Only two days before, the battalion had suffered its most recent casualty: Rifleman Joshua Lester, a 29-year-old former postman from Homerton in East London, who left behind a widow called Emily.

As the men struggled with a powerful mix of emotions, some of them were temporarily struck dumb, since to articulate all they had experienced seemed impossible. But through the mingled joy and sorrow, one feeling was paramount: an overwhelming sense of relief. For over four years, the entire world had held its breath – now, at last, the time had come for them to breathe again.

Perhaps appropriately for a battalion of former postal workers, the men of the Post Office Rifles received the final word on the end of the war in the form of a letter – scrawled by their commander, Lieutenant Colonel Derviche-Jones, on the last page of his Army correspondence book:

In the Field,
November 11th, 1918

To Officers and Men of the 8th Battalion City of London Regiment (Post Office Rifles),

I wish to congratulate the Battalion on the splendid spirit, courage, and endurance shown by all ranks, especially during the anxious days of the spring and early summer of this year, and the more stirring times of August, up to the 11th November – a day which will be for ever famous in history – and to thank all ranks for the consistent loyalty extended to me both personally and as Commander of the Battalion. The success which has always attended the efforts of this Battalion is due to the splendid co-operation between all ranks and to the indomitable spirit and devotion of each individual man.

I am indeed proud to have had command of such a splendid fighting force, and trust that the comradeship engendered by the War may endure during the years to come.

EPILOGUE

THE LAST POST

—

Ever in our thoughts
By his broken-hearted wife and family

Inscription on the grave of Rifleman A.R.
Butterfield, Oak Dump Cemetery, Belgium

OVER THE COURSE of the First World War,
approximately 12,000 men served in one of the three
battalions of the Post Office Rifles – some for a matter
of weeks or months, others for the full duration of the
conflict – and over 1,500 of them never came home
again. While that number is horrifying, it is far from
atypical, matching up almost perfectly with the
national average of 12.5 per cent. In addition to those
who lost their lives, a further 4,500 of the Post Office
men were left with injuries they had sustained during
the war, and many more spent the rest of their days
blighted by psychological damage, something that
might find an outlet through post-traumatic stress,
alcoholism, violence or depression.

No one could be entirely immune to the war's
mental after-effects, but for the majority of the men
who had faced the daily prospect of sudden
annihilation and watched countless comrades fall

along the way, the most remarkable thing of all was that somehow they had managed to survive it. They found themselves faced with a future that they had never expected to be granted, and many of them went on to lead long and fulfilling lives.

A large number of the rank and file returned to their old employer. Over 46 years of devoted service, Bill Howell worked his way up the ranks, until he was finally made an inspector at the King Edward Building. Thomas May, meanwhile, ended up running his own post office in Southgate – a cheerful, friendly place where his wife received regular bouquets of flowers from a team of contented postmen. On Christmas Day, Tom's family would wait for him at home as he went out on the delivery round. He loved nothing better than visiting the local families – laden with presents like Father Christmas – and he was not above working his own bit of festive magic, swapping the labels on food deliveries going to rich and poor neighbourhoods on the grounds that the wealthy could always afford to buy more.

Pat Patterson returned to his old job delivering parcels, based out of a depot at Mincing Lane in the City of London. One day, while out on his rounds, he ran into his former master, Percy Croysdale, who dashed across the road and gripped him tightly by the hand. The two men had by now returned to their different stations in life, but they reminisced about their time at the front with the genuine warmth of old comrades. In spite of its horrors, the war had forged some positive bonds, and had taught men from very different backgrounds to respect, and even love, one another.

Some men found that readjusting to life in the Post Office was more challenging than they had expected, especially after the life-and-death drama of the Western Front. When John Terrell returned to the Post Office as a junior sorter at Mount Pleasant, he requested to be put on the night shift. 'Oh no,' his supervisor told him, 'you can't do night work. You have to be over 21!' To John, who had spent 10 months in the front lines in France, up at all times of the day and night – and not to mention in mortal danger – the prohibition seemed positively ludicrous. But just like the Army, the Post Office had its rules and regulations, and John had no choice but to obey them.

Other Post Office men found a workplace that was very different to how they remembered it. Robert Nosworthy, the former messenger boy who had railed against the girls who took over his duties, returned to the Post Office after the war as a sorter. He could hardly believe his eyes when he arrived for his first day at work and a woman began showing him the ropes.

In the long run, however, it was Nosworthy and men like him who had the last laugh. In the years after the war, female workers were gradually weeded out of the Post Office. As the Postmaster General had always insisted, they had only ever been a 'war measure', and as peace returned and the men came home from the Continent, the women soon became surplus to requirements.

The officers who had served with the Post Office men throughout the war had never been postal workers themselves, and in peacetime they moved into a variety of different professions. Eric Gore Browne abandoned a promising pre-war career as a barrister for a life in banking – but he never forgot his old battalion. In 1921, after the Post Office Rifles had returned to its former status as a part-time Territorial unit, he was delighted to assume command once again, until the battalion was effectively disbanded in an amalgamation with the Shiny Seventh Londons. A lifelong churchgoer, in his retirement Gore Browne devoted himself to the finances of the Church of England, and he was heavily involved in the Christian Stewardship movement, which promoted charitable giving.

When Sir Eric – as he had become by then – died in 1964, his obituary in *The Times* described him as 'lucky' for having made it through the Great War in one piece – and that luck was something the survivors never forgot about. They had buried more than enough of their comrades on the battlefield to know that the chance to start their lives again was a precious one.

Gwendolen Peel, like so many widowed women, must have greeted the end of the war with mixed feelings. To the bereaved, every soldier happily reunited with his family was a reminder of someone who was never coming home again. Major Peel had died at the age of just 23, leaving behind a wife and two children. But he was only one of the 1,500-odd

Post Office Rifles who would remain forever in some corner of a foreign field.

After the war, the bodies scattered across the fields of France and Flanders began to be brought together. Under the careful supervision of the Imperial War Graves Commission, many hastily dug graves were reopened, and their contents moved to the new official cemeteries, where they could be reinterred in neat rows. In part, this was a money-saving exercise – fewer, larger cemeteries were less trouble to maintain than individual plots – but the symbolism was powerful too. The long lines of identical white headstones evoked the close bond between the troops at the front and embodied a powerful principle: no matter the wealth or rank of an individual, in death all men were equal.

Major Peel had been buried with care by the enemy soldiers who had found his body on the roadside. A few months later, when the advancing British troops had stumbled across his grave, they had replaced the wooden German cross with one of their own. But in the summer of 1919, Gwendolen Peel received a letter to say that her husband's body was about to be moved to an official War Graves Commission cemetery.

Gwendolen was evidently distressed at the thought of the grave being disturbed, since she wrote back to ask whether there was any way that they could leave Home where he was – she even offered to personally buy the land he was buried on from whichever French farmer it belonged to.

The Imperial War Graves Commission was familiar with Gwendolen's predicament, and had already reached a ruling on the matter, as described in the official report of a meeting from December 1918, which was attended by both Rudyard Kipling and the Secretary of State for War:

> *The Commission recognised the existence of a sentiment in favour of leaving the bodies of the dead where they fell, but in view of the actual conditions regarded it as impracticable. Over 150,000 such scattered graves are known in France and Belgium. In certain districts, notably those of Ypres and the Somme battlefields, they are thickly strewn over areas measuring miles in length and breadth. These areas will shortly be restored to cultivation, or possibly afforested, and the bodies cannot remain undisturbed. They must therefore be removed to cemeteries where they can be reverently cared for.*

Generally speaking, the War Graves Commission enforced its rules very strictly. At the same meeting they had discussed the desire of some wealthy families to ship their relatives' bodies back home for burial. The Commission had agreed that any such attempts should be absolutely forbidden, since 'to allow removal by a few individuals (of necessity only those who could afford the cost) would be contrary to the principle of equality of treatment'. But when it came to the request made by Gwendolen Peel, the officials were willing to bend the rules a little. They wrote back promising to speak to the local authorities and to do everything possible to accommodate her wishes.

As it turned out, however, Gwendolen's letter had arrived too late. On 17 September, she received an apologetic note from the office of the Director of Graves Registration. 'I regret very much to have to inform you that when the enquiry was made, the grave concerned had already been moved,' he told her. 'No time was lost, on the receipt of your instructions, to issue the necessary orders with a view to carrying out your wishes, and I regret that circumstance, over which I had no control, made this impossible.'

It was an honest mistake, although an embarrassing one, especially where a grieving widow was concerned, but perhaps in the long run it was for the best. Instead of a lonely grave by the side of the road, Peel's remains lie, to this day, alongside those of his countrymen, in the Guards' Cemetery on the outskirts of Lesbœufs. It's just a shame that, of the 1,500 men buried there, he is the only representative of the Post Office Rifles.

The Post Office men were granted their own cemetery in France – at Festubert, the site of their first major battle. A small graveyard by the side of the road with a modest stone sign, it holds the remains of 32 men of the First Battalion who died there, back in the spring of 1915. At the time their graves were first dug, that seemed a significant number of casualties, but as the years went by and the battalion's death toll mounted, they became just a tiny part of the awful bigger picture.

Many Post Office men were never afforded the reassuringly solid presence of a marked headstone, whether because their bodies were completely obliterated by horrors either manmade or natural – blown to pieces by shellfire or sucked under the mud of the battlefield – or because all that was left of them to be buried lacked any identifying features. The Post Office Rifles knew all too well how hard it could be recognising a mutilated body, and Major Peel was far from the only soldier who was identified thanks to letters found on his person. When two Post Office signallers were killed in an explosion in early 1917, their comrades found body parts strewn all over the nearby trees. One of the arms could only be identified thanks to a tunic pocket hanging from it, which contained the man's letters from home.

On the Western Front, over 150,000 unidentifiable bodies lie in graves marked 'Known unto God'. Their names are inscribed on the Menin Gate, and on the giant memorials at Thiepval, Tyne Cot and elsewhere – mingled with those of as many men again whose bodies have never been recovered. Among those commemorated in this way are more than 750 Post Office Rifles – around half the total number of the three battalions' war dead.

The men were gone, in some cases literally lost, but their comrades made sure they weren't forgotten. For over 70 years, starting in 1919, the Post Office Rifles Association provided a forum for the survivors to meet and reminisce about old times, to share memories of those less fortunate than themselves, and to recapture a little of the special camaraderie that had been forged amid the horrors of the trenches. In the Association newsletter they shared poems, jokes and songs, and compared notes on friends and foes alike. They also gathered twice a year – in March to celebrate the anniversary of the First Battalion's arrival in France, and in November to honour their fallen comrades in a service of remembrance. Over the years, the day that in 1918 had been so full of celebration and joy had come to stand in for the 1,500-odd days of misery that had preceded it.

In November 1991, at the King Edward Building in London, the final remembrance service was held for the Post Office Rifles. The commemoration had been a regular fixture for many decades now, but it had reached the stage where there seemed little point in continuing. Of the 12,000 men who had once passed through the battalion, only four were known to still be living, and none of them were well enough to attend.

Sir William Barlow, a former Chairman of the Post Office and the Patron of the Post Office Rifles Association, addressed the congregation. 'These men were ordinary men,' he told them:

Post Office workers who joined the army and with scant training were sent to fight in the front line in France. They found themselves in conditions of horror and indeed terror as both sides exchanged shells, mortars, bombs and machine-gun fire. They gave as good as they got, but always at the cost of men killed and wounded … In these conditions was created a comradeship extremely deep – far deeper than anything which would be created in normal life – and it lasted for a lifetime.

The incidents, the life, the battles, were shared memories of the veterans of the Post Office Rifles and they came each year to remember their comrades.

A hundred years after the start of the war, there are no more living memories – only the traces of lives lived long ago that have survived because they were written down on paper. Some are preserved in the vast archives of the Imperial War Museum, others held in pride of place at the British Postal Museum and Archive in Islington, just around the corner from Mount Pleasant Sorting Office.

The Post Office men knew better than anyone the importance of the written word, and how vital the right message could be to the person who received it. If they had ever doubted it in peacetime, the war had made this truth inescapable. They had seen the dead bodies on the battlefield, a last letter from home clutched desperately in their hands at the moment the spark of life had departed.

Today, those traces are all that remain of the thousands of men who served with the Post Office Rifles. We are left with the accounts they wrote down and shared with each other in later years, with the diaries they kept on the Western Front and the letters they sent home to their families. But the men from the Post Office are gone, and their extraordinary lives have crossed the threshold from memory into history.

ACKNOWLEDGEMENTS

—

THIS BOOK RESTS HEAVILY on the Post Office Rifles' own accounts, both letters and diary entries composed during the war and stories recounted in later years. For their care in recording and preserving this material, I would like to thank the Collections Department of the Imperial War Museum, whose supremely professional staff have been extremely helpful. Where possible I have sought permission to reproduce works from the relevant copyright holders, and I am grateful to those relatives who have corresponded with me – in particular Fanny Hugill, the daughter of Eric Gore Browne, and Anne Walsh, the granddaughter of Alfred Knight.

When quoting from diaries and letters I have made occasional corrections and standardised punctuation and spellings. I have tried as much as possible to corroborate what individuals have said, although with memories that were often recorded many years after the event, there are bound to be errors here and there.

I am grateful, too, to the extremely kind and helpful staff at the British Postal Museum and

Archive, who took time to talk me through their various files and artefacts and bore with numerous tedious requests. Thanks also to those at the National Archives and the National Army Museum. Of the many books that helped me to get to grips with the history of the First World War, first and foremost is Charles Messenger's *Terriers in the Trenches*, a brilliant account of the Post Office Rifles which sadly is now out of print.

For sterling research assistance I am grateful to Clara Jones and Sinéad Krebs, while Becky Barry, as always, provided extremely conscientious transcriptions. For sharing their professional expertise with me, I would like to thank Martin Brooks, Helen Glew and Will Irwin.

I am grateful to Helen Brocklehurst and Louise Stanley for shaping the initial idea for this book, and to Tom Bromley and Donna Wood for seeing it through to publication. Judith Forshaw, as copy-editor, brought a sharp eye for errors and made many helpful suggestions. My agent Jon Elek has, as ever, been a great source of encouragement.

It was my mother Michèle who first kindled my interest in the First World War, and who set me off on the train of thought that ultimately led to the Post Office Rifles. I am indebted to her for her expert advice, and for giving me the tour of France and Flanders.

My partner Nuala has been something of a war widow ever since I started work on the manuscript. For her patience and support throughout the process – not to mention her incisive suggestions on the text – I am incredibly grateful.

TIMELINE

—

4 AUGUST 1914	Britain declares war on Germany
NOVEMBER 1914	First Battalion arrives at Abbots Langley
17 MARCH 1915	First Battalion departs Southampton for Le Havre
15–25 MAY 1915	Battle of Festubert
25 MAY 1915	British Prime Minister Herbert Asquith forms coalition government
25 SEPTEMBER– 14 OCTOBER 1915	Battle of Loos
19 DECEMBER	Sir Douglas Haig replaces Sir John French as British commander-in-chief
24–27 DECEMBER 1915	First Battalion spends Christmas in the 'Hairpin'
27 JANUARY 1916	Britain introduces conscription
21 MAY 1916	First Battalion suffers box barrage at Vimy Ridge
5 JUNE 1916	Lord Kitchener dies when his boat hits a mine
1 JULY 1916	Battle of the Somme begins
15 SEPTEMBER 1916	First Battalion participates in successful capture of High Wood
7 OCTOBER 1916	First Battalion attempts to take Butte de Warlencourt
18 NOVEMBER 1916	Battle of the Somme ends

7 DECEMBER 1916	David Lloyd George replaces Herbert Asquith as British Prime Minister
27 JANUARY 1917	Second Battalion arrives in France
14 MARCH 1917	German forces begin retreating to the Hindenburg Line
6 APRIL 1917	United States declares war on Germany
27 MAY 1917	French Mutiny begins
7 JUNE	Battle of Messines Ridge
31 JULY 1917	Battle of Passchendaele begins
AUGUST 1917	Third Battalion works with D.W. Griffith at Blackdown Camp
20 SEPTEMBER 1917	Second Battalion fights at Wurst Farm Ridge, Alfred Knight wins Victoria Cross
7–8 NOVEMBER 1917	October Revolution in Russia brings Lenin to power
10 NOVEMBER 1917	Battle of Passchendaele ends
20 NOVEMBER – 7 DECEMBER	Battle of Cambrai
2 FEBRUARY 1918	First Battalion officially disbanded
3 MARCH 1918	Treaty of Brest-Litovsk signed between Germany and Russia
21 MARCH 1918	German Spring Offensive begins
21–22 MARCH 1918	Battle of St Quentin Canal
8 AUGUST 1918	Allied Hundred Days Offensive begins
11 NOVEMBER 1918	Armistice is signed and war comes to an end
28 JUNE 1919	Treaty of Versailles is signed

Q&A

WITH DUNCAN BARRETT

What drew you to the story of the Post Office Rifles?

Initially, I was intrigued by the idea of men who knew each other in peacetime signing up together – in particular those who had worked for the same organisation and therefore had seen each other every day in a very different context to the trenches. My own great-great uncle, Eric Layton, was one of thousands of men killed at High Wood on 15 September 1916 (the same day the Post Office Rifles fought there) and his former employer, the South Metropolitan Gas Company, honoured their war dead with a special remembrance service just as the Post Office did. Although peacetime colleagues often signed up and served together during the war, not many workplaces actually had their own battalion, so the Post Office Rifles was an obvious unit to focus on.

The Post Office is also a great national institution and inspires affection and nostalgia even today – perhaps all the more so since the recent privatisation of Royal Mail. Almost everyone knows their own local postman or postwoman, and postal workers do jobs that are easy to understand and relate to. I was fascinated by the idea of your friendly local postie being turned into a warrior. Writing about the Post Office also allowed me to consider the role of mail delivery in the war, and to pepper the book with lots of contemporary letters.

You've previously written about the Second World War. Was it very different writing about the First World War this time?

My books *The Sugar Girls* and *GI Brides* both dealt in part with women's experiences on the home front during the Second World War, so it was quite a challenge getting to grips with the ins and outs of the battlefield this time around. But the biggest difference for me was that those books were based on interviews I conducted myself with women who had lived through the Second World War, whereas when you're writing about the First World War there is no one left to interview. Fortunately, there is a lot of written material concerning the Post Office Rifles – letters, diaries, transcripts of oral history recordings, and so on – but there were many times I wished I could phone one of the Post Office men, as I often have the subjects of my other books, to find out exactly how they felt at a particular moment, or to ask them to explain something in more detail.

The book is written in quite a narrative style. Have you fictionalised any of the stories?

Occasionally I have added minor details based on my own research (for example, describing the weather on a particular day), but the stories in this book essentially belong to the Post Office men themselves. Many of them were gifted storytellers and fortunately recorded their memories before they died. I've reconstructed their stories in my own words, but the essence of them is the same. With my other books I've always run what I wrote past the interviewees to check I haven't got the wrong end of the stick – obviously that's not been possible in this case, but I hope that the men would agree that what I've written is a true account of what happened to them.

You mention that you visited France and Belgium. How did that inform the book?

It was very moving visiting the Post Office Rifles Cemetery and seeing the graves of some of the men I had read about – for example, Basil Moon, the brave lieutenant who was killed in the Battle of Festubert – as well as finding the final resting place of Home Peel near Lesbœufs. I also visited the Menin Gate, which lists the names of 146 men from the Post Office Rifles who died in Belgium, and the Thiepval Memorial to the Missing of the Somme, where another 177 are inscribed. But of all the cemeteries and memorials I visited, I was most struck by Warlencourt British Cemetery, where 95 of the First Battalion's dead are buried. What shocked me most is that the cemetery is only half a kilometre from the Butte de Warlencourt itself – and looking down from the Butte towards the hundreds of rows of white gravestones, it's hard to comprehend the number of lives that were lost attempting to capture such a small piece of ground.

As well as the official war cemeteries, I visited many of the battlefields where the Post Office Rifles fought. I tried to locate the site of the White Chateau, where Corporal Bottomley was killed, and found a modern house that appears to have been built on the same spot – although much of the surrounding area that the Post Office men fought over is now a golf course. The giant slag heaps near Loos are still standing, albeit a rather different shape and size than they were a hundred years ago – staggering breathlessly to the top of one of them gave me an insight into what difficult terrain they must have been to fight on. I was disappointed to find that although the trees have grown back at High Wood, the site is not open to the public – and when a local man told me the reason I was taken aback: visitors are forbidden not out of respect for the thousands of men who still lie buried there, but because it's now a popular spot for shooting pheasants.

How do you think the centenary of the First World War has affected people's understanding of the conflict?

The centenary has certainly brought more attention to bear on the war, and it's great that this has encompassed a broad range of approaches, beyond the traditional focus on the trenches of the Western Front. We've had Kate Adie writing about women in the war, and Jeremy Paxman's book and documentary series on experiences of the home front, as well as the BBC drama *The Crimson Field*, which dealt with the role of nurses. The centenary has also galvanized debate about the war, as both historians and politicians have argued over the ethics of the conflict: was it a senseless slaughter that could have been avoided, or a necessary evil in order to protect a free Europe?

Alan Clark described the British soldiers as 'lions led by donkeys' – an argument that has been much debated recently. Did your research shed any light on this?

There seems to be a backlash at the moment against the idea of the First World War as a futile and misguided tragedy, and partly this is connected to a reassessment of the generals who made the big decisions. I can't speak about the war as a whole, but as far as the battles I looked at are concerned, I found evidence of both considerate, compassionate leadership on the one hand, and on the other a bloody-minded refusal to heed good advice, which did cost a great many lives. Clearly some generals were better than others, but it's not true – as many people imagine – that the whole war was just one long battle of attrition. In fact, the British Army was constantly trying out new strategies and innovations in an attempt to gain the upper hand: from sniping and tank warfare to the use of gas and underground mines. Many attacks were planned and practised to the nth degree to maximise the chance of success. But even so, plenty of soldiers – from battalion commanders right down to the rank and file – became disillusioned thanks to decisions taken higher up the chain of command. As Home Peel wrote before he even set off for France in 1915, 'If one had any feeling of permanence or security, or any real trust in those set over me, everything would be all right; but everything is always changing, and the most ridiculous and stupid mistakes are continually being made by the great ones.'